Out

'art of this book is the argument that, the fact that so many post-ist French intellectuals have a strong 'colonial' connection, usually ,eria, cannot be a coincidence. The 'biographical' fact that so many itellectuals were born in or otherwise connected with French Algeria ı been noted, but it has never been theorised. Ahluwalia makes a con-case that post-structuralism in fact has colonial and postcolonial roots. in important argument, and one that 'connects' two theoretical currents ntinue to be of great interest, post-structuralism and postcolonialism.

T rereading of what is now familiar material against the background of o nial struggles demonstrates the extent to which it is this new condi-

U

n that prompted theory to question long-held assumptions inscribed in the ropean colonial enterprise. The wide-ranging discussion, ranging across uthors as different as Foucault, Derrida, Fanon, Althusser, Cixous, Bourdieu d Lyotard, enables the reader to make connections that have remained un-ticed or been neglected. It also brings back into view a history of struggles, h political and theoretical, that has shaped the landscape of critique in the social sciences and humanities.

This clear and lucid discussion of important and often difficult thinkers will be widely read and widely debated by students and academics alike.

Pal Ahluwalia is a Pro Vice-Chancellor and Vice President of the University of South Australia. He was previously Professor of the Politics Department, University of Adelaide, Australia, Professor with the University of California, San Diego, USA and Professor at Goldsmiths, University of London, UK. He is co-editor of the Routledge journals *African Identities*, *Social Identities* and *Sikh Formations*.

Postcolonial politics

'Postcolonial Politics' is a series that publishes books that lie at the intersection of politics and postcolonial theory. That point of intersection once barely existed; its recent emergence is enabled, first, because a new form of 'politics' is beginning to make its appearance. Intellectual concerns that began life as a (yet unnamed) set of theoretical interventions from scholars largely working within the 'New Humanities' have now begun to migrate into the realm of politics. The result is politics with a difference, with a concern for the everyday, the ephemeral, the serendipitous and the unworldly. Second, postcolonial theory has raised a new set of concerns in relation to understandings of the non-West. At first, these concerns and questions found their home in literary studies, but they were also, always, political. Edward Said's binary of 'Europe and its other' introduced us to a 'style of thought' that was as much political as it was cultural as much about the politics of knowledge as the production of knowledge, and as much about life on the street as about a philosophy of being, a new, broader and more reflexive understanding of politics and a new style of thinking about the non-Western world, make it possible to 'think' politics through postcolonial theory and to 'do' postcolonial theory in a fashion which picks up on its political implications.

Postcolonial Politics attempts to pick up on these myriad trails and disruptive practices. The series aims to help us read culture politically, read 'difference' concretely and to problematise our ideas of the modern, the rational and the scientific by working at the margins of a knowledge system that is still logocentric and Eurocentric. This is where a postcolonial politics hopes to offer new and fresh visions of both the postcolonial and the political.

The Postcolonial Politics of Development
Ilan Kapoor

Out of Africa
Post-structuralism's colonial roots
Pal Ahluwalia

Out of Africa

Post-structuralism's colonial roots

Pal Ahluwalia

LONDON AND NEW YORK

First published 2010 by Routledge
2 Park Square, Milton Park, Abingdon, Oxon, OX14 4RN

Simultaneously published in the USA and Canada
by Routledge
270 Madison Avenue, New York, NY 10016

Routledge is an imprint of the Taylor & Francis Group, an informa business

Typeset in Times New Roman by Glyph International Ltd
Printed and bound in Great Britain by TJ International Ltd, Padstow, Cornwall

British Library Cataloguing in Publication Data
A catalogue record for this book is available from the British Library

Library of Congress Cataloging in Publication Data
Ahluwalia, D. P. S. (D. Pal S.)
Out of Africa: post-structuralism's colonial roots / Pal Ahluwalia.
p. cm.
Includes bibliographical references.
1. Poststructuralism–Africa–Philosophy. 2. Structuralism–Africa–Philosophy.
3. Structuralism–Algeria–Philosophy. 4. French–Algeria–History.
5. Algeria–Colonization. 6. France–Colonies–Africa. I. Title.

B841.4.A37 2010
146′.960965–dc22 2009033335

ISBN 13: 978-0-415-57069-5 (hbk)
ISBN 13: 978-0-415-57070-1 (pbk)
ISBN 13: 978-0-203-85810-3 (ebk)

ISBN 10: 0-415-57069-7 (hbk)
ISBN 10: 0-415-57070-0 (pbk)
ISBN 10: 0-203-85810-7 (ebk)

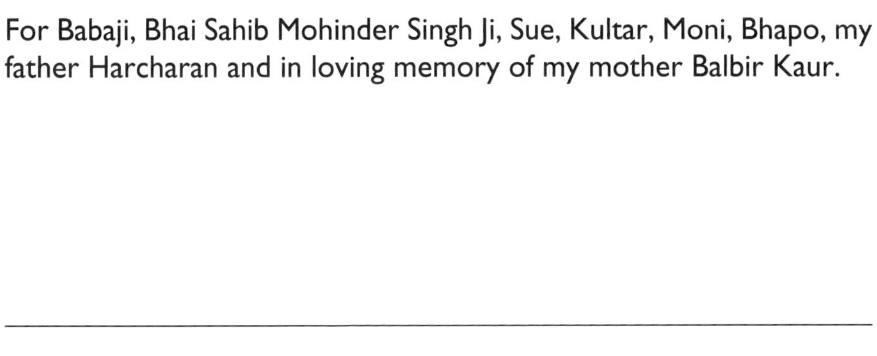

For Babaji, Bhai Sahib Mohinder Singh Ji, Sue, Kultar, Moni, Bhapo, my father Harcharan and in loving memory of my mother Balbir Kaur.

Contents

Acknowledgements

This book is an attempt to bring together the seemingly disparate worlds that I occupy. At its core, it is about bringing my work on Africa together with my interest in social theory. It is about moving away from an area studies approach where Africa is translated into European discourses by the specialist Africanist. In my work, I have persistently endeavoured to move from such a framework by deploying a postcolonial perspective, to offer a different rendering and account of the myriad complexities that mark both the continent and the African subject.

Perhaps the most profound influence on my intellectual project has been that of the cultural theorist, Edward Said. Said often claimed that he led two separate lives – that of an English Professor at Columbia University as well as that of perhaps the best-known Palestinian spokesman. He argued that in the classroom these two worlds were never brought together – that his political work did not bear on his work as an English professor. I have criticized Said for this, arguing that how could he make such a claim on the grounds that these two worlds were fundamentally linked. Yet, as I reflect on my own intellectual trajectory, I am struck at how I have tried to keep my two worlds separate – my most obvious Sikh identity and my work as a student of Politics. It is in this context that I have only recently recognized that this in fact is my 'uniquely punishing destiny' and hence, I find myself increasingly drawn into projects where these two worlds intersect.

This transition for me could be traced to a single event, that is, my meeting Bhai Sahib Mohinder Singh. This meeting served as a transformative encounter. I remain not only in awe of him but greatly indebted to him. My debts are wide ranging and I want to take this opportunity to thank many people who have helped me over the last few years as this book took shape. The Guru Nanak Niskam Sewak Jatha has become my extended family and to its members, especially Sukhbir Singh, I wish to express my deep gratitude. In London, I was adopted by Kultejwant Singh, Gurmit Kaur, Sukhdev, Jasvir, Onkar and Harpreet – many, many thanks. In Birmingham, I would like to acknowledge the friendship of Gurdev and Dr. Bob. My Aunt and Uncle Sawinder and Satinder Bajaj have been unstinting supporters for years, and I cannot thank them enough. I would like also to thank my colleagues and especially my students, from whom I learn so much each day. I wish to thank Abdul JanMohamed, Donald Moore, Abebe Zegeye, Toby Miller, John Hawley, Amritjit Singh, Paul Nursey-Bray, Peter Mayer, Greg McCarthy, Peter Burns, Carol Johhnson, Barry Hindess, Couze Venn, Ryan Bishop, John Phillips, Rob Hattam, Peter Bishop, Julie Matthews, Pam Christie, Ralph Premdas, Roberto Alvarez, Vanita Seth, Jeff Steeves, Philip Darby and Sanjay Seth for their most helpful comments. In the formative stages, this book benefited a great deal through the discussions I had with Bill Ashcroft. I would like to express my gratitude to him for these. I am also indebted to Craig Fowlie at Routledge who has been such a keen supporter for many years. I feel blessed to acknowledge the friendship and love that Michael Dutton has provided me over the years. At the University of South Australia, I am extraordinarily fortunate to have a very supportive network in Peter Høj and members of the senior management group. I am also extremely grateful to Lynda Edwards along with Simon Behenna for all their help.

During my stay in California, my parents Harcharan and Balbir, my brother Moni and sister-in-law Bhapo were always there for me. I lovingly acknowledge Jaswinder and Kulwinder, my beloved nephews with whom I share a special bond. My deepest and loving acknowledgements are to my wife Sue and son Kultar, who are my most ardent supporters and whose love sustains me in all my endeavours.

Chapter 1

Introduction

> I have been working to change the way I speak and write, to incorporate in the manner of telling a sense of place, of not just who I am in the present but where I am coming from, the multiple voices within me.
>
> (bell hooks)

The juxtaposition of the experience of Salman Rushdie, a Mumbai-born writer who now lives in Britain, with Jacques Derrida and Hélène Cixous, two French post-structuralists, is an important one when reflecting on their respective postcolonial identities. Rushdie writes that the 'formulation "Indian-born British writer" has been invented to explain me. But my new book deals with Pakistan. So what now? British-resident-Indo-Pakistani writer?' (cited in Welsh 1997: 56). In contrast, the identity of Cixous and Derrida has not been subjected to such scrutiny despite the fact that they were both born in Algeria. Their identity is not seen to be central to their respective projects; they are not thought of as Algerian-born French post-structuralists.

Is the difference between Cixous, Derrida and Rushdie traceable merely to race, or is there something unique about the manner in which the settler population from Algeria has been accepted in France and has had a profound influence on contemporary French theory and culture?[1] The impact of colonial Africa on French theory is pervasive, and its influence can be discerned in such diverse theorists as Louis Althusser, Hélène Cixous and Jacques Derrida, who were born in Algeria; Michel Foucault, who considered his time at the University of Tunis and its student movements as formative (Macey 1993; Miller 1993: 171; Young 2001a) as well as Michel Leiris, Pierre Bourdieu, Jean Francois Lyotard and Jean-Paul Sartre, amongst others. As Robert Young has pointed out, 'If "so-called post-structuralism" is the product of a single historical moment, then that moment is probably not May 1968 but rather the Algerian War of Independence' (Young 1990: 1).

This may well go to the heart of the differences between French and British colonialism and, in particular, the manner in which the former thought of its colonies as mere extensions of France itself and therefore proceeded to propound the attractive notion that all members of French territories were equal.

Aimé Césaire described the impact of this illusion: 'associated in our minds the word France and the word liberty ... bound us to France by every fibre of our hearts and every power of our minds' (cited in Hall 1995: 10). Yet, there are far too many examples of French colonial subjects, from the negritude writers to Frantz Fanon, who have illustrated the fictitious nature of this claim (Ahluwalia 2001a).

The colonisation of Algeria represented perhaps the best example of the illusion of the possibility of 'assimilation', with the colony being seen as inseparable from France. Indeed, Algeria was regarded as the most important French colonial possession. It was not only the oldest and largest colony but was also an icon of French greatness. In addition, the territory served as a launching pad for the control of the Maghreb.

Is it merely coincidental, then, that some of the most profound contemporary French theorists who have challenged the very precepts of modernity, as defined by the Enlightenment tradition, have been deeply affected in some way by France's African colonial project and their engagement with it as border intellectuals? Surely, it is more plausible that the questions that have become so much a part of the post-structuralist canon – otherness, difference, irony, mimicry, parody, the lamenting of modernity and the deconstruction of the grand narratives of European culture arising out of the Enlightenment tradition – are possible *because* of their postcolonial connection. As Azzedine Haddour points out, 'the problem of modernity and postmodernity has less to do with the decentering of the Cartesian subject than with the political realities of postcolonial France' (2001: 14).

Postcolonialism as a child of post-structuralism and postmodernism

There is now considerable agreement that Edward Said's pioneering work, *Orientalism* (1978), inaugurated the field of colonial discourse analysis, which in turn ultimately led to the development of postcolonial theory. Although Said moved on theoretically and jettisoned Foucault's methodology, postcolonialism remains beleaguered by charges that it is a by-product of post-structuralism and postmodernism (Ashcroft and Ahluwalia 2001). The debate surrounding the relationship between post-structuralism, postmodernism and postcolonialism is highly charged, with a considerable literature developed. There are a host of critics including Aijaz Ahmad (1992), Arif Dirlik (1994), Linda Hutcheon (1989; 1994) and E. San Juan (1998) who have a tendency to conflate these post-isms (see Ahluwalia 2001a). This conflation is made possible because of the many concerns that are shared by the different 'posts'. These common concerns have meant also that the language of postcolonial theorists is similar to that of both post-structuralism and postmodernism. The confusion is caused because a key aspect of postmodernism is the deconstruction of the logocentric metanarratives of European culture, which is much like the postcolonial project of breaking down the binaries of imperial discourse.

This leaves postcolonialism open to the charge that it is essentially a discourse of Third World intellectuals who operate from within their privileged position in the First World. Arif Dirlik goes so far as to claim that postcolonialism is 'a child of postmodernism' (Dirlik 1994: 348). He argues that this can be observed by the manner in which postcolonial critics acknowledge their debt to both postmodernist and post-structuralist thinking. This allows Dirlik to conclude that the most original contribution of postcolonial critics 'would seem to lie in their rephrasing of older problems in the study of the Third World in the language of post-structuralism' (352). By conflating the post-isms, Dirlik is able to argue that postcoloniality is appealing in the West primarily because postcoloniality 'disguises the power relations that shape a seemingly shapeless world and contributes to a conceptualization of that world that both consolidates and subverts possibilities of resistance' (Dirlik 1994: 356).

Aijaz Ahmad shares Dirlik's sentiments, declaring that the East 'seems to have become, yet again, a *career*—even for the "Oriental" this time, and within the "Occident" too' (Ahmad 1992: 94).[2] Ahmad argues that postcolonial theory merely reinscribes the very forms of domination that it seeks to deconstruct. This is necessarily so because postcolonial critics have 'themselves been influenced mainly by post-structuralism' (68). Ahmad's most trenchant criticism appears in an article in *Race and Class*, where he claims that postcolonialism is the progeny of postmodernism. He writes:

> ... the term 'postcolonial' also comes to us as the name of a *discourse* about the condition of 'postcoloniality', so that certain *kinds* of critics are 'postcolonial' and others not. ... the rest of us who do not accept this apocalyptic anti-Marxism, are not postcolonial at all ... so that only those intellectuals can be truly *postcolonial* who are also *postmodern*.
>
> (Ahmad 1995: 10)

Though I have written about the significant differences between postcolonialism, post-structuralism and postmodernism elsewhere, I am still struck by the manner in which this conflation continues to be dominant within postcolonial studies (Quayson 2000; Schwarz and Ray 2000; Goldberg and Quayson 2002). I have argued that postcolonialism is a counter-discourse that seeks to disrupt the cultural hegemony of the West, challenging imperialism in its various guises, whereas post-structuralism and postmodernism are counter discourses against modernism that have emerged within modernism itself (Ahluwalia 2001a). It is my contention that, in order to understand the project of French post-structuralism, it is imperative both to contextualise the African colonial experience and to highlight the Algerian locatedness, identity and heritage of its leading proponents. It is precisely the failure to confront or explicitly acknowledge the colonial experience that problematises the conflation of postcolonialism and post-structuralism.

There are important reasons for examining the centrality of Algeria to post-structuralist French theory. Algeria was the most significant and profitable of all French colonial possessions, being to France what India was to Britain. The importance of Algeria can be seen in the manner in which it was viewed as an extension of France. By the late nineteenth century, it had become both legally and constitutionally an important part of France. The settlers transformed the colony from an Arab and Berber country into *Algérie Française*.

It is important therefore to examine the relationship that most French post-structuralists have had with colonial Africa and, in particular, with Algeria. Why has there been a silence, suppression or, at best, a belated acknowledgement of the colonial roots and affiliations of these theorists? Is it because such an acknowledgement might well challenge the very belief in the superiority of the French on which the modern French nation has been constructed? For example, it is possible to simply read Derrida's work without acknowledging his colonial roots – as Derrida himself has noted, 'I do not believe that anyone can detect *by reading*, if I do not declare it, that I am a "French Algerian" ' (1998: 46). What happens when his Algerian locatedness is taken into account? What impact did his formative years have on his later work? What of deconstructive theory or Derridean logocentrism? Does his overall project reflect his colonial roots and the tensions that arise out of being relocated within a new culture? Is the fate of Derrida and Cixous as specular border intellectuals—of belonging and not belonging in both French and Algerian culture, of occupying that in-between space—part of their own alterity, which inevitably makes its way into their writings, and is it relevant to understanding their work? Does their profound influence on contemporary thought need to be contextualised against the backdrop of Algeria and the experience of colonisation? Is it their sense of exile, of being on the margins, that allows them to challenge Western theory?

It is surprising that postcolonial theory has often been characterised as being epistemologically indebted to both post-structuralism and postmodernism. Such a reading fails to acknowledge the centrality of the colonial encounter and its impact on producing the conditions necessary for the emergence of post-structuralism. This intervention seeks to challenge such assumptions and assertions. It strives to clarify and explain the colonial roots of post-structuralism in order to disrupt such readings of postcolonialism. The foregoing questions are explored in this book as it seeks to analyse the way in which the postcolony impacted upon the intellectual project of these border intellectuals.

Specular and syncretic border intellectuals

In order to understand the complexities that embody border intellectuals, Abdul JanMohamed makes an important differentiation between a 'specular' border intellectual and a 'syncretic' one. Both types of intellectuals are located in more than one culture, but the syncretic intellectual is generally more 'at home' in both cultures than his or her specular counterpart as a result of being able to combine the two cultures and articulate new syncretic experiences. The specular border intellectual, on the other hand, is either unwilling or unable to be at home in either culture. The specular intellectual questions both cultures and 'utilizes his or her interstitial cultural space as a vantage point from which to define, implicitly or explicitly, other, utopian possibilities of group formation' (JanMohamed 1992: 97). Wole Soyinka, Salman Rushdie and Chinua Achebe typify the syncretic intellectual, whilst the specular intellectuals include Edward Said as well as African-American activists and writers W.E.B. Dubois, Richard Wright and Zora Neale Hurston.

Although the idea of the specular border intellectual has limitations,[3] it is nevertheless a useful tool. JanMohamed argues that in someone like Edward Said, who is neither quite an exile nor an immigrant, we see the elements of a specular border intellectual precisely because of the discomfort caused by this ambivalent status. Said's work embodies the predicament of border intellectuals in that, 'first, his criticism is a "reflection", an indirect meditation, on the predicament; and, second, it occupies a specular position in relation to Western culture' (JanMohamed 1992: 101). He identifies four types of people who illustrate border crossings. These include the exile, the immigrant, the colonialist and the scholar who is typified by the anthropologist. The exile and the immigrant both cross borders between either a social group or a national one. The experience of the exile is generally a negative one, whilst that of the immigrant is usually positive. The immigrant often desires to discard the formative influences of his or her own culture in order to identify and merge with the new culture's collective subjectivity. It is this process that Edward Said finds disturbing and calls 'uncritical gregariousness'. For the colonialist and scholar, however, the host culture 'ultimately remains an object of attention'. The gaze of the colonialist 'is military, administrative and economic' whilst that of the scholar 'is epistemological and organizational'. These gazes differ from the perspectives of the exile and the immigrant in that they 'are panoptic and thus dominating' (JanMohamed 1992: 102).

Intellectuals like Edward Said and Richard Wright do not neatly fit into any of these categories but share elements with all, except for the colonialist. Hence, in the case of Said, 'he is able to provide in his writing a set of mirrors allowing Western cultures to see their own structures and functions' (JanMohamed 1992: 105). The position of border subjects such as Said and Wright is precarious, ambivalent, complicated and possibly even tenuous. Yet, when used productively as a site from which to reflect, 'such an appropriation can transform the predicament of the border intellectual into a fruitful and powerful asset' (118). It is precisely in this way that we can consider the examples of Jacques Derrida and Hélène Cixous as border intellectuals who, much like Said and Wright, do not fit neatly into these categories but are nonetheless able to reflect on the different worlds that they inhabit. The notion of the border intellectual is an important one when we think of the constellation of French theorists with an Algerian connection. The categories of the exile, the immigrant, the colonialist and the scholar all feature in the border crossings between France and Algeria, and these categories often overlap. Using a rather crude appropriation of JanMohamed's typology of border intellectuals and applying it to the Algerian case, it is possible to speculate that those border intellectuals born in Algeria, such as Derrida, Cixous and Althusser, might well be seen as specular border intellectuals. In contrast, Bourdieu and Lyotard, both with an extensive Algerian connection that was formative, might be classified as syncretic border intellectuals.

The worldliness of theory

For Edward Said, the world from which the text originated, the world with which it was affiliated, is crucial. For Said, 'every literary text is some way burdened with its occasion, with the plain empirical realities from which it emerged' (Said 1983: 35). The materiality, the locatedness, the worldliness of the text is embedded in it as a function of its very being. It has a material presence, a cultural and social history, a political and even an economic being (Said 1983; Ashcroft and Ahluwalia 2001).

Hence, by bringing together the world, the text and the critic, it is possible to highlight their affiliation. This means that the text is crucial to the way in which we 'have' a world, but the world exists as the text's location, and that worldliness is constructed within the text. The text has a specific situation that places restraints upon an interpreter, 'not because the situation is hidden within the text as a mystery but because the situation exists at the same level of surface particularity as the textual object itself' (Said 1983: 39). The text does not exist outside the world but is a part of the world of which it speaks, and this worldliness is itself present in the text as a part of its formation. For Said, theory can be effective only when it is located firmly within the world. He attacks theory that fails to do so on the grounds that for such theory:

> there seems to be no contact with the world of events and societies, which modern history, intellectuals and critics have in fact built. Instead, contemporary criticism is an institution for publicly affirming the values of our, that is, European, dominant elite culture and for privately setting loose the unrestrained interpretation of a universe defined in advance as the endless misreading of a misinterpretation. The result has been the regulated, not to say calculated, irrelevance of criticism.
>
> (Said 1983: 25)

It is precisely to the work of post-structuralists and postmodernists that Said's criticism is directed. The kind of suppression that occurs in someone like Derrida, and to a lesser extent Cixous, hides that very ambivalence that gives energy to the disruptive assertions of these thinkers. The suppression of the worldly origin of the theory, which might lead to the recognition of the actual effects of monolithic European discourses, establishes a chasm between the theory and its elaboration as the intellectually transformative discourse it aims to be.

Nevertheless, how do those affiliated with colonial Africa deal with their identity, especially given that the very space with which they are affiliated is highly contested in the colonisers' imagination. Edward Said has pointed out that, in the interplay between geography, memory and invention, it is invention that is central to processes of recollection. The idea of the geographical space, Palestine for example, as one that belongs to both Israelis and Palestinians is founded on two competing memories, two invented histories and two sorts of geographical imaginations. The suppression of colonial identity and recollection can be illustrated most vividly in the case of Frantz Fanon and Albert Camus. In the juxtaposition of Fanon and the French settler class in Algeria, we see this contestation being played out. This is not a simple matter of geographical displacement of the colonisers by the colonised but is 'more subtle and complex' in the 'unending cultural struggle over territory, which necessarily involves overlapping memories, narratives and physical structures' (Said 2000: 182). Both Fanon and the French colonial settlers were outsiders who had to invent themselves in the geographical space of Algeria. How is it that Fanon in a very short time came to identify himself as Algerian? How has Fanon subsequently become linked inextricably with Algeria? How has the French settler class that was present in Algeria for more than one hundred and thirty years suppressed its memory and reinvented itself? These processes show the interconnectedness of geography and space and illustrate how they can be manipulated to construct and reconstruct identity.

In the case of Fanon, we can see a particular form of suppression of colonial identity. As a Martiniquan brought up to think of himself as white and French, this identity had to be reconstituted painfully into that of a West Indian in Paris (Ahluwalia 2003). Camus, on the other hand, did the opposite. Although a French Algerian, Camus returned to France. However, the affiliations of his work already announce his failure to see the Algerian locality in which his books are set. 'Camus is a novelist from whose work the facts of imperial actuality, so clearly there to be noted, have dropped away; as in Jane Austen, a detachable *ethos* has remained, an ethos suggesting universality and humanism, deeply at odds with the descriptions of geographical locale plainly given in the fiction' (Said 1993: 208). In both Fanon and Camus, the worldliness of their texts announces the filiations and affiliations of their respective, albeit constructed, worlds.

The Algerian connection

Because of its proximity to France, Algeria remains deeply ingrained in the French imagination, with debate on the Algerian War of Independence (1954–62) continuing to the present day (MacMaster 2003; Prochaska 2003). It is France's closest Orient. But more than this, the experience of identity in those white settlers, who for generations regarded themselves as Algerian before leaving the country after the War of Independence, represents the most paradoxical, ambivalent and contested site of postcolonial identity. The nature of France's colonialism, with its strongly centripetal cultural pull, its insistence on colonies being identified as departments of France, and even sharing the same laws and administrative structures, meant that the identity of French settler Algerians, the nature of their emotional and psychological relationship to Algeria, was more than a little ambivalent. The rapidity and completeness with which the settler population left the country after the War of Independence demonstrates how poorly they were affiliated with Algeria in comparison to their filiative connection with France, their confident view of themselves as French. What it meant to be a settler Algerian, and in addition a Jewish Algerian as in the case of both Derrida and Cixous, lies at the heart of French Algerian intellectuals' pre-eminence in those movements that were most challenging to and disruptive of Enlightenment assumptions.

Algeria is an intensely imagined colonial space and the ambivalence of this imagined reality explains why Algerian intellectuals so quickly suppressed their origins and why those same intellectuals were responsible for producing some of the most radical challenges to the European philosophical tradition. There is considerable danger in assuming some causal connection between the events of an individual's life and the specific pattern of ideas and assumptions developed in their intellectual work. How would we then account for the differences in the thought of those with similar backgrounds? However, if we begin at the other end, at the site of intellectual work and move backwards to ask how it is situated in the world, we quickly discover that ideas are the product of lived experiences.

Exile and postcolonial identity

The profound influence of French post-structuralists with an Algerian connection on contemporary thought needs to be contextualised against the backdrop of Algeria and the experience of colonisation. It is their sense of exile, as border intellectuals, and of being on the margins that allows them to challenge Western theory from within its own intellectual heritage. This condition has been captured in perhaps the most insightful essay in *Representations of the Intellectual* (Said 1994), 'Intellectual Exile: Expatriates and Marginal', where Edward Said describes the fate of the exile. The question of exile is one that long preoccupied Said. Exile, he points out, is like the 'mind of winter'.[4] It embodies notions of decentring, dislocation and displacement. Exile in Western culture has occupied a much-celebrated position. The exalted status of the exile in the West, arising largely out of escape from fascism and communism, is a result of the contributions that exiles have made in defining modern Western culture. One has only to think of the influence and impact that exiles such as Einstein, Beckett, Conrad and Adorno have made in order to share Said's observation that 'the canon of modern Western culture is in large part the work of exiles, émigrés, refugees' (1994: 49). As Said points out,

> Exile … is 'a mind of winter' in which the pathos of summer and autumn as much as the potential of spring are nearby but unobtainable. Perhaps this is another way of saying that a life of exile moves according to a different calendar, and is less seasonal and settled than life at home. Exile is life led outside habitual order. It is nomadic, decentred, contrapuntal; but no sooner does one get accustomed to it than its unsettling force erupts anew.
>
> (Said 1994: 49)

Said's focus in this essay is on the exilic intellectual who is unwilling to make adjustments and remains an outsider, 'unaccommodated, un-coopted and resistant' (1994: 39). This allows him to argue that exile is not only an *actual* condition but also a *metaphoric* condition. Hence, exile for an intellectual in such a state is:

> … restlessness, movement, constantly being unsettled and unsettling others. You cannot go back to some earlier and perhaps more stable condition of being at home; and, alas, you can never fully arrive, be at one with your new home or situation.
>
> (1994: 39)

It is not surprising, then, that Said sees this state as allowing the intellectual to be happy with the idea of unhappiness.

Said claims that Adorno is the quintessential intellectual, for he hated '*all* systems, whether on our side or theirs, with equal distaste' (Said 1994: 41). While celebrating Adorno, Said goes on to argue that he fails to capture the pleasures of exile. These entail an element of surprise, 'of never taking anything for granted' (1994: 44). It is this that gives the intellectual the critical edge. This standpoint allows the intellectual to examine situations as contingent,

> … not as inevitable, look at them as the result of a series of historical choices made by men and women, as facts of society made by human beings, and not as natural or god-given, therefore unchangeable, permanent, irreversible.
>
> (1994: 45)

To adopt such a position, one need not be an actual exile but one must adopt the perspective of the outsider, to think on the margins. In the case of the thinkers under consideration in this book, for example, it is their postcolonial identity as well as their condition of exile that allows them to disrupt and challenge theory. It is this reading of post-structuralism and postmodernism that must be confronted in order to recognise the centrality of the post-colonial condition.

Modernity, ambivalence and the postcolonial condition

The task here is not to consider merely the question of origins but rather to examine the contingent circumstances that gave rise to a certain critical constellation of border intellectuals arising out of the colonial condition. This process is embedded deeply within notions of progress, civilisation, modernity and reason that underpinned the colonial project. The West's success was based upon the exploitation of the colonies, which were necessarily portrayed as inferior. As Bruce Knauft notes, 'in ideational and ideological terms, correspondingly, non-Western areas typically served as the primitive Other against which European Enlightenment and colonialism were elevated and justified' (2002: 6). The colonial condition characterised by the 'civilising mission' was linked inextricably to notions of modernity.

The very notion of modernity suggests a temporal separation, a rupture with tradition. Hence, it was necessary to delimit the concept and to render colonial peoples as nonmodern. As Dipesh Chakrabarty points out, 'Western powers in their imperial mode saw modernity as coeval with the idea of progress. Nationalists saw in it the promise of development' (2002a: xix). What the colonial powers promised their subjects was the opportunity to be modern, to be like them. France, the birthplace of the very ideas of liberty, equality and fraternity, was at the forefront of promoting such modernity in its colonies and among its colonial subjects. It was a promise, however, that was infinitely deferred given the orientalist imperative that underpinned the European colonial project. Nevertheless, the nationalists were seduced also by these very notions of progress and development, and convinced their citizens that they were better equipped to deliver these cherished ideals.

This resulted in a rage for European modernity, a modernity that wreaked havoc with so many lives through colonial domination, world wars, racism, fascism, as well as violent decolonisation. All of these 'made Western modernity highly suspect as a model for general improvement and world progress' (Knauft 2002: 11). It was modernity that the border intellectuals understood was deeply flawed. It was precisely this recognition that gave rise to the crisis of Western humanism that the post-structuralists and postmodernists so clearly articulated.

Mahmood Mamdani argues that in the African context the colonial state governed by racism, established the distinction between settler and native by demarcating different rights for a minority White settler and majority Black 'native' population. On the one hand, it functioned on the rule of law and rights when it came to settlers who were defined as citizens and, on the other hand, it was a state that ruled over subjects who were not entitled to any of the rights associated with the settler population. It was only at the moment of decolonisation that the boundaries of civil society were extended to create an indigenous civil society. However, Mamdani points out that this was of limited significance, because independence merely de-racialised the state without doing the same in civil society (Ahluwalia 2001a; Mamdani 1996). However, in the Algerian case, the question of the settler was more complicated than the simple binary of settler and native. The Jewish settler community, for example, was often denied the very rights that the French settlers were accorded.

Subaltern studies, provincializing Europe and postcolonial studies

The Subaltern Studies project began as a result of several scholars' dissatisfaction with the ways in which traditional Indian historiography erased histories of subordinated groups. Since then, Subaltern Studies has gained a much wider audience across the world and has developed a broad interdisciplinary following.[5] A great deal of the global interest in Subaltern Studies comes from the ways in which the project is affiliated with, and constitutes part of, a larger 'postcolonial' critique. The Gramscian category of 'subaltern' as it has been deployed by Ranajit Guha and other members of the Subaltern Studies collective has become an important explanatory tool.

The 'postcolonial' affiliation of Subaltern Studies, which has no doubt led to its immense popularity, has resulted also in much critique. For example, Arif Dirlik argues that the historical innovations of the Subaltern Studies group may have appeared novel in the context of Indian historiography but were essentially an adaptation of the methods of British historians such as E.P. Thompson and Eric Hobsbawm who pioneered 'history from below' (Dirlik 1996). Dipesh Chakrabarty takes Dirlik to task for this suggestion. In an essay that documents the history of Subaltern studies, Chakrabarty traces how the Subaltern studies project developed out of dissatisfaction with modern Indian historiography into a project in which history itself as a European form of knowledge has been severely questioned. In its latest manifestation, it has further engaged with colonial discourse analysis and with the work of Homi Bhabha, Gayatri Spivak and Edward Said and has come into direct conversation with postcolonial studies. As Chakrabarty explains:

> *Subaltern Studies* was not a case of the application to Indian material of methods of historical research already worked out in the metropolitan Marxist tradition of history from below. It was in part a product of that lineage, but the nature of political modernity in colonial India made this project of history writing nothing short of an engaged critique of the academic discipline of history itself.
>
> (Chakrabarty 2002a: 19)

The Subaltern Studies project was aimed at conceptualising political modernity in India and its variegated effects on the colonial subject, such as the dual role of the peasant as a citizen. In the first role, the peasant has 'to be educated into the citizen and who therefore belongs to the time of historicism' and in the second role, the peasant, despite the lack of formal education, is already a citizen (Chakrabarty 2000: 10).

Dipesh Chakrabarty's *Provincializing Europe* grew out of the tradition of Subaltern Studies and is an attempt to 'provincialize or decenter' an 'imaginary figure that remains deeply embedded in *clichéd and shorthand forms* in some everyday habits of thought that invariably subtend attempts in the social sciences to address questions of political modernity in South Asia' (2000: 3). He argues that the very idea of ' "political modernity" – namely, the rule by modern institutions of the state bureaucracy and capitalist enterprise – is impossible to think of anywhere in the world without invoking certain categories and concepts, the genealogies of which go deep into the intellectual and even theological traditions of Europe' (3–4). These traditions and genealogies were universalised through the impetus of colonial rule even though the colonial subjects were in practice denied these much-cherished ideals. Despite this denial, it is this heritage that has not only been universalised, but has become global.

Political modernity outside Europe, in the postcolonial world, Chakrabarty argues, entails the rethinking of the conceptual gifts of nineteenth-century Europe – historicism and the idea of the political—both central to modernity itself. 'Provincializing Europe' in the postcolony means that 'European thought has a contradictory relationship to such an instance of political modernity. It is both indispensable and inadequate in helping us think through the various life practices that constitute the political and the historical' (2000: 6).

Chakrabarty is well aware of the critiques of historicism that have emanated from within the 'Western' tradition. Yet, what disturbs him is that little attention is paid to the 'deep ties that bind together historicism as a mode of thought and the formation of political modernity in the erstwhile European colonies' (2000: 7). He is careful to point out that, despite the impact of thinkers like Michel Foucault, it would be incorrect to think of 'postcolonial critiques of historicism (or the political) as simply deriving from critiques already elaborated by post-modern and post-structuralist thinkers of the West. In fact, to think this way would itself be to practice historicism, for such a thought would merely repeat the temporal structure of the statement, "first in the West, and then elsewhere" ' (6).

Provincializing Europe is not about 'native' rage and the repudiation of all things European – a type of postcolonial cleansing that entails the rejection of European thought and the return to some pure precolonial thought. Rather, it is about recognising that 'European thought is at once both indispensable and inadequate in helping us to think through the experiences of political modernity in non-Western nations, and provincializing Europe becomes the task of exploring how this thought – which is now everyone's heritage and which affects us all – may be renewed from and for the margins' (Chakrabarty 2000: 16).

Chakrabarty insists that historicism has always been conceptualised as historical time that measures the cultural distance between the West and non-West. The key purpose is not simply to dehistoricise or provincialise Europe but rather to look at the effects the former colonies have had upon European thought. Chakrabarty's problematic is to ascertain the manner in which 'we think about the global legacy of the European Enlightenment in lands far away from Europe? How do we envision or document ways of being modern that will speak to that which is shared across the world as well as to that which belongs to human cultural diversity?' (Chakrabarty 2002a: xxi).

Provincializing Europe is not only about Europe's success, its dominance over the world, but also about the manner in which that success has been checked by imperialism and postcolonial nationalism. It is in short a mode of challenging European universalism. As Chakrabarty puts it in a recent interview:

> My point in *PE* was that being modern did not involve us in thinking universals (though it may find us using universal-sounding words pragmatically and rhetorically). Yet thinking about political modernity is impossible to do without engaging some universals of 'European thought'. The problem with these universals is this: they, as thought concepts, come packaged as though they have transcended particular histories in which they were born. But being pieces of prose and language, they carry intimations of histories of belonging, which are not everybody's history. When we translate them – practically, theoretically – into our languages and practice, we make them speak to other histories of belonging, and it is how difference and heterogeneity enter these words. Or, in thinking about them and self-consciously looking for places for them in life-practices we have fabricated using them, we sometimes rediscover their own plural histories in the history of European thought.
> (Chakrabarty 2002b: 865)

The project of 'provincializing Europe', Chakarbarty points out, is one that does not as yet exist. In order to establish what it must be, he argues that it is important to see what it is *not*. It is certainly not a project of cultural relativism and it is important that it does not begin with the idea that those tropes that make Europe modern are not simply seen as being the very domain of European cultures. The point is 'not that Enlightenment rationalism is always unreasonable in itself, but rather a matter of documenting how – through what historical process – its 'reason', which was not always self-evident to everyone, has been made to look obvious far beyond the ground where it originated' (2000: 43).

Provincializing Europe is similar to Couze Venn's *Occidentalism*, in which he seeks to understand the processes through which modernity itself is refigured differently in two critical projects: post-structuralism and postcolonialism. For Venn, Occidentalism:

> … is the conceptual and historical space in which a particular narrative of the subject and a particular narrative of history have been constituted; these have become hegemonic with modernization, having effects throughout the world because of the universal scope of the project of modernity and the global reach of European colonization.
>
> (Venn 2000: 2)

In a trenchant critique, Vasant Kaiwar (2004) has argued that there are real difficulties with Dipesh Chakarbarty's analysis, in particular his claim that he is influenced by Marxism. This critique is reminiscent of the attacks on Laclau and Mouffe (1985) and the argument that it is difficult to ascertain how they continued to argue that they were Marxists when they had abandoned the Marxist project (for example, see Geras 1987). For Kaiwar, the problem is much broader than Chakarbarty enunciates it. He believes that postcolonialism itself is problematic in the way in which it renounces the universalist pretensions of Marxism and the Enlightenment project. This is all the more so in Chakarbarty's case, given the manner in which he appropriates the language of post-structuralism.

If this is the case, it is important to ask why postcolonial theory, criticism and critics have found post-structuralism and postmodernism so attractive. Is it simply that they share a similar language and that they have many concerns in common? Or is it, as the Algerian case illustrates – that, rather than European thought being provincialised in the way Chakarbarty suggests, it might well be that the border intellectuals who questioned the universality of European modernity are intimately connected with the colony itself. So, rather than assuming that it is European thought that has been provincialised, in fact the post-structualist and post-modern project has its deepest affiliations in the colony. It is in Algeria that we find the most radical disjuncture between the promise of European modernity and the reality, which demonstrated the very pitfalls of the universality of those ideas. It is here that the very antecedents of the critique of European thought can be located. This is the very site that makes post-structuralism and postmodernism fundamentally postcolonial. This does not mean that these post-isms can simply be conflated. It is important to understand how postcolonialism has developed and the manner in which the political modernity of the postcolony took on a rather different trajectory.

Alternative modernity

Arjun Appadurai (1996) and Paul Gilroy (1993) have been at the forefront of mapping out the notion of 'alternative modernities'.[6] Gilroy has suggested that Afro-modernism and the Black Atlantic need to be seen as a counterculture of modernity (117). In The Black Atlantic, he uses the ship as a metaphor to rethink modernity through the history of the Black Atlantic and the African diaspora.[7] The ship not only connects the triangular trans-Atlantic trade but also adds cultural and political dimensions that allow for a reconceptualisation of the relationship between modernity and slavery through a re-examination of the 'problems of nationality, location, identity and historical memory' (Gilroy 1993: 16). This reconceptualisation allows him to expose the limitations of post-Enlightenment thought and his project not only questions 'the credibility of a tidy, holistic conception of modernity but also ... argue[s] for the inversion of the relationship between margin and center as it has appeared within the master discources of the master race' (1993: 45). Gilroy suggests that there has been an occlusion of a black sensibility contributing to notions of modernity. He argues:

> ... that the concentrated intensity of slave experience is something that marked out Blacks as the first truly modern people, handling the nineteenth-century dilemmas and difficulties which would only become the substance of everyday life in Europe a century later.
>
> (Gilroy 1993: 221)

He is concerned to connect three nodes of the slave trade – Africa, Europe and the Americas – through a refusal to accept that slavery is merely a problem for the slaves. In short, Gilroy suggests a rethinking of modernity, because it has been linked inextricably with slavery. Michael Hanchard (1999) questions if this modernity is simply an appendage of Western modernity or whether it points towards several divergent paths of modernity.

In contrast, Hanchard suggests the conception of Afro-modernity as a means of understanding modernity as well as modern subjectivity for people of African descent. Afro-modernity, he suggests,

> ... consists of the selective incorporation of technologies, discourses, and institutions of the modern West. ... It is no mere mimicry of Western modernity but an innovation upon its precepts, forces, and features. Its contours have arisen from the encounters between people of African descent and Western colonialism not only on the African continent but also in the New World, Asia, and ultimately Europe itself.
>
> (Hanchard 1999: 247)

African modernity is intertwined with the very history of colonialism. Since then, the complicity between modern knowledge and modern regimes of power has meant that African subjects have been represented as mere consumers of universal modernity. As Partha Chaterjee has pointed out, it is because of this that 'we have tried for over a hundred years, to take our eyes away from this chimera of universal modernity and clear up a space where we might become the creators of our own modernity' (1997: 14). It is in the postcolony that we can see an alternative modernity, a modernity that is not simply a mimicry of some universal modernity but a modernity with its own peculiarities. In the age of globalisation, in the postcolony, it is a modernity fuelled by consumption.

In any number of African cities from Cape Town, Dakar, Kampala, Kinshasha, Johannesburg to Nairobi, it is evident that there is a rage for modernity. These decaying postcolonial cities are, as Alessandro Triulzi describes them, underpinned by 'street buzz'. Not only is this street buzz the new centre for politics but also a product of the chaos of everyday life marked by small traders and peddlers engaged in different ways in the practice of urban survival (1996: 79). Nowhere is this rage captured better than in the markets, which aim to lure potential customers with the latest modern commodity, fashion, or fad.

> Those who submit to that rage for modernity are not naive; they are not unaware of its Western origins, its colonial designs, its capitalist logic and its global reach. In haphazardly naming everything modern, they are exercising one of the few privileges that accrue to the latecomer: license to play with form and refigure function according to the exigencies of the situation.
>
> (Goankar 1999: 17)

However, Albert Paolini points out, 'modernity is consumed, not merely as some fetishized commodity but as an appropriated, hybridized feature of everyday life. It thus becomes as much part of the local and particular as the traditional and "indigenous" ' (1999: 169). As such, 'the alternatively modern is the social and discursive space in which the relationship between modernity and tradition is configured' (Knauft 2002: 25–26).

Decolonising forms of knowledge and postcolonial futures

Sanjay Seth has noted that reason, one of the central tenets of European modernity, has not been displaced under the weight of the attacks marshalled against it by feminism, queer theory, postmodernism, postcolonialism and a host of other contemporary theoretical currents (Seth 2004: 85). Seth calls for a pluralizing of reason so that it moves out of its Western frame. As he puts it:

> To pluralize reason is not to abandon reasoning; to deny that there is an Archimedean point from which one can criticize is not to call for an end of criticism. But it *is* to call for a reconsideration of what we think we are doing when we redescribe the past(s) of peoples that are alien to them. If there is not Reason but traditions of reasoning, not History and its representation in history writing but rather many pasts

> re-presented in many ways, then we cannot write with any presumption of epistemic privilege.
>
> (Seth 2004: 97)

In a similar vein, David Scott has pointed out that '... one way of reformulating the claim of criticism so as to answer the antifoundationalist critique of the Enlightenment without at the same time reinscribing a new rationalism is to understand criticism as a *strategic* practice' (1999: 5).

What both Seth and Scott are grappling with is the manner in which postcolonial theory problematised the certainty and universality of Western categories firmly embedded within the Enlightenment tradition. As the promise of decolonisation and liberation rapidly unravelled and the much-cherished ideal of freedom and independence seemed to be highly questionable, postcoloniality emerged out of the chaos of the late 1970s and 1980s as an alternative. This reconceptualisation was undoubtedly triggered by the publication of Edward Said's magisterial *Orientalism*. As David Scott so aptly puts it, 'Of especial concern to the new theoretical discourse was the dependence of the anticolonial nationalists on certain epistemological assumptions regarding culture, class, subjectivity, history, knowledge and so on. *This* is the moment – and political-theoretical problem-space – of postcoloniality' (1999: 11).

Postcoloniality has been concerned with disrupting Western representations of the rest of the world and in particular, to challenge the manner in which the rest was made part of the history of the West. Its central concern has been the 'decolonization of the West's theory of the non-West' (Scott 1999: 12). Whilst postcolonial theory has made major strides, a growing sense of crisis looms. This crisis suggests that the secular modern project ushered in by colonialism and the promise of 'development' is being challenged by new forms of hegemony and a critical engagement with the geopolitical machinations that drive the contemporary global condition. As Couze Venn points out,

> Humanisms, since the Enlightenment, had promised the realization of a cosmopolitan we, a *sensus communis*, secure in the ability to determine the future on the basis of consensus and reason. Modernity has failed to deliver on this and other promises, unable to reconcile the diversity of cultures, for it could not separate its avowed goal of universal emancipation and liberation from its own history of subjugation.
>
> (Venn 2000: 15)

This crisis renders a new role for postcolonial criticism and demands that it engages in a 'critical interrogation of the practice, modalities and projects through which modernity inserted itself into and altered the lives of the colonized' (Venn 2000: 17). David Scott's intervention is somewhat different from Dipesh Chakrabarty's project of provincialising Europe. For Scott, what is important is not the mere 'decentring' of Europe but rather a 'critical interrogation of its practices, modalities and projects through which the *varied forms of its insertion* into the lives of the colonized were constructed and organized' (Scott 1999: 26).

Scott urges a new approach to colonialism, one in which Europe is historicised in a different way in order to 'bring into focus the differentia in the political rationalities through which its colonial projects were constructed' (1999: 51). He argues that the Left is currently embroiled in a theoretical impasse that impacts on postcolonial criticism. This impasse is particularly marked by the absence of the political. Two discursive contexts, postcommunism and post-structuralism, frame the manner in which we approach the present. In the aftermath of the collapse of communism, the defining tropes of resistance that were at the core of much anticolonial resistance appear to be inadequate. We are, Scott argues, inhabiting a world without alternatives, which necessitates that what the 'criticism of our present ought to be about is re-examining the normative vocabulary of our social and political hopes' (134). He notes:

> ... postcolonial criticism, like other orientations of the cultural Left, has ... privileged the "responsibility to otherness" over the "responsibility to act" – the opening up of cognitive space for the play of difference over the affirmation of institutional frameworks that embody normative political values and normative political objectives.
>
> (Scott 1999: 135)

Postcolonial criticism has focused far too often on the epistemological rather than on strategy, and it is because of this that 'the political *as such* does not appear' (Scott 1999: 141). Postcolonial criticism has been implicitly dependent upon the spectre of socialism, which was posited as a real alternative to capitalism in the anticolonial struggles of the twentieth century. It is the lack of alternatives and the triumph of neoliberalism that renders postcolonial discourses as lacking a political project. In response to this crisis, postcolonialism has necessarily to mark its distance from the 'Enlightenment project of both Marxism and liberalism' and construct 'a problematized relation to the claims and categories of our political modernity' (149).

Scott points out that the politics of liberation that confronted Frantz Fanon and the postcolony are no longer appropriate for the current epoch. The present configuration necessitates that we question the fundamental premises of the politics that underpinned notions of emancipation and resistance. As Scott puts it,

> We stand, I suspect, in an historical predicament in which the old languages of Left politics – that is to say, the oppositional languages of emancipation – are no longer effective. And therefore the question that arises for us (or which *ought* to arise for us) is: What is the yield and

> what is the limit of the Fanonian narrative of liberation in the cognitive-political present?
>
> (1999: 199–200)

What Scott is pointing towards is the failure of the middle-class nationalist project that brought decolonisation to the postcolony. What is required now, Scott argues, is an amalgamation of Fanon and Foucault. This is necessary because:

> … it is possible to fissure the Fanonian narrative of liberation and the alienation/realization model of the political subject it depends upon without foreclosing the possibility of a politics of imagining the project of politics/ethics more generally …
>
> (1999: 219)

The amalgamation of Fanon and Foucault is only possible because of the impact of the postcolony in defining their very theoretical precepts. They are indeed the products of the postcolonial condition.

The sense of departing but not arriving in the case of border intellectuals, such as Cixous and Derrida, illustrates the transformative nature of postcolonial societies. It shows how the trace of the colony remains within the postcolonial subject. It further demonstrates the difficulty of being located within a single culture and the opportunities that such a specular position offers. It occludes the distinctions between the coloniser and colonised. It speaks of the kind of globalisation that implicates different cultures within each other. It helps to break down binaries such as metropolitan–colonial, developed–underdeveloped and civilised–primitive. By drawing on what I have elsewhere termed 'postcolonial inflections' (Ahluwalia 2001a), we will see how postcolonial subjects confront their colonial legacy and define their postcolonial future.

For me, mapping the Algerian connections in this book is not an exposé, or an attempt to bring these post-structuralists to account, or even to reclaim a colonial legacy that has been suppressed. As a postcolonial subject, I am all too aware of the manner in which one can be dehumanised by practices of othering. Rather, I am concerned with how these strategies are being deployed to marginalise the very enterprise of postcolonial studies as merely an adjunct, progeny, by-product or offshoot of post-structuralism. How are we to treat the criticisms of Ahmad and Dirlik? It is the failure of post-structuralism to confront or acknowledge the colonial experience, the locatedness of Algeria that has allowed such a conflation. Furthermore, postcolonialism's concerns about identity and the disruptive effects of colonisation enable us to understand the source of inspiration of the post-structuralist project. Is it not proper to see Althusser, Bourdieu, Cixous, Derrida, Fanon, Foucault, Lyotard and Memmi as Franco-Maghrebians who have sought to challenge the very epistemology of French colonialism and its ideas of cultural superiority? In the writings of these Franco-Maghrebians who had, or have, a foot firmly planted in Algeria, we see their impact on socialism, humanism, Marxism, post-structuralism, postmodernism, postcolonialism and the project of modernity itself. Above all, it is the spectre of Algeria that sharpened their focus and forced them to challenge the orthodoxy that sustained the cultural practices of the French imperial project.

Scope and organisation

This book is divided into six chapters. The next chapter (Chapter 2) examines the French colonial project in Algeria, a country which it is argued, is most significant to the formation of France's belief in its own cultural superiority. The writings of Alexis de Tocqueville illustrate the way in which the importance of Algeria became an important precept for all subsequent administrations. Algeria was conceived simply as an extension of France. In order to understand the complexities of the French colonial project, it is juxtaposed to British colonialism.

Chapter 3 considers the influence of the postcolony on three thinkers whose names are inseparable from Algeria – Jean-Paul Sartre, Frantz Fanon and Albert Camus. Each, in his own way, was insider and outsider to both Algeria and France. The manner in which they conceptualised their views of liberation and emancipation was integrally linked to their politics and inevitably influenced their entire corpus of work. Their politics was necessarily born within the context of Algeria and the struggle for liberation. Critically, Sartre's role in fissuring the grand narrative of humanism and his influence on Fanon is considered.

Chapter 4 discusses the effects of Derrida's colonial origin upon his theory and considers, the implications, for his theory, of the suppression of that origin. The chapter examines his Algerian locatedness. It questions the impact of his formative years on his later work and the implications of this for deconstructive theory or Derridean logocentrism. It questions whether his overall project reflects his colonial roots and the tensions which arise out of being relocated within a new culture. Is the fate of Derrida of belonging and not belonging in both French and Algerian culture, of occupying that in-between space, part of his own alterity which inevitably makes its way into his writings, relevant to understanding his work? It considers his profound influence on contemporary thought and argues that it needs to be contextualised against the backdrop of Algeria and the experience of colonisation.

In Chapter 5, the work of the Algerian-born, French feminist scholar Hélène Cixous is considered. Cixous' work has been highly influential within feminism and is embedded firmly between theory and fiction. She has been deeply influenced by her Maghrebin colleague, Jacques Derrida. Her work is intimately associated with écriture feminine, feminine writing. Her writing methodology seeks to create a social space and community. For Cixous, the text has a great deal of power and it is through the text that she seeks to imagine another world – a world informed by the other that she first encountered in Algeria.

In the final chapter, the work of perhaps the most influential thinkers of the twentieth century: Louis Althusser, Pierre Bourdieu, Michel Foucault and Jean-François Lyotard is examined. These thinkers were all influenced by their experiences in the postcolony. The Algerian War of independence deeply influenced a whole generation of scholars who were disillusioned by the promise of the French colonial project and the violence and dehumanisation that ensued. In each of their works, we see the influence of the postcolony and its impact on modernity and its discontents. All the thinkers in this book are doubly inscribed as both insiders and outsiders to France and the postcolony. Hence, they are well placed to subvert the anthropological and ethnographic gaze. Algeria was, and remains, in the French imagination its most significant other.

Chapter 2

Algeria and colonisation

> I have no doubt that we can raise on the coast of Africa a great monument to the glory of our country.
>
> (Alexis de Tocqueville)

> In Algeria, however inconsistent the policy of French governments since 1830, the inexorable process went on to make Algeria French. First the land was taken from the natives and their buildings were occupied; then French settlers gained control of the cork-oak forests and mineral deposits. … For several decades after 1830 'booty capital' ran the economy, the native population decreased, and settler groups increased … while France reproduced itself in Algeria, Algerians were relegated to marginality and poverty.
>
> (Edward Said)

Algeria is located directly across the Mediterranean from France's south coast and has been linked to France since at least the early 1500s as part of its commercial activities. Algeria came under French rule in 1830 as a way to recover lost pride and to gain national glory when Algiers was forcibly seized from the Ottomans. The French monarchy of Charles X was in disarray and an invasion of Algiers was considered as an effective means to bolster a monarchy in crisis. The French had blockaded Algiers for three years after what was considered an insult by the Dey of Algiers to the French consul. In 1830, the failure of the blockade was the pretext for a military invasion. Although the unpopular monarchy could not be saved, French rule of Algeria continued, despite opposition, on the grounds that it was necessary for national glory and prestige. In 1834, France annexed and occupied the territory and placed it under the administrative control of a Governor-General. Initially, French rule in Algeria was restricted to the coastal areas of Oran and Bône. From its inception, there was a great deal of resistance to the French occupation. One of the most well-known challenges came from Emir Abd al-Kader, the head of a Moroccan force, who gained hero status in 1832 for trying to defeat and remove the French from Oran (Stone 1997: 30). However, by 1851, the French had established rule over three civil territories that included Algiers,

Oran and Constantine, all of which were deemed to be integral parts of France and under the rule of the French administration.

Over the next forty years, France was able to pacify resistance and control the country albeit at a huge cost of nearly a million lives. From the beginning of colonisation, there was a concerted effort to expropriate land and encourage settlement. This was by no means a unique conception for, throughout Europe's domain, colonial rule was premised upon the notion that a colony was to serve the interests of the metropole. Colonies were to be ruled at a minimal cost whilst they were expected to return profits through both raw materials as well as new markets for metropolitan goods. The search for these new colonies was predicated on the belief that European nations had a right to rule foreign lands given the superiority of European civilisation over non-Europeans. As Victor Hugo put it, 'conquest … is civilization marching against barbarousness. It is an enlightened people finding a people in the night. We are the Greeks of the world; it is up to us to illuminate the world' (cited in Naylor 2000: 16). It was in this spirit that Prime Minister Ferry stated in 1885:

> Can you deny, can anyone deny that there is more justice, more material and moral order, more equity, more social virtue in North Africa since France carried out its conquest? … Is it possible to deny that in India, despite the unfortunate episodes which have been encountered in the history of its conquest, there is today infinitely greater justice, enlightenment, order, public and private virtue since the English conquest?
>
> (cited in Aldrich 1996: 98)

Algeria and the French colonial project

In the nineteenth century, France's instability as a result of its domestic regime meant that imperialism was seen, even by many liberals, not only as a way to unite the nation but also as a form of glorification. Alexis De Tocqueville in his first writings on Algeria, when he was trying to get elected to Parliament, envisaged precisely such a role for Algeria. His ideas were no doubt influenced by the example of the British who 'seemed to show that empire could help secure a sense of national identity and cohesion during difficult periods of political transition' (Pitts 2000: 302). At the same time, he envisioned a colony where disparate peoples, the Arabs and the French, could be united into a single national identity. Tocqueville's belief that colonisation was a solution to France's domestic crisis illustrates 'certain ill-known contours of his liberalism: its susceptibility to the notion of national glory as a substitute for political virtue; its willing exclusion of unfamiliar peoples from moral consideration for the sake of national consolidation' (Pitts 2000: 298; Kohn 2008; Richter 1963).

Tocqueville eventually made two visits to Algeria in order to see the colony firsthand, first in 1841 and then again in 1846. Based on these visits, his writings provide an insight into France's colonial project. Mary Lawlor points out that Tocqueville's work on Algeria was 'on the one hand quite unethical and on the other rather enlightened' (Lawlor 1959: 175). This ambivalence is a reference to his avowed imperialism coupled with his liberalism. Tocqueville's commitment to the colonisation of Algeria was based on the belief that it was part of a national project that would unite a divided France and gain the nation respect in Europe. His initial vision of Algeria was to establish a colony that was 'a great monument to the glory of our country' (Tocqueville 2001: xx). He argued:

> We should set out to create not a colony properly speaking in Algeria, but rather the extension of France itself across the Mediterranean. It is not a matter of creating a new people, with its own laws, its customs, its interests, and sooner or later its separate nationality, but of implanting in Africa a population that resembles us in everything. If this goal cannot be attained immediately, it is at least the only one for which we should constantly and actively strive.
>
> (Tocqueville 2001: xxvii)

Tocqueville's concern for the indigenous population, however, was short-lived as colonialism became integrally tied to the idea that the colony had to serve France's economic interest as well as give it a sense of prestige. After his first visit, he came to believe that if France was to maintain its rule it had to accept the reality that violence and resources were essential to consolidate a French hold on Algeria. He became convinced of the futility of racial integration and concluded that relations would be characterised by violence. His earlier plans for assimilating the Arab population and establishing European civilisation in Algeria gave way to the idea that the French at best could 'hope to weaken indigenous hostility to French rule and win the population's support not through ideas or integration but by demonstrating their common interests through effective imperial governance' (Tocqueville 2001: xxvii). Nevertheless, Tocqueville remained firmly committed to France's colonial project and throughout his life believed that Algeria's colonisation was central to France's reputation and interest. It was a commitment that all subsequent French governments strongly adhered to, and is best captured by Charles De Gaulle's assertion that its loss 'would produce a decline which could cost us our independence. To keep it … is to stay great' (cited in Sorum 1997: 187).

Above all else, what underpinned the colonial project was the belief in French civilisation's superiority and its assumed right to rule foreign lands. The colonialists believed that 'Europeans bore a responsibility to bring civilisation to the uncivilised; this mission civilsatrice (civilising mission) provided a moral mandate for expansion' (Aldrich 1996: 92). In the case of Algeria, this was all the more important given its proximity. Algeria was France's most significant other, the very site that confirmed France's belief in its superiority. In all the various European projects of colonialism during the nineteenth and twentieth centuries, the French colonisation of Algeria came closest to the idea of France overseas through the policy of 'assimilation'. For France, the 'civilising mission' of colonialism became more of a reality with the view that its overseas colonies had to be subjected to the same laws and values as that of France.

Assimilation was a policy that, Jean Martin argues, was 'directed at removing all the differences between colonies and the metropole by endowing them with the same administrative, fiscal, judicial, social and other regimes as the metropole and at giving their inhabitants full civic rights and obliging them to the same duties as citizens in France itself' (cited in Aldrich 1996: 110). It was the assimilation policy that was to determine the relations between the coloniser and colonised. In practise, however, as Michael Crowder points out, 'the French when confronted with people they considered barbarians, believed it their mission to convert them into Frenchmen' (cited in Khapoya 1998: 120). The implication of such a policy were that education had to be in French because it was seen to be the key to civilisation itself. Indeed, so rigidly was this rule applied that Arabic itself was banned for the Algerians.[1]

Colonial Algeria: the consolidation of the settlers

Algeria, however, remained largely outside the configurations that governed the bulk of the French colonies because it was seen as an extension of France, making it perhaps the most prized of all French colonial possessions. It rapidly became both constitutionally as well as legally an important part of France. In 1848, Algeria officially became a part of France in the form of three départements. As Benjamin Stora notes:

> An Algeria made up of three French departments would forever 'Gallicize' the territories of the central Maghreb. … Its aim was to ensure the absolute and complete subjugation of the population to the needs and interests of colonization. The colons enjoyed full rights, the colonized were 'subjects' not 'citizens', liable to special provisions: tallage, corvee, and detention without due process.
>
> (Stora 2001: 6)

From the beginning of colonisation, there was a concerted effort to expropriate land and encourage settlement. The settlers, the colons or *pieds-noirs* were mostly peasant farmers or had working-class origins. By the end of the nineteenth century, the colons had established farms and vineyards and with 'French-style cities and European settlers, Algeria was well on its way to becoming Algérie française. The indigenous Berbers and Arabs had been relegated to the background, a picturesque population living on the fringes of their own country' (Aldrich 1996: 28).

It was this belief that Algeria was an integral part of France that rendered decolonisation so problematic, making it both protracted and violent.

Algeria was the most important and profitable of France's colonies and was equivalent perhaps to what India was for Britain. It rapidly attained an influential role in virtually all aspects of French life and remains even today an important part of the French imagination. As Philip Naylor points out, since the inception of Algerian colonialism in 1830:

> France often identified its power and potential, its grandeur, and independence, in relation to Algeria. This profoundly differentiated Algeria, even with its obvious strategic geopolitical significance, from the métropole's other overseas territories. Algeria particularly appealed to France's imagination of itself as a great power, an acutely sensitised national identity.
>
> (2000: 12)

It is not surprising, then, that the nature of French intellectuals' relationship with French identity is tied to the very different nature of British and French colonialism. The French colonial political system 'which placed a premium on standardisation of laws and institutions throughout the country and centralisation of power in Paris, was not congenial to British-style self government' (Aldrich 1996: 110). In the British colonies, there was little pretence that colonial subjects had to be treated as equals or that they enjoyed the same rights as their metropolitan counterparts. As Edward Said pointed out, 'France's empire, according to one of its most famous historians, though no less interested than Britain's in profit, plantations and slaves, was energized by "prestige"' (Said 1993: 204).

In the French Empire, Algeria was significant not only because of its proximity but also because it was deemed to be a colony of settlement. Nevertheless, the colonisation of Algeria was no different from other settler colonies. Once Marshal Bugeaud had successfully invaded Algeria, he argued before the Chamber of Deputies that, 'wherever good water and fertile land are found, settlers must be installed without questioning whose land it may be' (cited in Davidson 1978: 119). Although settlement was not carried out immediately, the French inevitably paved the way by challenging and imposing their conceptions of land ownership. By 1856, an official French text recognised that 'natives' unable to prove ownership 'have been treated as mere users of the land, or tenants who may have been displaced at will, so as to free land for colonisation' (119).

A series of resettlement programmes with land-owning inducements were introduced to encourage French settlement in the colony. There was a concerted effort to 'modernise' the colony with the introduction of new systems of infrastructure, educational and governmental institutions. The initial migrants to Algeria were mostly military personnel who had little experience in agriculture and most of them returned to France. Between 1842 and 1846, 198,000 Europeans arrived in the colony but 118,000 departed. In addition, the colony was plagued by disease, especially cholera, which had a deleterious effect on the nascent settler population. The French government also used Algeria as a penal colony, much like the British did with Australia, and many of these prisoners chose to remain in the colony.

Despite the push for settlement, nineteenth-century France was not suited to a great deal of emigration as a result of falling birth rates as well as an abundance of land. Napoleon III, however, was attracted to the idea of establishing a colony with a significant settler presence. A number of French settlers eventually moved to Algeria lured by the prospect of a better life. In addition, a large number of settlers came from around the Mediterranean with France's encouragement. The settlers were seen as the drivers of modernisation, and it was their sweat and labour that became legendary. Algeria was rapidly being developed as the site from which agricultural goods could be supplied to French consumers.

The idea that Algeria was an extension of France really gained prominence after the German occupation of Alsace and Lorraine in 1870. For example, Cardinal Lavigerie, speaking to the Christians of the region, extolled the benefits of Algeria: 'Algeria, French Africa, opens its doors and its arms to you. Here you will find for yourselves, for your children, for your families, lands wider and more fertile than those you have left in the hands of the [German] invader' (cited in Davidson 1978: 97). It was this loss that fuelled the idea of the colonies as an extension of the French nation. It was this that led to the idea of assimilation with the implied suggestion that this was different to the British idea of indirect rule. The notion that the French did not have to resort to indirect rule because the colonies were an extension of the French nation is one that needs to be considered along with the emphasis that both systems gave to the civilising mission. Nevertheless, there were considerable differences:

> Where the British model supposed nation-building in Africa as the gateway to equality of rights, the French model called for assimilation to the nation already built, the French nation sacred and eternal, guarantee of all virtues, source of all culture worth the name and mother of every admissible ambition.
>
> (Davidson 1978: 187)

The loss of Alsace and Lorraine had a major effect on the French psyche and led to a renewed interest in French geographical societies and questions of empire. The linkages between knowledge and power in the development of French imperialism were exemplified by the address of the President to the second international congress of geographical sciences:

> Gentlemen, Providence has dictated to us the obligation of knowing the earth and making conquest of it. The supreme command is one of the imperious duties inscribed on our intelligences and on our activities. Geography, that science which inspires such beautiful devotedness and

> in whose name so many victims have been sacrificed, has become the philosophy of the earth.
>
> (cited in Said 1993: 205)

Despite these calls for the French to settle in Algeria, a large number of settlers continued to come from other European countries. By 1886, 219,000 French citizens resided in Algeria with an additional 211,000 other Europeans, mostly from Spain and Italy. Algeria, at least in terms of its settler population, 'provided refuge to a heterogenous population held together by the desire to make a new life in better conditions' (Aldrich 1996: 145). What united this rather heterogeneous settler population was their belief that they were superior to the indigenous population as well as their links to France, which was seen as the guardian of all Europeans within the colony.

Under French rule, Algerian lands were confiscated under the Warnier Law of 1873 in order to accommodate a growing settler population. The French authorities assumed power through various forms of legislation which usually meant the disenfranchisement of the indigenous population. This land was then redistributed as the authorities wished to the settler population. An 1895 official enquiry reported that indigenous Algerians had lost more than five million hectares of land. This figure had increased to 7.7 million hectares by 1936, representing more than 40 per cent of the land dispossessed as a result of French colonialism. Critically, this was the most productive land in the country. Inevitably, this resulted in 'the pauperisation of Algerians, increasing possibilities for settlers to enrich themselves, and rising hatred of the French' (Aldrich 1996: 218).

It was the aggrandisement of land by such methods that transformed Algerian agriculture. This meant that a predominately cereal-producing country providing for its population was transformed into an export enclave and became an integral part of the French imperial system. Basil Davidson points out that the impact of this transformation was so acute that by the middle of the 1950s cereal production remained at the levels of the 1880s: 'with cereals a staple of Algerian diet, this meant deepening hunger. If each inhabitant in 1871 could have five quintals of cereal a year, according to another informed guess, this total had been halved by 1940' (1978: 119). This transformation of Algerian agriculture was centred on producing wine, a drink that was not consumed locally, which was to have severe implications for the food resources of the local population. As Robert Aldrich points out, 'although metropolitan France was a major producer of wine, the North African colonies provided vin ordinaire; wine accounted for four-fifths of Algeria's export earnings' (1996: 165).

This transformation of Algeria was driven by the privatisation of land in the colony often through political, economic and military means. The increase in land prices was the direct result of the development of viticulture aimed at serving bourgeois tastes in France. This adverse affect on land prices meant a heightened exploitation of indigenous labour. This further exploitation of the indigenous population meant that they 'were forced to increase their production, to obtain a sufficient financial return to gain further access to the use of marginal land, simply to ensure their survival' (Samers 1997: 40).

The colonial myth that Algeria was built on the sweat and hard labour of the French pioneers toiling on the soil was thus highly problematic. The agriculture system was based on large corporate or large individual landholders who were dependent upon indigenous labour. This meant that:

> ... the typical European colon did not become a farmer but became instead a small businessman, a tradesman, or government employee, or he involved himself in the construction or other support industries. A typical European who came to Algeria expecting to become a farmer might well end up opening a bar to serve wine and absinthe to French soldiers. The hard labour in both the rural and urban economies was supplied by the dispossessed Arabs and Berbers.
>
> (Rudey 1992: 72)

Formal colonisation entailed the heightening of political identities within the country. Relations between the settler population and the French government were based on the notion that these settlers were 'Algerians' who placed demands on the colonial government (Zack 2002). There was also a small Jewish population that had been resident for centuries and recognized as an official minority under the Ottoman Empire.[2] However, they were not recognised by the French settlers as equal and tensions between the communities remained throughout the colonial period.

In 1870, the French state in Paris replaced the military regime that had ruled in Algeria since the advent of colonization with a civil government dominated by the French settler minority. From that point onwards, Algeria became firmly entrenched in the hands of the colons who had settled in the country. They were now able to determine the future and had a huge impact on metropolitan policy towards Algeria. The army, which had dominated affairs until then, 'was no longer allowed to impose its will; the rule of the saber had to end. As an instrument of conquest, it had no choice but to hand over responsibility to those who could make the colony profitable' (Stora 2001: 5).

During the 1870s and 1880s, the central government pursued an official policy of assimilation, with the expressed intention of folding Algeria into France, and facilitated all sorts of economic development. Nevertheless, the ideas of superiority that the settlers held over the Arab and Berber population meant that the notions of assimilation that were prominent in theory rapidly gave way to the interests of the settler population on the ground. As Edward Said so aptly put it, 'natives and their lands were not to be treated as entities that could be made French, but as possessions the immutable characteristics of which required separation and subservience, even though this did not rule out the mission civilisatrice' (Said 1993: 206).

In its attempts to make Algeria 'French', the French government gave citizenship rights to the 35,000 Jews in Algeria in 1870 after the passing of the Crémieux laws and, in 1889, to the European settlers from other countries. At the time, the majority of the 300,000 settlers were not of French origin but migrants from other southern European countries (Wood 1998). The effect of granting citizenship was that the colons now had an ally community. Ian Clegg has argued that because of the *pieds-noirs'* different backgrounds they had a 'desperate need for identity'. They discovered 'their basic unity in the defence of the privileges accorded them by the French administration and their hostility to the Muslims. This appeared in an assertion of their basic Frenchness, in fervour for things that far surpassed its equivalent in the metropolis' (Clegg 1971: 27–28). If there were differences between the different migrant communities initially, over time these diminished as they came together against the Arabs whom they had dispossessed. These diverse migrant groups forged a common identity, so that by the time of the Algerian War of Independence these settlers saw themselves as 'French Algerians' who wished to protect their way of life. As Pierre Bourdieu pointed out, 'the European gradually created an environment that reflected his own image …, a world in which he no longer felt himself to be a stranger and in which, by a natural reversal, the Algerian was finally considered to be a stranger' (Bourdieu 1962: 131).

The 1870 Crémieux laws which granted French citizenship to Algeria's Jews evoked a great deal of opposition from the Arabs, who were not allowed to obtain citizenship unless they renounced their traditional Islamic legal status and fulfilled other stringent requirements. This placed the Jewish population in an ambivalent position where they were legally granted French citizenship but were in reality often marginalised. It further disenfranchised the predominantly Muslim indigenous population who were treated as inferior and every aspect of their lives problematised with even the most basic of rights denied to them. They were denied citizenship unless they renounced Islam and embraced Christianity and even then, they were not accorded the same rights and privileges accorded to the French settler community. The distinction between citizen and subject was important, with the Arab and Berber population accorded the latter status. This distinction between citizen and subject has been extensively explored by Mahmood Mamdani in his analysis of civil society in Africa:

> The division between the citizen and subject, the non-native and the native, was characteristic of all colonial situations. It was not unique to Africa. Specific to Africa, though was the closeting of the subject populations in a series of separate containers, each under the custody of a Native Authority …
>
> (1996: 49)

Although Mamdani is talking about British rule, this distinction was just as relevant to French Algeria. Although in theory, indigenous locals were eligible to obtain citizenship, it was rare, and meant a renunciation of their own culture and religion. The local population was subject to a system of indirect rule under the Code de l'indigénat. This code allowed a coercive legal system to operate in which the police and the judicial administrative structure were accorded free rein in ensuring compliance on the part of the Arabs. Ironically, the code that was established in 1834 became more repressive at the very time that the settlers were provided with greater autonomy and accessibility to basic rights.

By the 1890s, while there was a sizable French settler population in the country, nevertheless the identity that people adopted at different times was highly contingent and it was not always clear what the terms 'French' or 'Algerian' meant in different political contexts. As Zack points out, the manner in which one chose to identify oneself in relation to others:

> ... as 'Jew', 'French', 'neo-French', 'Algerian', 'native' – were becoming formally embedded within the conditions, practices, interactions, and institutions of every day political life in Algeria. A settler may have been 'French' when requesting aid at the public assistance office in central Algiers, a 'Valencian' at the café in his local Bab-el-Oued neighborhood, and an 'Algerian' around election time.
>
> (2002: 65)

Although the Jewish population had gained citizenship, the French settler population remained largely hostile towards them. Antagonism escalated in the mid-1890s after the Dreyfus Affair, the famous scandal in which a Jewish army captain was convicted of spying on behalf of the Germans. In Algeria, the Dreyfus Affair paved the way for rabid anti-Semitism. The anti-Jewish fervour began in Oran and culminated in riots there in May 1897. This anti-Jewishness was marked by persecutions in both everyday as well as official life. The ascendancy of the movement in '1897–98 in Algiers got settlers with closer ties to France to identify as "French antijuifs" and those of other backgrounds to identify as "Algerian antijuifs." For the moment, hatred of the Jews made them allies' (Zack 2002: 68). The identity 'French' now became associated with metropolitan France, the administration and Republicanism, whilst 'Algerian' was considered to be coterminous with antijudaisme, and antirepublicanism. The direct intervention of the French state was necessary to bring about an end to the anti-Jewish campaign. Nevertheless, a strong anti-Jewish element remained albeit that it was muted. It was this anti-Jewish movement that helped to consolidate identities:

> The crise did accomplish the task of setting the 'French' apart from all who were not – 'Algerians', 'Jews', 'native Muslims', 'criminals', 'subversives', and 'clerics'. Even if the crise antijuive did not draw a clear line around the group of 'French', it helped consolidate a boundary between the 'French' and other groups.
>
> (Zack 2002: 74)

By the 1900s, the policy of assimilation gave way to the idea of 'association', which allowed 'greater flexibility for administrative, legal, and financial policy' (Aldrich 1996: 110). Although in theory this policy of equality was promoted, in reality it only applied to the white French settlers. Indeed, it was not until 1914 that the first black African was elected to represent Senegal under the system that granted some colonies representation in Paris (Chamberlain 1985: 56). In 1946, France reorganised its colonies into the French Union with a number of colonies designated 'Associated States'. Under this configuration, the distinction between citizens and subjects in the Union was to be abolished. Despite the rhetoric, the distinction remained until 1958 when Charles de Gaulle returned to power. Under de Gaulle, the union was replaced by the French Community. However, the community did not last long, as the 'winds of change' that were blowing through the British colonies affected the French colonies and a rapid process of decolonization ensued across the French empire.

In Algeria, however, the settlers had a stronghold on the government and any notion that the indigenous population was to have any role to play in the government was vehemently denied. Furthermore, as Algeria was considered to be an integral part of France, these machinations were seen as being irrelevant. Not only were the Arabs and Berbers denied a role but also the relations between the communities continued to be based on the notion of French superiority and a hierarchy of races and civilisations. It was not surprising then that in 1910 the ardent supporter of French colonialism Jules Harmand continued to argue that:

> … we belong to the superior race and civilization, still recognizing that, while superiority confers rights, it imposes strict obligations in return. The basic legitimation of conquest over native peoples is the conviction of our superiority, not merely our mechanical, economic, and military superiority, but our moral superiority. Our dignity rests on that quality, and it underlies our right to direct the rest of humanity. Material power is nothing but a means to that end.
>
> (cited in Said 1993: 17)

This meant that Algeria continued to be seen as a colony of settlement with new settlers being encouraged by the French government. The European settlement of the colony, however, was predicated on the confiscation of the country's most productive resources and the destruction of the indigenous political, cultural, social and economic system. Algeria had to be restructured to meet the ever-growing needs of a colonial economy that increasingly demanded a cheap reservoir of labour to meet the needs of the settler population in both rural and urban locations. In this, the colony was no different from other settler colonies. As Benjamin Stora points out, from 1871 to 1919 more than 215 million acres of land were expropriated from the indigenous population which the state, colons and major companies had divided up among themselves (2001: 7). The colons in the department of Algiers managed to quadruple their holdings during that period (from 250,000 to 1 million acres).

The rise of nationalism and decolonisation

As in other colonial situations, Algerian writers were at the forefront of the struggle. Through their writings, they imagined and paved the way for a new liberated world. They began by proving their competence in the French language, in a desire to demonstrate that they were capable of emulating the coloniser's language. This, however, gave way to a new wave of writers who were keen to discover a pure precolonial Algerian personality. The evolution of these writers can be traced along much the same lines as Kwame Anthony Appiah (1993). By the 1950s, a newfound spirit emerged and writers began to establish a new national consciousness that they were keen to liberate from colonialism itself. In contrast, metropolitan literature presented Algeria as a tabula rasa: 'as a virgin, even vacant, territory offering spectacular opportunities for France' (Naylor 2000: 15). These writers' actions were paralleled in the politics of the day.

In Algeria, although French colonialism was strongly resisted from its inception, the antecedents of modern nationalism arose from within the French colonial system – the product of the education that emphasised notions of equality, justice and liberty. As in other colonial enterprises, the French cultivated a small indigenous elite who, infused with French values and education, eventually challenged the very foundations of the colonial system of rule. At the same time, they became the champions of the Algerian nationalist demand for independence. Initially, this resistance was linked inextricably with Islam and the call for more Koranic schools as well as the push for the recognition of Arabic as an official language in schools in conjunction with French, a demand that was resoundingly denied. However, it was in France itself, in the heart of the metropole, that Arab immigrants began to push for independence. At a small public meeting in Paris in 1924, Hadj Ali shouted, 'It's our complete independence we want. We've had enough of your sympathy, we want to be masters in our own home' (cited in Davidson 1978: 195).

The full-blown Algerian nationalist movement developed between the two World Wars, initially demanding basic civil rights for all indigenous peoples. Not surprisingly, this challenge to colonial rule occurred at the very time that the settlers were reaping massive economic benefits from the development of the colony. Although the colonial state attempted to give the nationalist movement certain concessions, the French settlers, who had attained political representation in the National Assembly, effectively prevented these concessions from being granted. Nevertheless, support for the notion of independence continued to grow amongst Arab immigrants as they encountered a great deal of racism in France. This nascent nationalism found expression in 1926 in the formation of the Étoile Nord-Africaine led by Messali Hadj with the support of the French Communist Party. They eventually split over the claim that the French communists had little ability to understand the colonial situation from other than a French perspective. In May 1936, when the Popular Front government came to power in France, there appeared to be some progress. The new government promised to improve conditions in Algeria for the entire population and even contemplated granting citizenship to a small elite Muslim population. Predictably, the proposal was met with strong opposition by the settler population.

The party was eventually banned in 1937 following protests by the Algerian government. Messali and his colleagues immediately formed another political party, the Parti du Peuple Algérien (PPA). The party's aims were to seek 'neither assimilation nor separation, [from France], but emancipation' (Davidson 1978: 196). This agenda allowed Messali to organise in Algeria with some 4000 supporters demonstrating for the PPA in Algiers. However, the party was banned on the eve of the Second World War.

In the aftermath of the Second World War, the colonial state tried to draw Muslims into the structures of administration, but by that time strong oppositional views of the French as the oppressors, coupled with the widespread belief in the need for armed resistance, meant that such token gestures were no longer enough to placate the demands for liberation. By the 1950s, the Algerian nationalist movement had organised itself and was promoting change through violence. At the centre of the ensuing cycle of violence was the settler population, which was unwilling to voluntarily relinquish the privileges they had gained over more than a century at the expense of the local population. As Benjamin Stora puts it:

> The rift had widened between the majority of Muslim Algerians and the European minority. Plebeians form the cities (the underclass, the unemployed), the proletariat, and the Algerian peasantry had experienced the power of collective action; a new generation was making its entrance, one that would make armed struggle an absolute principle. Nine years later, the Algerian War would begin.
>
> (Stora 2001: 22)

The Algerian War

By the time the War of Independence broke out in 1954 there were nearly a million Europeans in Algeria, with a significant number being naturalised citizens. Nearly 80 per cent of them were born in Algeria and they strongly identified themselves as 'Algerian-French' in contrast to the indigenous Algerians. Above all else, they were absolutely committed to retaining Algeria as French. This inevitably pitted the nationalist movement against the colonial state and set the stage for a protracted Algerian War of Independence led by the National Liberation Front (Front de Libération Nationale, FLN) and the National Liberation Army (Armée de libération nationale, ALN).

In March 1954, Ahmed Ben Bella set up a revolutionary committee in Egypt and in November, the FLN declared war on the French, launching attacks on key government positions. The response of the French government was to launch a massive counteroffensive that ultimately led the FLN to engage in a guerrilla war, fighting nearly 400,000 French troops who were deployed to the colony to quell the resistance. The large deployment of troops was clearly a recognition that Algeria was different from any other colonial possession; it was a legal extension of metropolitan France and it was that 'fact that made it possible, in contrast to Indochina, to send French soldiers as part of their national military service. Nearly an entire generation of Frenchmen from all walks of life performed their required service in Algeria' (Derderian 2002: 29).

The most protracted violence occurred after the Battle of Algiers, when three FLN women bombed a popular café. The war of independence meant, inevitably, that reprisals and counter-reprisals were directed at the population at large. The Algerian War had an immense cost, with both sides encountering heavy losses. As Robert Aldrich points out:

> In 1962, Paris admitted that 12,000 soldiers fighting for the French (including 9000 Frenchmen, 1200 Legionnaires and 1250 Muslims) had been killed, as well as 2500 other French sympathisers who had taken arms. French authorities estimated the Algerian death toll at 227,000 soldiers (including those killed by the ALN for collaboration with the French) and 20,000 civilians; the FLN claimed that one million Algerian Muslims had been killed. More recent estimates have settled on a death toll, including the French and Algerians, of about half a million.
>
> (Aldrich 1996: 297)

Regardless of the huge human cost of the war, it had the effect of uniting the indigenous population against France's continuing occupation. France maintained its rule through extreme violence during the war with the inevitable outcome that the nationalists would not permit the restoration of an economic and political system that privileged the settlers, who were after all a minority of the overall population of the colony. In addition, Arab nationalism was reinforced by a resurgence of Islam that gathered momentum particularly after World War I. Nevertheless, the ensuing debate raised the question of whether an 'Algerian' identity was coterminous with the majority Muslim population. This debate was clearly not settled at the outbreak of World War II. However, by 1954 and the outbreak of the insurrection that eventually escalated into a full-scale war, these identities were firmly entrenched between 'French' and 'Algerians'. As Zack explains, the reason for this hardening of identity was a result of the conflict that 'activated another important and durable difference – one's relationship to the metropole—and compelled people to identify with one of two communities, those more closely tied to the metropole and those more oriented to local Algerian life' (2002: 87).

In 1958, the colonial and French armies joined forces to lead France to a victory over the FLN. Although General De Gaulle returned to power with the support of the extreme right, he was aware of the fragility and the inability of the French government to sustain colonial rule. Consequently, he announced a referendum in which Algerians were to choose their future. De Gaulle's policy was met with further violence by a militant organisation composed of settlers (the Organisation Armée Secrete, OAS). The OAS was formed to carry out a ruthless campaign of violence against the FLN, the Algerian people and the French government. De Gaulle's representatives began negotiating with FLN delegates and the Evian Accords began in March 1962, resulting in the official ending of the Algerian war three months later with a ceasefire agreement. In the subsequent referendum, the Algerian people overwhelmingly voted for independence. In the wake of the referendum, the remaining French settlers left the colony in droves and by the end of the year, almost all colons had departed. Nevertheless, the Algerian War left a legacy of economic and social disorder. As Samers points out:

> The destruction of factories, farms, and homes through wholesale burning by the French (the famous terre brulée campaigns), capital flight linked with the departure of Europeans, massive un- and underemployment (measured unemployment stagnated at 45 per cent), eventual difficulties with worker autogestation, concentration of large tracts of land in the hands of the few, widespread malnutrition, and poor housing, all plagued the country.
>
> (Samers 1997: 54)

Remembering Algeria

In 1962, the Algerian War ended with the Evian Peace Accords and effectively brought an end to a 132-year colonial occupation. Lizabeth Zack has summarised the manner in which the Algerian War has been explained by three schools of thought – the state-centred, nationalist-centred and settler-centred – all of which ascribed fixed binary identities such as 'French' and 'Algerian' (Zack 2002: 56). The first takes the perspective that the French state failed in the distribution of rights and privileges, which led the native population into armed insurrection.[3] The second school argues that it was the repressive nature of French colonialism that brought together disparate communities to fight a common enemy in the quest for Algerian independence.[4] The third view squarely lays blame on the settler population, whose behaviour polarised the population, culminating in a colonial war.[5] These accounts, Zack argues, 'simply assume the existence of "French" and "Algerians", of "settlers", "natives", and "the state" at the onset of war and build their explanations on top of these categorical frameworks' (2002: 86). What they fail to realise is that these identities were contested, highly contingent and consolidated after much debate. Drawing on postcolonial theory, Zack (2002) problematises the binary 'French' and 'Algerian', arguing that it fails to capture the multiple identities deployed by the various groups who lived in Algeria.

In recent years, a debate about the Algerian War of Independence has opened in France largely around the question of whether torture was used, a claim that the French state has denied vehemently. The reason for revisiting the Algerian war and the question of terror is that there is now an ever-growing presence of those who have linkages to Algeria within France, an estimated six million, 'who in one way or another have a direct and personal link to the Algerian war: the retired soldiers, the *pieds-noirs,* the harkis, the Algerian migrants and their immediate descendants' (MacMaster 2002: 451).

The issue came to a head in 1997–98 when the torture issue was raised during the trial of Maurice Papon for crimes against humanity committed during the Second World War. It was in that context that Papon's repressive role in the Algerian War as Chief Administrator of Constantine from 1956 to 1958 and as Prefect of Police during the Paris massacre of 17 October 1961 was raised. The effect of the trial was that the French government finally passed a law acknowledging the Algerian War and the war was finally discussed with a new openness. In 2000, the publication of Louisette Ighilahriz's allegations of torture and interviews with Generals Jacques Massu and Marcel Bigeard led to them acknowledging the use of torture during the Algerian War. In 2002, General Paul Aussaresses admitted to torture but showed little remorse when he was convicted for not repudiating war crimes. The reconsideration of the Algerian War and France's role were now reinvested in the issue of colonial repression and violence which were part of 'the national psychic energy that had gone into the long and heated battle over French collaboration during the Second World War and the deportation of Jews' (MacMaster 2002: 450).

David Prochaska argues that there is an 'Algerian syndrome', which is analogous to the 'Vichy syndrome', 'both defining moments of twentieth century French history, both historical blind spots, freighted combinations of willed forgetfulness, collective denial, misremembering and, first for Vichy and now increasingly for Algeria, the return of what has been repressed, occluded, ignored, put away' (Prochaska 2003: 133).

Despite the very large numbers of Arabs who are now located in the metropole, French society in the postcolonial period seemed almost incapable and indeed numb to the plight of its repatriated and displaced communities. The *pieds-noirs* were often represented as oddities, racists and even fascists who did not belong within the new French nation. They represented 'France's inability to resolve, on social, cultural, even epistemological levels the decolonisation of Algeria' (Naylor 2000: 264). It was for this reason that the debate over the conduct of the war and the terror controversy was carried out with such vitriol: not only because it was such a terrible conflict but also 'because the confrontation regarding torture was a substitute for a truly national debate about the wisdom of maintaining empire' (Cohen 2003: 229). At least in France there appears to be a new mood to consider and to face up to a difficult past. However, given the outbreak of violence in Algeria during the 1990s and the FLN's own repressive conduct, there has been a silence about this most traumatic period of Algeria's history after independence.

Conclusion

The French colonisation of Algeria in 1830, which was justified ultimately in the name of the civilising mission (la mission civilisatrice), remained the ideological basis of the colonial project. However, the theory was never put into practice and the indigenous Algerian population was from the outset treated as the barbaric 'other'. The very foundations of that society were disrupted and reshaped at an enormous cost, both economic and human. Algeria became France's most valued colonial possession and its centre for the Maghreb and the Eastern Mediterranean. For several generations, French leaders regardless of their political persuasion were convinced that the retention of Algeria was crucial to French greatness. The Algerian colonial project was about French prestige, and it was for this reason that it was so difficult for the indigenous Algerians to attain liberation. Algeria became 'an iconic symbol of French power. Just as it was strategically seen as the lynchpin of the French empire, in the same way, the French experience of Algeria now provides for most Frenchmen [sic.], rightly or wrongly, a concentrated vision of their imperial past' (Cohen 2003: 227).

Colonisation was, and continues, to be viewed in different ways by both the colonisers and the colonised. They interpret the events and common history they share from different perspectives and different registers. For example, if we juxtapose a contemporary Algerian intellectual with a French counterpart what the former remembers of the colonial situation, Edward Said points out, are:

> … France's military attacks on villages and the torture of prisoners during the war of liberation, on the exultation over independence in 1962; for his French counterpart, who may have taken part in Algerian affairs or whose family lived in Algeria, there is chagrin at having 'lost' Algeria, a more positive attitude toward the French colonizing mission – with its schools, nicely planned cities, pleasant life – and perhaps even a sense that 'troublemakers' and 'communists' disturbed the idyllic relationship between 'us' and 'them'.
>
> (Said 1993: 11)

The decolonisation process in France's African colonies was very different from that in British colonies, as the massive withdrawal of French settlers from Algeria indicates. This was a result of French colonies being conceived as an extension of France overseas. The Algerian War deeply affected French public life and for eight long years dominated political debate within the nation. The war had a huge cost, both in terms of revenue as well as the large number of lives that were lost. It caused destruction and devastation on an unprecedented scale, which divided the population and left deep scars that continue to haunt the French imagination.

Chapter 3

Sartre, Camus and Fanon

> This suspect individual *represents* nobody; but, since he *is* everybody at once, he is the best of witnesses.
>
> (Jean-Paul Sartre)

> This was the very country into which he felt he had been tossed, as if he were the first inhabitant, or the first conqueror, landing where the law of the jungle still prevailed, where justice was intended to punish without mercy what custom had failed to prevent – around him these people, alluring yet disturbing, near and separate, you were around them all day long, and sometimes friendship was born, or camaraderie, and at evening they still withdrew to their closed houses, where you never entered, barricaded also with their women you never saw …
>
> (Albert Camus)

> I find myself suddenly in the world and I recognize that I have one right alone: that of demanding human behavior from the other. One duty alone: that of not renouncing my freedom through my choices.
>
> (Frantz Fanon)

Introduction

Jean-Paul Sartre, Albert Camus and Frantz Fanon are all border intellectuals. However, whilst Camus and Sartre can be characterised as 'syncretic' border intellectuals, Fanon may be seen as the exemplary 'specular' border intellectual (JanMohamed 1992). All three, though, are accorded the status of border intellectuals on the basis of their filiation and affiliation with Algeria. Whilst both Camus and Fanon were associated directly with Algeria, with the former being born there and the latter choosing to live there, Sartre was deeply implicated by his unswerving support for its liberation. Although they are not directly linked to French post-structuralism, they each occupy a pivotal role not only because they embody disparate ideological positions but also because of their influence on whole generations of French theorists. Neither Sartre nor Fanon had a simple relationship to Marxism or existentialism – the movements with which they are linked inextricably. Rather, it is through the ambivalences and complexities of their own positions that we begin to glean the beginnings of the radical disruptions of the Enlightenment made by post-structuralist theory. They were reacting to the triumph of reason and the promises of the French empire that, at least theoretically, accorded its colonial subjects the same rights as in the metropole. In the end, it was the pervasive and excessive colonial violence, the shattered bodies of the colonised, that forced a rethinking of the humanism that underpinned the Enlightenment project (Bataille 1985).

In the case of Camus and Fanon, we can see how they were outsiders and insiders to both Algeria and France, and this ambivalence has a profound effect on their identity, commitment, politics and conceptualisation of Algerian colonialism and liberation. Both Camus and Fanon were outsiders to France, with the former born in Algeria and the latter in Martinique. And yet, in some unique ways, they were also outsiders to Algeria. Nonetheless, in the case of Fanon, an obvious outsider, his commitment and alignment with the Algerian cause led to his being seen as an insider and his name remains intertwined with the Algerian struggle for liberation. It is interesting that Fanon's name is linked inextricably with Algeria rather than the Caribbean, where he spent his formative years. Paget Henry argues that Fanon needs to be contextualised against the early period of Caribbean philosophy which was almost exclusively European. His intervention was nothing short of a challenge to the very world in which he had been brought up where there was a 'complete disenfranchisement of African philosophy on the grounds that philosophy was not a practice engaged in by "primitive" peoples' (Henry 1996: 230). Camus, on the other hand, an insider by the very nature of his birth, a *colon*, eventually was cast as an outsider as a result of his inability to see a future for independent Algeria without a French presence.

Edward Said's notions of filiation and affiliation are particularly useful in understanding how Algeria is inextricably bound with these border intellectuals. For Said, the worldliness of texts is linked to patterns of filiation and affiliation. Filiation is about heritage, tradition or particular forms of lineage, which were dominant modes of social relationships until peoples' lives became complex and had to be replaced by forms of affiliation. Said explained this transition:

> If a filial relationship was held together by natural bonds and natural forms of authority – involving obedience, fear, love, respect, and instinctual conflict – the new affiliative relationship changes these bonds into what seem to be transpersonal forms – such as guild consciousness, consensus, collegiality, professional respect, class, and the hegemony of a dominant culture. The filiative scheme belongs to the realms of nature and 'life', whereas affiliation belongs exclusively to culture and society.
>
> (1983: 20)

The transition from filiation to affiliation is akin to that of a move from nature to culture. The centrality of the family and its hierarchal forms of authority gives way to a 'system of thought no less orthodox and dominant than culture itself' (Said 1983: 20). Although Said was advocating that the critic recognise this transition and read texts affiliatively to ensure their worldliness, the very characteristic is important in understanding how Camus, Fanon and Sartre are themselves filiatively and affiliatively associated with Algeria. Affiliation itself forces us inevitably to the very location and the *locatedness* of the text's production.

Sartre

Jean-Paul Sartre was born in 1905 in Paris. At a very early age he graduated from the École Normale Supérieure (ENS). It was at the ENS that he first met Simone de Beauvoir and the two became inseparable and remained lifelong companions. Upon graduation, he taught philosophy and, in 1933–34 studied under Husserl and Heidegger in Berlin. In 1939, he was drafted into the French army but was soon captured by German troops. Subsequently, in 1940, he spent nine months as a prisoner of war. During this period of captivity, Sartre began to compose plays for his fellow prisoners. In 1941, he was released and he took up a position at the Lycée Condorçet in Paris. Sartre's captivity as a prisoner of war was a profound experience and led to his early politicisation and radicalisation. Upon his release, he joined the Paris resistance movement where he contributed by writing for several underground newspapers. His political commitment eventually led to his resignation from the Lycée Condorçet in 1942, when he decided that it was no longer possible for him to be independent whilst holding an academic position. In 1965, he was awarded the Nobel Prize for Literature, a prize he declined on the grounds that as a writer he could not allow himself to be transformed into an institution.

As a philosopher, Sartre was best known as an existentialist and one of the founders of the French postwar left-wing intellectual movement and was, perhaps, France's most famous public intellectual. Together with Maurice Merleau-Ponty and Simone de Beauvoir, in 1945, he launched the journal *Les Temps Modernes*. Although Sartre was, as John Gerrasi (1989) has argued, the 'hated conscience of his century', his anticolonial work has far too often been overlooked. For example, his classic work *Colonialism and Neocolonialism*, first published as *Situations V* in French in 1964, only became available in English in 2001.

Despite his phenomenal influence on the negritude writers as well as Frantz Fanon and Albert Memmi, Sartre's work has been largely ignored within postcolonial studies. This is particularly surprising because his work was preoccupied with the colonial world from the 1940s onwards. He was concerned fundamentally with ethical issues and it was his engagement with the colonial world that further politicised his work. His early concern with ethics, issues of freedom and with questions of responsibility was most probably a result of his growing up in a Christian household with a cleric as a grandfather. As Sartre noted, 'I was a cleric from childhood; I had the unctuousness of the princes of the Church and the hearty manner of the priesthood' (cited in Zaborowski 2000: 51). As a Marxist, colonial oppression became a central focus of his political agenda, which was all the more remarkable given that the Left at that time had largely ignored colonialism and its debasing effects.

Ironically, as Robert Young has noted, Fanon and his Marxism inspired by Sartre has been a pillar of postcolonial studies whilst the thrust of French Marxism since the 1960s has sought to refute Sartrean existentialism (2001b: xix–xx). Indeed, Sartre has been rendered invisible in the postcolonial canon largely due to his 'tendency to reduce the colonial problematic to a notion of class struggle and to seek to resolve this problematic in a Marxist eschatology' (Haddour 2001: 11). The work of Levi-Strauss and Althusser and their critiques of Sartre 'made the effective openings that enabled the later postcolonial deconstruction of the ethnocentric premises of European philosophy', and yet, it was Sartre's work in the 1940s that was particularly inspiring for those engaged in the French anticolonial movement (2001b: xx). In recognition of this influence, Valentin Mudimbe has dubbed Sartre a 'Negro philosopher' because he was deeply aware that anticolonial resistance and the 'pursuit of political liberation had been accompanied by the development of new forms of knowledge, a counter-modernity set against that of the West' (Young 2001b: xxii).

Sartre's existentialism is most evident in his magisterial *Being and Nothingness* (1943), which was a phenomenological exposition into the very nature of what it meant to be human. Here, Sartre subverted Marx's notion that consciousness is determined by the world. Rather, he argued that freedom was the very essence of being human. The individual became central to Sartre's thought, with individuals coming together to alter the course of history. As Robert Young notes, 'Sartre thus anticipates the performative basis of today's identity politics by several decades – except that for Sartre politics begins rather than ends with identity' (Young 2001b: x).

The idea that the individuals had a capacity to change their very conditions, that they had agency, was of course one that was highly appealing to French colonial subjects who had witnessed the German occupation and saw their own oppression in analogous terms. It was the Second World War as well as his own particular situation that led Sartre to champion the cause of liberation for the colonies. In particular, he was struck by the irony of the oppressive nature of French colonialism, a nation that itself had been liberated by the allies. What is particularly interesting about Sartre's position is that his stand on colonialism was a product of his thinking through ethical issues rather than politics. Although it is difficult to separate the two, this focus can be discerned by the manner in which he sought to understand the very nature of racism in phenomenological terms. It was these concerns that allowed him to consider the phenomenology of race within the system of colonialism.

As Robert Young points out, inspired by Richard Wright's statement that 'there is no Negro problem in the United States, there is only a white problem', Sartre wrote 'it is not the Jewish character that provokes anti-Semitism but, rather, … it is the anti-semite who creates the Jew' (2001b: xi). The anti-Semite had created a Manichean world in which there was no possibility of reconciliation, only the triumph of one over the other. Sartre had written this to understand and to expose the collusion of the French in the Nazi project, but it clearly had reverberations with his own work on the oppressive nature of colonialism and with anticolonial theorists such as Fanon and Memmi.

Sartre's critical stance on Algeria, which was counter to the prevailing orthodoxy of his time, was a product of his disagreements with the French Communist Party and, in particular, his 'dislike and distrust of Stalinism but also his disagreement with the Communist Party line on the French colonies, particularly Algeria' (Young 2001b: xvi; also see Birchall 2004). Indeed, his concern can be discerned in *Black Orpheus* where he confronted the issue of race consciousness and recognised that it was the 'unique suffering of blacks, not shared with the proletariat, namely being victimized *because of racial features*, that requires the correlative remedy of race-consciousness' (Barber 2001: 95).

The degrading effects of colonialism and the failure of the Communist Party to deal with race had also troubled Aimé Césaire, who resigned from the party in protest. Césaire's position had great resonance with a whole generation of thinkers including Fanon, Guevara and Castro. They challenged the very precepts of humanism or tried to 'articulate a new antiracist humanism, which would be inclusive rather than exclusive, and which would be the product of those who formed the majority of its new totality' (Young 2001b: xiv). As Michael Lowy pointed out, the Marxist humanism of Guevara is 'a revolutionary humanism which finds expression in his conception of the role of men in the revolution, in the communist ethics and in his vision of the new man' (Lowy 1973: 17). The issue of identity is thus transmitted into a new humanity and a society which will support the existence of this new species.[1] For Fanon and Guevara, revolution was only authentic, only worthwhile, to the extent that it created the basis for a new humanity, for a new human identity provides conditions that will succour it. As Donald Wehrs has noted, Sartre's 'ethical reflection was displaced into a politics governed by the assumption that since Marxist revolution would bring justice, whatever promoted revolution was ethical' (Wehrs 2004: 763).

Sartre's account of colonialism as a system based on his understanding of the Algerian situation was aimed at making the general point that colonialism was a calculated and systematic type of exploitation. It was this basic formulation that Fanon developed 'so that Sartre's Manichean system provided the fundamental model for his much more abstract account of colonialism and anticolonial resistance in *The Wretched of the Earth*' (Young 2001b: xviii).

In his essay 'Colonialism is a System', Sartre pointed out that the Algerian colonial situation was fundamentally based upon a system whereby there was a real concentration of European land at the expense of the indigenous Algerian population as well as ensuring that there was a cheap labour supply to work the European farms. As he aptly put it:

> Nothing demonstrates better the increasing rigour of the colonial system. You begin by occupying the country, then you take the land and exploit the former owners at starvation rates. Then, with mechanization, this cheap labour is still too expensive; you finish up taking from the natives their very right to work. All that is left for the Algerians to do, *in their own land*, at a time of great prosperity, is to die of starvation.
>
> (Sartre 2001: 39)

The effect of this internal displacement was that Algerians had to move out of their country in order to seek jobs in France. As a worldly response to the colonial system, the formative struggle for an Algerian self sought not simply to end the oppression and dehumanisation of the colonised, but also to end the oppression and dehumanisation of the colonisers by the system itself. Sartre pointed out that when addressing the colonial system it was important to be precise about its meaning, to recognise that it was an infernal cycle that was ingrained in over a million colonists, 'who think, speak, and act according to the very principles of the colonial system. For the colonist is fabricated like the native; he is made by his function and his interests' (Sartre 2001: 44).

For Sartre, the violence of the Algerian revolution had its roots in colonialism. Hence, the only possible way out of colonial oppression was to battle against the colonial others' very praxis of violence. He was concerned to show the totalising essence of history and used the ' "Other" to explain the colonists' capitalistic exploitation of Algerian "natives" ', and he argued that 'this exploitation permanently suspended the colonial situation in a dialectic of violence' (Le Sueur 2001: 229). In *Colonialism and Neocolonialism*, Sartre set out to challenge the very precepts upon which French colonialism was structured. The very ideas of liberty, equality and fraternity championed by the French were shown to be wanting in the colonies; hence the necessity for decolonisation. The essence of his argument is an elaboration of the dialectical relationship between the oppressor and the oppressed.

The prefaces that Sartre wrote to Fanon's *Wretched of the Earth* and Memmi's *The Colonizer and the Colonized* were the important beginnings that 'marked the fissuring of the grand narrative of Western Humanism and anticipated its deconstruction' (Haddour 2001: 8). This anticipation can be exemplified by the manner in which Sartre argued that 'the moment that they overthrow a language consecrating the priority of white over black, not only do they overturn the hierarchal coupling of this binary and all the conceptual oppositions which perpetrate the rhetoric of difference, but they poeticize this language' (Haddour 2001: 10).

In his preface to Memmi's book, Sartre wrote about the binding relationship between the coloniser and the colonised. The bond between the colonised and coloniser was one that at the same time constrained even as it united them. He argued that, in the case of France, the colonial project in Algeria was costing the nation more than it benefited it and that 'we know that we will abandon the war, without victory or defeat, when we are too poor to pay for it' (Sartre 2001: 53).

The colonial system about which Sartre wrote was based on the desire to obliterate the indigenous population. However, he recognised that, despite the ruinous conditions the Algerians had endured, they were defiant and fought for their freedom albeit at a very high cost.

> The land lies abandoned, the *douars* have been obliterated by bombing, the livestock – the peasants' meagre wealth – has disappeared. After seven years, Algeria must start from scratch: first of all win the peace, then hang on with the greatest difficulty to the poverty we have created: that will be our parting gift.
>
> (Sartre 2001: 132)

In 1961, the OAS (*Organisation de l'Armée Secrète*), comprised of far-right radicals committed to maintaining colonial rule, initiated a campaign of bombings to try to block the Evian peace accords. Sartre's support for the Algerian cause incurred a huge personal cost, as he was targeted and his apartment building bombed. As David Macey put it:

> Sartre's position on Algeria was no secret, but associating himself publicly with Fanon meant going further than he had ever gone before. *Le Figaro's* Thierray Maulnier had challenged him to take the risk of supporting the FLN with a bomb in hand. In literary terms, that was precisely what he now did.
>
> (2001: 462)

The first bomb, in 1961, was misplaced on the floor above his apartment from which he narrowly escaped. In January 1962, a second bomb was detonated whilst Sartre and Beauvoir sought refuge elsewhere. Remarkably, his mother who was in the bathroom at the time escaped unhurt. This was all the more poignant given the controversy in which Sartre and Albert Camus were embroiled and the latter's public declaration of the fear he held for his mother's safety given the anticolonial violence of the FLN in Algeria. As Ronald Aranson points out, violence became a key issue not because 'Camus was nonviolent and Sartre was violent, but the one was preoccupied with keeping his hands clean, and the other with the necessity of getting his hands dirty' (Aranson 2004: 218).

Camus

Albert Camus was born on November 7, 1913 in Mondovi, Algeria to a settler colonial family. His father was a *pied-noir* while his mother, from the Sintes family, was of poor Spanish peasant background. His father, Lucien Auguste Camus, belonged to the group of French soldiers from Alsace-Lorraine who were sent to settle in Algeria after France lost the province to the Prussians and where there was a great deal of unemployment. He initially served in the army that had invaded Morocco in 1907 but subsequently worked for a wine company. Albert never knew his father, as he died in 1914 whilst serving in the First World War only a few months after Albert was born. Camus grew up under difficult financial circumstances in a household that included his grandmother, uncle, his mother Catherine Hélène and older brother Lucien. The family lived in a working-class area of Algiers where the young Camus experienced at firsthand the severe inequalities that existed between the Arab and French populations. It was this experience that no doubt left an indelible mark on him and one that is consistently found in his writings.

Camus was greatly influenced by Germain Louis, a teacher at the École Communale in Algiers, and it was through his help that he won a scholarship at the Lycée of Algiers in 1923 which was the necessary prerequisite for his further study at the University of Algiers and subsequently in France. In 1930, Camus was infected with tuberculosis and was sent to live with his uncle and aunt, Gustave and Antionette Acault, where he was able to live in some domestic comfort. By the age of nineteen, Camus had left his uncle's residence and fallen in love with Simone Hié whom he married in 1934. The marriage was short-lived and they were divorced in 1936 in part due to her drug addiction. It was around this time that Camus began to explore ideas and began to write intensely. In order to survive he decided to become a journalist. At the same time, he ran the Theatre de L'Europe from 1935 to 1938. It was also around this time that he joined the Algerian branch of the French Communist Party (PCF) only to be expelled for his courageous stand opposing the placing of Algerian Arab concerns second to the goal of establishing the widest possible antifascist front that included as many *pieds-noirs* as possible (Aranson 2004: 25). In 1938, just as he was being recognised as a leading writer, he moved to Paris where he eventually joined the French resistance and served as editor for the left-wing newspaper *Combat.* It was whilst working at the newspaper that he became very close friends with Jean-Paul Sartre and Simone de Beauvoir. By the end of 1945, both Camus and Sartre had gained a great deal of notoriety and fame and 'the two were ubiquitous, writing philosophy, criticism, novels, plays, stories, and essays, and their journalism added to that body of work almost by the day' (Aranson 2004: 44).

From his early writings, Camus was deeply aware of his Algerian identity and conscious of the conditions that the Arab Algerian population endured. In his own way, he pushed for Franco-Arab reconciliation on the basis that this could only be attained if the French extended to its colonial subjects the very universal rights that it accorded its metropolitan population. In 1945, he wrote a series of articles that outlined the socioeconomic and political conditions that prevailed in Algeria and the manner in which this affected the Arab population. Although Camus wrote that the Arabs did not desire assimilation, he ended 'with a vague demand for justice, for giving Algeria not the discourse of democracy but its reality' (Aranson 2004: 62).

However, as violence was becoming prevalent in Algeria, Camus believed that it was a result of the intransigence of the French settlers to accord the assimilation of the Arab population as a priority. Despite recognising the escalation of state violence, what was astonishing was that he was not prepared to accept that the colonial population had a legitimate right to oppose such violence. As Le Sueur points out, for Camus, 'just as repression has sparked the rebellion, terrorism ran the risk of becoming 'racist'. Terrorism was not exposed to political control and was susceptible to becoming a 'crazy weapon of elementary hate' (2001: 97).

Camus remained remarkably consistent from his earliest writings until his death in 1960 in arguing that the survival of the French-Arab community in Algeria was dependent upon the assimilation of the Algerians. His belief in the centrality of assimilation was highly paternalistic and based on the notion that the French presence was necessary, because it aided the Algerians. He argued:

> … we have an obligation in that country, it is to permit one of the proudest and most human populations in the world stay true to itself and its destiny.
>
> The destiny of this people, I do not think I am wrong in saying, is to simultaneously work and think, and through these actions to give lessons of wisdom to the troubled conquerors that we are. Lets us know, at least, how to pardon ourselves for this fever and need of power, so natural for mediocre people, in taking it upon ourselves to care for the needs of a wiser people, in order to deliver them, in their entirety, to their profound grandeur.
>
> (Le Sueur 2001: 92)

Camus's paternalism allowed him to speak favourably for the Algerian population but not to the point where they could break free from France. Ironically, he could not sense the urgency and need for liberation for a people who had endured colonial rule for decades. This was all the more striking given his role in the French resistance and his position on the need to fight Nazi occupation and oppression. In his 1943 *'Letters to a German Friend'* he wrote:

> It taught us that, contrary to what we sometimes used to think, the spirit is of no avail against the sword, but that the spirit together with the sword will always win out over the sword alone. That is why we have now accepted the sword, after making sure that the spirit was on our side …

> We have paid dearly, and we have not finished paying. But we have our certainties, our justifications, our justice, your defeat is inevitable.
>
> (Le Sueur 2001: 93)

In contrast, Camus's orientalism was most apparent in his claim that it was not 'by the Orient that the Orient will physically save itself, but by the West, which in the end, will find nourishment in the civilization of the Orient' (cited in Le Sueur 2001: 100). Above all, what was evident was that Camus could not foresee a future for Algeria without the French. In short, he was convinced of the centrality of France's civilising mission in Algeria.

The paradox of Camus's position can be discerned in the very public manner in which his friendship with Jean-Paul Sartre ended. The split was simply the parting of ways but in their own way, each represented one side of the chasm that had arisen in response to the Algerian question. At the centre of the dispute was the question of violence, with Sartre embracing the right of the colonised to oppose state violence and Camus committed to resolutely denouncing any form of violence. As Aranson puts it, 'in occupied France, the child of privilege was dramatically comfortable with dirty hands at a time when the *pied-noir* from Algiers was determined to enter and leave the struggle with clean hands' (2004: 34). Despite growing up in relative poverty, what Camus failed to understand was that the poorest of settlers still led a life of privilege when compared to the indigenous population. This was, of course, obvious to Fanon who saw the Manichean nature of colonial rule.

In Camus's celebrated *L'Etranger*, the settler and the native share the same physical space, and yet, they appear to live in completely separate worlds. The Arabs, Camus observed, stared 'at us in silence, but in that way of theirs, as if we were nothing but stones or deaf trees' (Camus 1989: 48). The settlers also fail to acknowledge the Arabs. Indeed, all the Arab characters in Camus's novel remain nameless. As Said pointed out, 'Meursault kills an Arab, but this Arab is not named and seems to be without a history, let alone a mother or father; true also, Arabs die of plague in Oran, but they are not named either …' (1993: 212).

In his work, Camus presented 'colonial unease in a metaphysically abstract worldscape' (Apter 1997: 503). Under the piercing Algerian sun, the very boundaries between life and fiction, imagination and fact were uncertain. As Aranson points out,

> In the great novel of French Algeria, Camus's Meursault revels in its sensuous reality, bonding with its sun and sea, its heat and landscape. On the other hand, Meursault's violent and inexplicable murder of the anonymous Arab, following on his complicity with Raymond's beating of the young man's sister, conveys without the slightest sentimentality Algeria's texture of colonial brute force. And in both *The Stranger* and *The Plague* Camus re-creates the settlers' personal and political worlds

> as strangely devoid of non-Europeans, portraying the original occupants as occasional, silent, brooding, and threatening presences.
>
> (2004: 218–19)

In his advocacy for Algeria, Camus remained convinced of the efficacy of 'our justice', which entailed a process of assimilation for the Algerians. As he put it, 'infinite force of justice, and that alone, which should help us reconquer Algeria and its inhabitants' (cited in David 1997; Dubey 1998; Le Sueur 2001: 94). He was never prepared to understand that for the Algerians the French were an occupation and colonial presence that needed to be defeated. Camus's position became less credible when Algerian writers challenged the legitimacy of his position and, in particular, the very absence of Algerians in his fiction. Mouloud Feraoun, a Kabyle and Muslim, wrote:

> … among all your characters there was not one indigenous person and that Oran was in your eyes nothing but a banal police headquarters. Oh! This is not a reproach. I simply thought that, if there were not this gulf between us, you would have known us better, you would have sensed yourself capable to speak to us with the same generosity that benefits everyone else. I will always regret, with all my heart, that you do not know us sufficiently and that we have no one who understands us, to make us understood, and who helps us understand ourselves.
>
> (cited in Le Sueur 2001: 95)

As Algeria descended into further violence and as the cause for liberation gained momentum, Camus tried to intervene as a 'voice of reason' arguing for a civilian truce only to find that his position appeared all the more out of touch with events on the ground. He characterised the Arab revolt as an act of 'despair', which was resoundingly viewed as further evidence of his paternalism and exceedingly patronising. It appeared as if 'Camus was still interpreting Arab Algerians to French readers even after the FLN had enabled Algerians to take matters into their own hands' (Aranson 2004: 187). It was Mouloud Feraoun who reprimanded Camus for failing to stand up for the Algerian cause:

> … in the end this country is indeed called Algeria and its inhabitants are called Algerians. Why sidestep this evidence? Are you Algerians, my friends? You must stand up with those who fight. Tell the French that this country does not belong to them, that they took it over by force, and that they intend to remain here by force. Anything else is a lie and in bad faith.
>
> (cited in Le Sueur 2001: 101)

What was particularly difficult was the celebration of Camus as a figure who stood for justice and as an outspoken critic of the Nazi occupation. At the same time, he was speaking out against the injustices taking place as a result of the Soviet occupation of Hungary without recognising the contradictions in his stance on Algeria. In addition, he was strongly opposed to capital punishment and state repression. His critics were quick to point out the inconsistencies of his position when juxtaposed to Algeria (Apter 1997).

Camus received the Nobel Prize in 1957 and his work was widely celebrated. However, he was rapidly engulfed in a crisis the day after receiving the Nobel Prize whilst he was still in Sweden meeting students at Stockholm University. The meeting was marred by an Algerian student who heckled him about his silence on the Algerian question. Camus responded in exasperation:

> I said and I repeat that it is necessary to do justice to Algerians and to give them a fully democratic regime, until one or another type of hate has become such that it no longer prevents an intellectual from intervening, his declaration no longer aggravating terror. It seems better to wait until the proper moment in order to unite in place of dividing. I can assure you, nevertheless, that you have comrades who live today because of actions that you know nothing about. It is not without certain repugnance that I give my reasons like this in public. I have always condemned terror. I must also condemn a terrorism which is exercised blindly, in the streets of Algiers, for example, and which one day could strike my mother or my daughter. I believe in justice, but I would defend my mother before justice.
>
> (cited in Le Sueur 2001: 111)

Camus, the figure celebrated for his stance on justice, was immediately marked by severe criticism. One of the most trenchant critiques came from the French-Spanish-Algerian Jean Sénac, who argued that Camus's European paternalism and his sympathy with the European minority in Algeria only helped 'maintain Europe in its illusory intellectual supremacy' (cited in Le Sueur 2001: 114). Simone de Beauvoir met Camus's self-imposed silence on the Algerian question with particular disdain:

> … I was revolted by Camus' refusal to speak. He could no longer argue, as he had done during the war in Indochina that he didn't want to play the Communists' game; so he just mumbled something about the problem not being understood in France. When he went to Stockholm to receive his Nobel Prize, he betrayed himself even further. He boasted about the freedom of the press in France: that week, *L'Express*, *L'Observateur*, and *France-Nouvelle* were all seized. In front of an enormous audience, he declared: 'I love Justice; but I will fight for my mother before Justice', which amounted to saying that he was on the side of the *pieds-noirs*. The fraud lay in the fact that he posed at the same time as a man above the battle, thus providing a warning for those who wanted to reconcile this war and its methods with bourgeois humanism.
>
> (cited in Aranson 2004: 383–84)

Camus, although widely discredited, did not completely withdraw from the debate. He argued that Algerian nationalism was closely tied to Nasserism and pan-Arabism in a brief essay titled 'Algeria 1958'.

As Camus's critics gained momentum, he withdrew from active debate on Algeria and adopted a silence that has marked him since that time. This silence was the result of his belief that any further intervention on his part would result in increased violence against French settlers and in particular his mother who remained in Oran. Nevertheless, he steadfastly held on to his conviction that his role in Algeria never was and 'never will be to divide, but rather to use whatever means I have to unite. I feel solidarity with everyone, French or Arab, who is suffering today in the misfortune of my country' (cited in Le Sueur 2001: 109).

Although Camus maintained his silence, Algeria and the war remained a central concern. He spoke about it privately to friends and in March 1958 met with de Gaulle to convince him of the importance of his middle way if he returned to power (Aranson 2004: 215).

Camus prematurely died in a car accident in January 1960 at the age of 46. His death has meant that his silence on Algeria remains open to debate. While his brilliance and humanism was widely celebrated, his position on Algeria has remained problematic. As Le Sueur puts it:

> In many ways, Camus represented one of the central paradoxes of French liberal intellectuals during the war. As spokesmen for the oppressed, the liberals as a whole felt it their obligation to speak out against the injustices of the French government in Algeria. Camus did not hesitate to accompany other liberals along this path, but he stopped where others continued. As a French-Algerian, Camus never allowed his attachment to Algeria to be separated from his attachment to France. For him such a separation would only provoke the destruction of both communities.
> (2001: 126)

Nevertheless, Camus's preoccupation with Algeria became all the more evident when his semiautobiographical last novel was found in the car in which he died. *The First Man* is more than an autobiography; it is an insightful account of the *pied-noir* experience and the paradoxes that marked the colonial situation. In this novel, the protagonist intimately describes the lives of the French settlers and the reality of the effects of the Algerian War of Independence. Camus captures their heritage and painful legacy:

> … and so it was with their sons. And the sons and grandsons of these who found themselves on this land as he himself had, with no past, without ethics, without guidance, without religion, but glad to be so and to be in the light, fearful in the face of night and death. All these generations, all those men come from so many nations, under this magnificent sky where the

> first portent of light was already rising, had disappeared without a trace, locked within themselves. An enormous oblivion spread over them.
>
> (Camus 1996: 193)

Camus's first and last novels, *The Stranger* and *The First Man,* capture how for the settler *pieds-noirs* Algeria was both a stark and harsh land where they had no past but at the same time, a glorious land that was full of hope and love. As Emily Apter puts it, 'the paternal void, and the loss of personal genealogy, undergird the narrator's bizarre affirmation that Algeria "has no history" ' (1997: 506). The *pieds-noirs* were outsiders, not quite at home and not fully alien. The Algerian indigenous population, on the other hand, were alienated in their own home by the oppression of the colonisers who had rendered them, the other, not yet fully human. What Camus failed to see was the two competing nations. He steadfastly held on to the utopian belief in France's civilising mission, one that would result in the 'pan-Mediterranean man'. But, as Connor Cruise O'Brien has pointed out, even as Camus 'wishes to affirm the unity of the Mediterranean world, the marriage of East and West, he reveals himself as incapable of thinking in any categories other than those of a Frenchman' (1970: 9).

O'Brien's attack on Camus came at a time when Camus was celebrated as the universal harbinger of justice, the one figure who stood out in his generation as a critical conscience. As Said has so aptly noted, Camus's choice of the Algerian locale now appears incidental 'to the pressing moral issues at hand' and 'his novels are thus read as parables of the human condition' (Said 1993: 212). Indeed, such a view of Camus continues to the present day (Bartlett 2004; Kritzman 1997; Salgado 1997; Todd 1997). Sascha Talmor claims that,

> … both in his life and his work, Camus has tried to answer the essential question: *how should one live*? It is this question which informs all his *oeuvre*, from his first book *L'Etranger* to his last, *Le premier homme.* He not only was but also saw himself as, above all, a moralist, whose life and work showed an attitude of personal revolt and defiance against life's meaninglessness.
>
> (1995: 684)

Connor Cruise O'Brien, however, exploded the myth of the universal French subject that Camus held so dearly, illustrating its Eurocentric limitations. For him, Camus was particularly disturbing, because he recognised that he was 'a stranger on the African shore, and surrounded by people who are strangers in that France of which they are legally supposed to be a part' (O'Brien 1970: 11; also see Macey 2001: 472–73). Camus was, as Edward Said points out, a 'very late imperial figure' but one who 'survives today as a "universalist" writer with roots in a now-forgotten colonialism' (1993: 208).

It is clear that Camus's position was more than ambivalent but what was striking was his steadfast belief that France had the ability to forge a different kind of nation even at the height of the Algerian War. Edward Said has argued that it is a mistake to read Camus's works without locating them within the imperial context as well as against the background of Algerian resistance because of the 'affiliations with the facts of power which informed and enabled them' (1993: 195).

Fanon

The name Frantz Fanon has become synonymous with anticolonialism. By the time he reached Algeria, his focus on race, which had motivated his psychiatric studies in the first place, was subsumed into a much broader critique of colonialism and its dehumanising effects on the Algerian population. It is important to link Fanon's work on race with his writings on Algeria. Fanon was deeply influenced by Jean-Paul Sartre and the notion of nausea had a particular resonance for him. Fanon's nausea was manifested clearly in his recognition of the absurdity of the colonial world. However, this became enabling, forcing him to consider the possibilities of a new society in which both the coloniser and colonised are transformed through a new humanism, one that is by no means the humanism of the Enlightenment. It is this possibility of transformation that is pertinent to postcolonial societies.

In their introduction to *Fanon: A Critical Reader*, Gordon *et al.* (1996) have pointed out that since his death, a form of intellectual production has emerged which they label 'Fanon studies', which can be divided into four stages. The first stage encompassed the variety of ways in which his work could be applied and reactions to his work. The second entailed exploring biographical material whilst the third was a period of intensive research on his significance in political theory. The final stage, which they see as ongoing, is linked to postmodern, cultural and postcolonial readings. However, they point out that a fifth stage inaugurated by their work 'consists of engagements with the thought of Fanon for the development of original work across the entire sphere of human studies' (Gordon, Sharpley-Whiting and White, *et al.* 1996: 6).

Fanon's doubts about the 'Pitfalls of National Consciousness' and his suspicions concerning the monologic tyranny of nationalism offer insights into the way forward – particularly that of transformation where simple racial binaries are no longer sustainable. Leonard Harris and Carolyn Johnson have questioned whether Fanonism should be likened to Derrida's understanding of Marxism in *Specters of Marx*. Is it, they ask, 'a quaint collection of interesting theory, a historical memory, available as enriching discourse without a further presumption of its direct applicability, explanatory power, or predictive efficacy? Is Fanonism a feature of our haunting past, an apparition, a skull?' (Harris and Johnson 1996: xvi).

Frantz Fanon was born in Martinique on July 20, 1925 and grew up in the capital of Fort-de-France. Fanon was part of a very small percentage of black Martinicans who were able to be educated at the *Lycée*. Growing up within the French system of education had a profound influence on Fanon and no doubt paralleled the experience of Aimé Césaire, who described the education he received as one that 'associated in our minds the word France and the word liberty, and that bound us to France by every fiber of our hearts and every power of our minds' (cited in Hall 1995: 10).

It was this idea of France and the notion of liberty that made every French colonial subject believe that they were linked inextricably to France. Roland Barthes captures the essence of the myth that was promulgated in his discussion of a photographic image of a young black solider in a French uniform saluting the tricolour. Barthes illustrated how this image served to reinforce colonial ideology and the idea that French colonies were a mere extension of the metropole:

> 'that all her sons, without any colour discrimination, faithfully serve under her flag, and that there is no better answer to the detractors of an alleged colonialism than the zeal shown by this Negro in serving his so-called oppressors'.
>
> (cited in Young 1990: 123)

It was against this background that Fanon joined the Free French Army in 1944 when he fled Martinique and joined the Allied forces fighting against Germany in North Africa and Europe. The war had a profound effect on Fanon's identity. He had grown up in Martinique thinking that he was French. However, he experienced a great deal of racism not only in the French Army but also from the French population during the war. When he returned to Martinique as a decorated war veteran, having received the *Croix de Guerre* for bravery, Bulhan notes that he 'brought with him not only memories regarding the horrors of war, but also serious doubts about his identity as a Frenchman' (1985: 28).

This identity had to be reconstituted painfully into that of a black West Indian when he moved to Paris to study, taking advantage of the scholarships that were available to war veterans.[2] Fanon studied medicine at the University of Lyons, and defended his medical thesis in 1951 before undertaking a residency programme in psychiatry at the Hôpital de Saint-Alban. This period of study was highly influential for Fanon because the community was 'a hot bed of radical politics and in the midst of heated racial tension' (Gordon *et al.* 1996: 2). In October 1952, he married a French woman whom he had known throughout his studies, Marie-Josèphe Dublé. Upon completing his studies, Fanon wrote to Léopold Sédar Senghor about the possibility of working in Senegal. Senghor never replied and instead Fanon went to Algiers in November 1953 as medical director of the Blida-Joinville Hospital, the largest psychiatric hospital in Algeria. It was through practising in this hospital that he came into close contact with Algerians fighting for independence as well as French police officers, both victims of the colonial experience. Algeria, Fanon noted, was situated at 'France's gateway' and 'reveals to the Western world in detail, and as though in slow motion the contradiction of the colonial situation' (1970: 75). Colonialism also affected the colonisers, who become alienated by the very brutality that was inflicted on the colonised. Fanon records the effect on the French police:

> They hit their children hard, for they think they are still with Algerians. They threaten their wives, for 'I threaten and execute all day long'. They do not sleep, because they hear the cries and moans of their victims.
>
> (1970: 77)

It was here that he eventually decided to join the Algerian freedom fighters in their struggle for independence from French colonisation. In 1956, Fanon resigned from his position at the hospital. This was an important juncture where his French upbringing and training itself was under attack from his conscience. It was the beginning of the world turning upside down. He published his letter of resignation, addressed as 'Letter to the Resident Minister' in *Toward the African Revolution*:

> For nearly three years I have placed myself wholly at the service of this country and of the men who inhabit it. I have spared neither my efforts nor my enthusiasm. …
>
> If psychiatry is the medical technique that aims to enable man no longer to be a stranger to his environment, I owe it to myself to affirm that the Arab, permanently an alien in his own country, lives in a state of absolute depersonalization.
>
> What is the status of Algeria? A systematized de-humanization. …
>
> For many months my conscience has been the seat of unpardonable debates. And their conclusion is the determination not to despair of man, in other words, of myself.
>
> (Fanon 1970: 62–64)

In January 1957, Fanon received a letter of expulsion from the Algerian government ordering him to leave the country within forty-eight hours. As an active member of the FLN by this time, he was the target of several assassination attempts. Fanon served the FLN in a variety of capacities at its headquarters in Tunis, including being editor of the movement's newspaper, *El Moudjahid*, as well as working as a doctor. In 1960, during a visit to Mali as a FLN representative, Fanon suddenly fell ill and by the end of that year, he was diagnosed with leukaemia. He went to Moscow for initial treatment but it was suggested that he should seek further treatment in the United States. Fanon returned to Tunis and remarkably wrote his last book, *The Wretched of the Earth* (1967), in a mere ten weeks. He finally reluctantly went for treatment in the US and travelled to Washington through an arrangement with the CIA. His short stay in the US remains clouded by uncertainty and rumours that suggest that he was left in a hotel room for several days where he was interrogated before being admitted to hospital when it was too late. Fanon died in the US on December 6, 1961 at the age of 36. His body was returned to Tunisia and then 'smuggled across the border to Algeria, where he was buried in an FLN cemetery with full military honors' (Alessandrini 1999: 4).

Fanon's Algerian locatedness is critical. Through his personal experiences, he began to reject the universalism that had been ingrained in him through the French system. His sense of personal alienation enabled him to question the humanism of the Enlightenment which had been promised to him through the idea that the colonies were a mere extension of France. The precursors to his theorising about a new humanism were his experiences in Martinique and the process of self-discovery and realisation that he undertook in his first book, *Black Skin, White Masks*. Here, Fanon subverted Freud's 'what does woman want?' by asking the question, 'What does the black man want?' (1986: 10).

The desire to be white

In response to this rhetorical question, Fanon observed, 'There is a fact: White men consider themselves superior to black men. There is another fact: Black men want to prove to white men, at all costs, the richness of their thought, the equal value of their intellect' (1986: 12). This was best demonstrated in the way that mastery of the French language in Martinique was a way to climb the social ladder. Ngugi Wa Thiong'o's (1993) claim that the power of language is central to the maintenance of a culture is clearly inspired by Fanon's writings about language and the way in which French occupied a central place in Martinique. It is not surprising that Ngugi has argued that the early post-independence literature should be read as 'a series of imaginative footnotes to Frantz Fanon' (Wa Thiong'o 1993: 66). Fanon argued: 'the Negro of the Antilles will be proportionately whiter – that is, he will come closer to being a human being – in direct ratio to his mastery of the French language' (1986: 18). It was this desire to master the French language that led many middle-class Antilleans to abandon Creole. Fanon noted that, 'In school the children of Martinique are taught to scorn the dialect ... Some families completely forbid the use of Creole, and mothers ridicule their children for speaking it' (20).

However, in France, Fanon noted, the 'European has a fixed concept of the Negro', one where there is 'nothing more exasperating than to be asked: "How long have you been in France? You speak French so well" ' (1986: 35). The command of the French language, however, gave the black person 'honorary citizenship'. Fanon narrated his experience in Lyon where in a lecture he drew a parallel between black and European poetry, only to be told by a French acquaintance that 'at bottom you are a white man' (38). In a further incident, Fanon pointed out that in the 1945 election campaign, Aimé Césaire was giving a speech during which a woman fainted, and the next day an acquaintance commented that she had fainted because she was overwhelmed by his French refinement of style. What remained significant for the Antillean was there was always a qualifying phrase, which signalled a deep-seated racism, such as 'great black poet' or André Breton's description of Césaire: 'Here is a black man who handles French language as no white man today can' (39).

For the Antillean, the world was divided into two poles, white and black, 'a genuinely Manichean concept of the world' (Fanon 1986: 44–45). This division gives rise to the desire to be white and is deeply manifested in the manner in which a black woman 'whether in a casual flirtation or in a serious affair, is determined to select the least black of the men' (47). This desire to be white pervades relationships between blacks and whites. Fanon noted that 'the Negro enslaved by his inferiority, the white man enslaved by his superiority alike behave in accordance with a neurotic orientation' (60). In his discussion of the autobiographical novel by René Maran, Fanon tried to make sense of the relationship between the black man and the white woman. Through the character John Veneuse, who was born in the Antilles but who had lived in Bordeaux, we gain an insight into the Manichean world and the internal conflict that arises: 'The Europeans in general and the French in particular, not satisfied with simply ignoring the Negro of the colonies, repudiate the one whom they have shaped into their own image' (64).

Fanon was acutely aware of the negritude writers and their project, which aimed to illustrate that they had a cultural heritage that was of equal or greater importance to the French.[3] It is possible to make sense of the Manichean structure of Fanon's world and his desire to transcend it in his discussion of negritude. Indeed, he accused Sartre of blocking the source of negritude. He wrote that at the very moment when he was 'trying to grasp my own being, Sartre, who remained The Other, gave me a name and thus shattered my last illusion' (1986: 137). This illusion of being able to find yourself by reclaiming your past African heritage, of being black, was shattered and Fanon wrote: 'Not yet white, no longer wholly black, I was damned. Jean-Paul Sartre had forgotten that the Negro suffers in his body quite differently from the white man' (138).

Fanon's relationship to negritude can at best be described as ambivalent (Parry 1994). He was conscious of the essentialised nature of the identity that was being advanced by negritude but at the same time recognised its necessary positive effects. He recognised the need for the affirmation of black identity. In this context, negritude was not only necessary but also unfeasible. It was necessary because it effected 'a shift between black–white relations', offering the black person a source of pride, while at the same time a white person 'recognises in the Negro qualities that he now experiences himself as lacking, such as closeness to nature, spontaneity, simplicity' (Kruks 1996: 130). In this process, there is finally a sense of recognition. Through this affirmation of identity, the black person at last gains recognition.

Whilst recognising negritude's importance and rebuking Sartre, ultimately Fanon adopted a stance akin to Sartre. He documented the alienation entailed in not belonging in either culture and saw that the only way out was 'to reject the two terms that are equally unacceptable, and through one human being, to reach out for the universal' (1986: 197). He criticised negritude's search for a black identity in some distant African past as irrelevant, because it is not possible to achieve freedom without looking toward the future. In short, Fanon recognised that it was important to celebrate and affirm one's black identity but that in itself was not enough to change the course of history, a task to which he was fundamentally committed in the struggle for Algeria.

Fanon's position on negritude is much like Gayatri Chakravorty Spivak's notion of 'strategic essentialism', where essentialist forms of native identity are seen to be important in order to transcend the assimilationist phase of colonialism and to develop a decolonised national culture.[4] In other words, it is an important phase in the process of decolonising the mind. Chinua Achebe recognised this 'strategic essentialism' when he wrote:

> You have all heard of the African personality; of African democracy, of the African way to socialism, of negritude, and so on. They are all props we have fashioned at different times to help us get on our feet again. Once we are up we shall not need any of them any more. But for the moment it is in the nature of things that we may need to counter racism with what Jean-Paul Sartre has called an anti-racist racism, to announce not just that we are as good as the next man but that we are better.
>
> (cited in Moore-Gilbert 1996: 179)

Ultimately, however, the methodology employed by Fanon was what he had been taught at medical school. He looked for symptoms that would allow him to diagnose a particular disease and it was from such a diagnosis that he sought a cure. He wrote, 'I believe that the fact of the juxtaposition of the white and black races has created a massive psychoexistential complex. I hope by analyzing it to destroy it' (1986: 14). Fanon sought to understand the processes that forced the black person to want to become white.

Fanon was particularly apt at showing how all identity was relational. Drawing upon Jean-Paul Sartre's statement that, 'it is the anti-Semite who *makes* the Jew', he concluded that, 'the feeling of inferiority of the colonized is the correlative to the European's feeling of superiority. ... *It is the racist who creates his inferior*' (1986: 93). Fanon explained how a whole system of racism operates on the basis of colour and establishes a hierarchy:

> The Frenchman does not like the Jew, who does not like the Arab, who does not like the Negro ... The Arab is told: 'If you are poor, it is because the Jew has bled you and taken everything from you'. The Jew is told: 'you are not the same class as the Arab because you are really white because you have Einstein and Bergson'. The Negro is told 'you are the best soldiers in the French Empire; the Arabs think they are better than you, but they are wrong'.
>
> (1986: 103)

Fanon's nausea

Sartre's *Anti-Semite and Jew* (1965) was highly influential for Fanon and this is evident clearly in *Black Skin, White Masks*, where he extends the notions of recognition and nonrecognition through the trope of racial identity. However, what is significant about the two is that Sartre was not writing as a Jew whereas Fanon was writing from the lived experience of being black. Sonia Kruks sums up Fanon's project in this book as being 'less to account for white negrophobia than to explore the lived-experience and moral possibilities open to a black living in a negrophobic world' (Kruks 1996: 128). The major lesson that Fanon learned from European existentialism was the 'basic concept of nonbeing that he used to describe the conditions of aridity and paralysis that often follow ego collapse' (Henry 1996: 234). At that point, Fanon addressed the absurdity of the colonial world and here the idea of nausea became paramount. 'Fanon saw that there could be no transcendence of the (white) ego without transcendence of the 'lived experience of the black'. The transcendence of both represented the transcendence of the racialized ego and its object' (Turner 2002: 47–48).

Fanon's notion of nausea can be discerned in the oft-quoted encounter between a white child and Fanon himself in *Black Skin, White Masks*. It is possible in this encounter to decipher Fanon's project. He demonstrated how the effects of colonialism permeated the black body and created a desire to wear a white mask, to mimic the white person in order to survive the absurdity of the colonial world. Fanon wrote about the sense of alienation, of being an object in a world of objects created by colonisation. Ronald Judy points out that the principal task of *Black Skin, White Masks* is 'to understand what the consciousness of and for the black is by understanding how it is, its process of becoming'. The entire book can be seen as an 'attempt to understand the forms of consciousness that occur in history' (1996: 54). This book needs to be seen as more than a social psychology of racism; it is about the lived experience of being black.

This encounter, which is played out in three stages, epitomised for Fanon the fact that, 'not only must the black man be black; he must be black in relation to the white man' (1986: 110).

The first stage is the sighting of Fanon by the white child, possibly at a railway station.

> 'Look a Negro!' It was an external stimulus that flicked over me as I passed by. I made a tight smile.
>
> 'Look a Negro!' It was true. It amused me.
>
> 'Look a Negro!' The circle was drawing a bit tighter. I made no secret of my amusement.
>
> 'Mama, see the Negro! I'm frightened! Frightened! Frightened!' Now they were beginning to be afraid of me. I made up my mind to laugh myself to tears, but laughter had become impossible.
>
> (1986: 112)

Unable to laugh, Fanon noted the manner in which the black man's 'corporeal schema' is replaced with an 'epidermal schema'. This gives way to the second stage.

> In the train it was no longer a question of being aware of my body in the third person but in a triple person. In the train I was given not one but two, three places. I had already stopped being amused. It was not that I was finding febrile coordinates in the world. I existed triply: I occupied space. I moved toward the other … and the evanescent other, hostile but not opaque, transparent not there, disappeared. Nausea.
>
> (1986: 112)

This transition, the recognition that he has no control over the white child's gaze, illustrates that the gaze is not neutral but a 'racially saturated field' (Butler 1993: 17). This recognition leads to revulsion, to a feeling of sickness, to nausea. The nausea forces him to conclude that he had indeed interpreted the gaze correctly: 'It was hate; I was hated, despised, detested, not by the neighbours across the street or my cousin on my mother's side, but by an entire race' (Fanon 1986: 118). The nausea makes way for the third stage.

> On that day, completely dislocated, unable to be abroad with the other, the white man, who unmercifully imprisoned me, I took myself far off from my own presence, far indeed and made myself an object. What else could it be for me but an amputation, an excision, a hemorrhage that spattered my whole body with black blood? But I did not want this revision, this thematization. All I wanted was to be a man among other men.
>
> (1986: 112)

In this third stage of the encounter the mood changes from being disempowered by nausea to the recognition of being trapped, injured and most importantly of the possibility to break out of that condition, to be a 'man among other men'. Fanon's nausea, obviously indebted to Jean-Paul Sartre,[5] however, is different because as he says he 'rejected all immunization of the emotions. I wanted to be a man, nothing but a man' (1986: 113).

Humanism and colonialism

Black Skin, White Masks was an important point of departure for Fanon. Here, we gain an insight into the Manichean world of his formative years. He was desperate to understand and transcend the nauseating banality of this world. As he pointed out at the end of the book:

> Was my freedom not given to me in order to build the world of *You*?
>
> At the conclusion of this study, I want the world to recognize, with me, the open door of every consciousness.
>
> (1986: 232)

Fanon's account of the Manichean world of colonialism, Homi Bhabha argues, needs to be seen as the 'image of the post-Enlightenment man tethered to, *not* confronted by his dark reflection, the shadow of colonized man' (1986: xiv). This realisation led to his desire to change the madness of the colonial world, a task that became critical for him when he moved to Algeria.

In Algeria, Fanon was forced to conceptualise a new humanism. The tenuous hold he had on cultural certainty led to a weakening of the hold of humanism and the conception of a new humanism, a disruption of humanism that previewed the post-humanism of post-structuralism. Colonialism created the conditions that necessitated the new humanism. The new humanism was not a radical break with Enlightenment humanism, because of the way in which he drew on Marxism and existentialism. The old categories were, however, becoming problematic primarily because the issue of race problematised Marxist universalism.

Although there are many types of humanism and the term is highly contentious, it nevertheless signifies that there is something universal and given about human nature and that it can be determined in the language of rationality. These ideas of human nature and rationality underpin the Enlightenment humanism that post-structuralist and postmodernist antihumanists find objectionable on the grounds that these notions are historically contingent and culturally specific. Leela Gandhi points out: 'the underside of Western humanism produces the dictum that since some human beings are more human than others, they are more substantially the measure of all things' (1998: 30). In this context, Aimé Césaire observed that the only history is white (1972: 54). As Dipesh Chakrabarty points out:

> For generations now, philosophers and thinkers shaping the nature of social science have produced theories embracing the entirety of humanity; as we well know, these statements have been produced in relative, and sometimes absolute, ignorance of the majority of humankind i.e., those living in non-Western cultures.
>
> (1992: 3)

There is little recognition, however, of the origins of antihumanism. In general, it is thought that the movement was initiated in an exchange between the Marxist humanism of Lévi-Strauss and Althusser and the existential humanism of Sartre and others in the French Communist Party.[6] But, as Robert Young points out, this fails to take into account the attempts by Sartre, Lukács and others to found a 'new historical humanism' which challenged the idea of man's unchanging nature on the grounds that it was important to see 'man as a product of himself and of his own activity in history' (1990: 121). It was, of course, this idea of humanism that Fanon and Césaire challenged. Their 'version of anti-humanism starts with the realization of humanism's involvement in the history of colonialism, which shows that the two are not so easily separable' (Young 1990: 121–22). Decolonisation, apart from the displacement of colonial rule, has been about decolonising European thought and history, which marks that 'fundamental shift and cultural crisis currently characterised as postmodernism' (119). It is important to recognise that Frantz Fanon was firmly ensconced in this project.

Colonial violence and new humanism

In his preface to *The Wretched of the Earth*, Jean-Paul Sartre pointed out the manner in which a new generation of colonial subjects challenged their European masters: 'You are making us into monstrosities; your humanism claims we are at one with the rest of humanity but your racist methods set us apart' (Fanon 1967: 8). In Fanon, Sartre found the voice of the Third World which did not speak to Europe but spoke to itself. He pointed out that Fanon's book did not need a preface, because it was not directed at the coloniser but that he had written it to bring the argument to a conclusion:

> ... for we in Europe too are being decolonized: that is to say that the settler which is in every one of us is being savagely rooted out ... we must face that unexpected revelation the strip-tease of our humanism ... It was nothing but an ideology of lies, a perfect justification for pillage; its honeyed words, its affectation of sensibility were only alibis for our aggressions.
>
> (Fanon 1967: 21)

Fanon recognised that above all else, decolonisation was a violent phenomenon, because it entailed 'quite simply the replacing of a certain 'species' of men by another 'species' of men ... there is a total, complete, and absolute substitution' (27). Irene Gendzier has pointed out that Fanon was deeply influenced by Hegel's account of the master–slave dialectic (Gendzier 1973: 23). His reading of Hegel's *'Lordship and Bondage'* had a profound influence on his advocacy of violent decolonisation. For him, violence became a means to attain self-knowledge and a way of dealing with the problem of the self and the other.

Through decolonisation a new people are created and a new humanity emerges.[7] As Fanon pointed out, decolonisation puts into practice the sentence: 'The last shall be first and the first last' (1967: 28). What makes putting this sentence into practice violent is the compartmentalisation of the Manichean colonial world, which Fanon captured in his description of the spatiality of the colonial urban site:

> The zone where the natives live is not complementary to the zone inhabited by the settlers. The two zones are opposed, but not in the service of a higher unity ... they both follow the principle of reciprocal exclusivity.

> No conciliation is possible, for the two terms, one is superfluous. The settlers' town is a strongly built town, all made of stone and steel … a well-fed town, an easy-going town; its belly is always full of good things. The settlers' town is a town of white people, of foreigners.
>
> The town belonging to the colonized people, or at least the native town, the Negro village, the medina, the reservation, is a place of ill fame, peopled by men of evil repute. They are born there, it matters little where or how; they die there, it matters not where, nor how. It is a world without spaciousness … a hungry town starved of bread, of meat, of shoes, of coal, of light … a town of niggers and dirty Arabs.
>
> (1967: 39)

Abdul JanMohamed captured the paradoxes of colonialism where on the one hand the 'native' is completely denigrated and on the other hand is absolutely necessary to maintaining the superiority of the settler. The colonial system, he pointed out, 'simultaneously wills the annihilation and the multiplication of the natives' (1983: 4). A necessary part of colonialism is the process whereby the colonisers problematise the culture and the very being of the colonised, where the latter come to accept the 'supremacy of the white man's values' (Fanon 1967: 43). During the period of decolonisation, this very acceptance is repudiated. Fanon detailed the oppressive nature of the colonial system and pointed out that the only way that it can be overcome is through violence. Colonialism forces violence to become a cleansing agent which has the cathartic effect of creating a new identity both at the individual and collective levels:

> … for the colonized people this violence, because it constitutes their only work, invests their characters with positive and creative qualities. The practice of violence binds them together as a whole, since each individual forms a violent link in the great chain, a part of the great organism of violence which has surged upwards in reaction to the settlers' violence in the beginning.
>
> (1967: 87)

The question of violence in Fanon's project, Lewis Gordon (1996) points out, arises out of the very condition of colonialism.[8] For the coloniser, his or her place in the colony is not unjust, but the idea that they might be replaced constitutes an injustice. From the perspective of the colonised, prior to the arrival of the coloniser his or her place was just and their replacement is what constitutes an injustice, which entails living under a system of violence. As Gordon puts it, 'the situation begins to take on tragic dimensions when the discourse on method – mediation – emerges with teleological import: "the last shall be first"' (Gordon 1996: 304). In this context, the call for nonviolence by the coloniser is seen to constitute violence, because it is a continued way of ensuring that colonialism is preserved. This notion of losing can be seen to constitute violence. In this way, both the coloniser and colonised can be seen to 'converge as sufferers during the period of liberation' (305). The price of a new humanism lies in the 'tragedy of the colonial and racist situation' (305).

Ato Sekyi-Otu (1996) has pointed out that those who label Fanon as primarily a theorist of violence often forget that he was concerned to show that the colonial situation was much like a state of nature where there was no civil and political sphere. As David Macey points out, Fanon

> does not glorify violence and in fact rarely describes it in any detail ... The violence Fanon evokes is instrumental and he never dwells or gloats on its effects. In a sense, it is almost absurd to criticize Fanon for his advocacy of violence. He did not need to advocate it. The ALN was fighting a war and armies are not normally called upon to justify their violence.
>
> (2001: 475)

Fanon was suggesting 'with the most classical of political philosophers that where there is no public sphere, there is no political relationship, only violence, "violence in a state of nature"' (Sekyi-Otu 1996: 86–87). Richard Onwuanibe has pointed out that above all else, Fanon should be seen as humanist despite the role of violence in his work. This assertion is made on the basis that above all else, Fanon sought to extend the full development of humanity to all those who had been exploited, especially through the processes of colonialism. Violence in this context was a just and legitimate means to end colonialism so that a new society could be inaugurated (Onwuanibe 1983). It served a rehabilitative and healing function and had much to do with his training as a medical doctor. The goal of violence was cleansing, akin to solving a medical condition. In an article in 1957, Fanon made the explicit connection between colonialism and disease when he noted: 'the independence of Algeria is not only the end of colonialism, but the disappearance, in this part of the world, of a gangrene germ and the source of an epidemic' (cited in Presbey 1996: 284).

This equation of colonialism with disease is the driving force behind Fanon's desire to end the oppression of colonialism as soon as possible by violent means if necessary. As Presbey points out, Fanon was well aware of the trauma that the colonial situation produced on the colonisers, many of whom were his patients, but he was prepared to risk saving the majority at the expense of the settler colonial minority (1996: 288). The medical metaphor is an important one in order to understand the place of violence in Fanon's thought. Violence is like surgery: quick and brief so that in its aftermath a process of healing can begin. For Fanon, violence was not simply about revenge; it had to be followed by education and political organisation to ensure that the entire society was liberated. As Presbey points out, for Fanon, 'there may be cases in which brief surgery is the quickest and surest way to health' (1996: 292). Through decolonisation a new humanism can emerge. As Fanon points out, 'the "thing" which has been colonized becomes man during the same process by which it frees itself' (Fanon 1967: 28).

In an interesting reading of Fanon and Gandhi, Presbey suggests that the ideas of violence and nonviolence have much in common as opposed to alternative strategies for achieving decolonisation. In both cases, the tactics are dependent upon the colonisers giving up the battle despite their ability to obliterate the colonised. Presbey notes that 'neither can force the hand of the opponent equipped with superior technological weaponry; but people's actions can make the colonizers' actions seem more and more ridiculous to themselves' (1996: 295).

Fanon's notion of humanism can also be found in his discussion in 'Racism and Culture', where he argues that in order to attain liberation, 'the inferiorized man brings all his resources into play, all his acquisitions, the old and the new, his own and those of the occupant' (1970: 53). However, through decolonisation racism itself is brought to an end. A new humanism, a new society, is born in which:

> The occupant's spasmed and rigid culture, now liberated opens at last to the culture of the people who have never really become brothers. The two cultures can affront each other, enrich each other.
>
> In conclusion, universality resides in this decision to recognize and accept the reciprocal relativism of different cultures, once the colonial status is irreversibly excluded.
>
> (1970: 54)

The humanism Fanon wishes for can also be gleaned in his 'Letter to the Youth of Africa' where he pointed out that it is necessary for oppressed peoples to link up with 'the peoples who are already sovereign if a humanism that can be considered valid is to be built to the dimensions of the universe' (1970: 125). Fanon described a new society that was only possible through the end of colonialism. He noted that, at 'the same time that the colonized man braces himself to reject oppression, a radical transformation takes place within him which makes any attempt to maintain the colonial system impossible and shocking' (1965: 159). The revolution, he argued, 'changes man and renews society … this oxygen which creates and shapes a new humanity' (154).

Postcolonial transformation

If Fanon has touched a chord with contemporary postcolonial studies, it is precisely because of this recognition that the end of colonialism necessitated the end of the coloniser and the colonised.[9] This process would be 'complete only with the disappearance of racism, if not as a shedding of skin, at least as a shedding of what skin colour has come to mean in a world defined by colonialism' (Bernasconi 1996: 113). Fanon's critique of old humanism was indebted to Jean-Paul Sartre, who noted that 'for us there is nothing more consistent than a racist humanism since the European has only been able to become a man through creating slaves and monsters' (Fanon 1967: 22). Fanon was more than aware of the ironies of such humanism when he noted:

> Bourgeois ideology, however, which is the proclamation of an essential equality between men, manages to appear logical in its own eyes by inviting the sub-men to become human, and to take as their prototype Western humanity as incarnated in the Western bourgeoisie.
>
> (1967: 131)

For Fanon, the disarticulation of always being a French subject rather than being accepted as French highlighted how the old humanism could only be universal in theory. The humanism that he sought to expound was meant to bring theory and praxis together. Robert Young, however, has suggested that Fanon's new humanism can be seen as a theoretical antihumanism which is rooted in 'the realization of humanism's involvement in the history of colonialism, which shows that the two are not so easily separable' (Young 1990: 122).[10] Young questions whether it is possible to articulate a new humanism and if it is possible to 'differentiate between a humanism which harks back critically, or uncritically, to the mainstream of Enlightenment culture and Fanon's new 'new humanism' which attempts to reformulate it as a non-conflictual concept no longer defined against a sub-human other' (125).

Young does not explore Fanon's new humanism. Rather, he is content to note that the challenge that Fanon mounted was enough to expose the limitations of Western ethnocentricity which have the 'effect of decentring and displacing the norms of Western Knowledge' (1990: 125). However, the implication that Fanon simply reversed the binary in his formulation of new humanism so that it was a nonconflictual concept does not tally with Fanon's line of argument. In the preface to *A Dying Colonialism*, Fanon pointed out the task for his new humanism:

> The new relations are not the result of one barbarism replacing another barbarism, of one crushing of man replacing another crushing of man. What we Algerians want is to discover the man behind the colonizer; this man who is both the organizer and the victim of a system that has choked him and reduced him to silence.
>
> (1965: 20)

The new humanism that Fanon evoked here has the task of liberating both the coloniser and the colonised. He articulated it at the end of the book when he proclaimed that the true revolution 'changes man and renews society', which 'creates and shapes a new humanity' (1965: 160). This new humanism was to be achieved through violence, a violence that brought to an end the very process of colonialism. As Bernasconi points out, 'a new humanity could arise only through the creative praxis of the colonized. Theirs was a violence that would not only destroy the old order, but produce a new one' (1996: 121).

In the following passage in the *Wretched of the Earth* we begin to see that Fanon's new humanism was not simply a humanism of the European Enlightenment. We can see linkages here between Fanon and the post-structuralists:

> The west saw itself as a spiritual adventure. It is in the name of the spirit, in the name of the spirit of Europe, that Europe has made her encroachments, that she has justified her crimes and legitimized the slavery in which she holds four-fifths of humanity. Yes, the European spirit has strange roots.
>
> (Fanon 1967: 252)

He recognised the failure of this European spirit in the colonial context where humanism was not universal. Despite this recognition, Fanon was caught in a paradox: he rejected European humanism but remained committed to the idea that 'all the elements of a solution to the great problems of humanity have, at different times, existed in European thought' (1967: 253). The paradox for Fanon was that he not only critiqued European humanism but he was also aware of its importance. As Azar points out, Algeria 'becomes the name of the historical subject, the spirit, that Fanon invokes to transcend the antinomies that have marked the history of mankind' (1999: 22).

It is important to recognise the disjuncture between the Antilles, France and Algeria which gives rise to what Alessandrini has termed a 'transnational humanism' in Fanon's thought. This transnational humanism is very much a product of Fanon's relationship to the Algerian Revolution: he felt that he was affiliated to the world, as suggested by Edward Said (1983) and also Ashcroft and Ahluwalia (1999). Azar points out that the quest to transcend the Manichean logic was based on a dislocation of Fanon's own universe, where an Antillean and French identity was replaced by an Algerian one, which became the foundation of his new humanism (Azar 1999: 23). In Algeria, Fanon recognised the paradox of French colonialism with its civilising mission and desire for exploitation which meant that the line between the 'master' and the 'slave' could never be crossed. Fanon was not alone in recognising this fundamental contradiction in French colonialism. Camus had also recognised this contradiction in the aftermath of massacres in Sétif and Guelma in 1945 when he urged that France take responsibility for the 'natives'. Azar points out the difference between Fanon and Camus is that 'Camus never takes the crucial step from "Frenchman" to "Algerian": in fundamental respects, he remains a spokesman for *L'Algérie Française*' (1999: 24). For Camus, there was no alternative way for Algeria but that of France. In short, Camus was never able to transcend the myth of French colonialism with all its pretensions of universal humanism. For Camus, French colonialism was vital, because he had internalised the myth that Fanon sought to deconstruct:

> The settler makes history; his life is an epoch, an Odyssey. He is the absolute beginning: 'This land was created by us'; he is the unceasing cause: 'If we leave, all is lost, and the country will go back to the Middle Ages' … And because he constantly refers to the history of his mother country, he clearly indicates that he himself is the extension of that mother country.
> (Fanon 1967: 50)

In his articulation of a new humanism, Fanon set himself the task of replacing France with Algeria without succumbing to the antinomies of the Manichean structure of colonialism. As Azar points out, this entails 'nothing less than a 'right to citizenship' in a world of "reciprocal recognitions" ' (Azar 1999: 31).

From decolonisation to liberation

This possibility of transformation has resonance for postcolonial societies. Through decolonisation, the colonised country begins to construct a history. This can be conceived only as a result of the war of liberation whereby the colonised nation is able 'to rediscover its own genius, to reassume its history and assert its sovereignty' (Fanon 1970: 94). In order to reclaim their history, it is not enough that the colonial power be defeated. A new consciousness that is part of the national culture is required. There is no returning to an old culture. Rather, a national culture arises out of the struggle in the fight against colonialism. This national culture 'is the whole body of efforts made by a people in the sphere of thought to describe, justify and praise the action through which that people has created itself and keeps itself in existence' (Fanon 1967: 188). This process of forging a national culture is ongoing and in many cases predates the struggle itself. Fanon observed: 'Everything works together to awaken the native's sensibility and to make unreal and unacceptable the contemplative attitude, or the acceptance of defeat. … His world comes to lose its accursed character' (196).

The revolutionary struggle, for Fanon, was paramount. Both a new consciousness and a new society are restructured through such a struggle. This new consciousness can arise only by destabilising the colonial order and, through the struggle, 'there is not only the disappearance of colonialism but also the disappearance of the colonised man' (Fanon 1967: 197). Political education is central to forging a new consciousness. Fanon pointed to the centrality of educating the masses for they are integral to the process of transformation:

> To educate the masses politically … is to try, relentlessly and passionately, to teach the masses that everything depends on them; that if we

> stagnate it is their responsibility, and that if we go forward it is due to them too, that there is no such thing as a demiurge … but that the demiurge is the people themselves and the magic hands are finally only the hands of the people.
>
> (1967: 157)

Through this process of education the cultural domination of the colonial power can be eradicated and a new national culture established in which the mass of the people can be integrated. The restructuring of consciousness becomes central to the decolonisation process. Fanon demonstrates that it is not enough to merely attain decolonisation but that it is important to decolonise the mind. He argued that it 'is not possible to take one's distance with respect to colonialism without at the same time taking it with respect to the idea that the colonised holds of himself through the filter of colonialist culture' (1970: 114). As Sekyi-Otu has noted, Fanon's message can be starkly stated as:

> the moral credibility of the fight against the white man, the legitimacy of the postcolonial age, the justice of transactions among its citizenry and of the forms of governance under which they live – all this rests on the degree to which the independence of persons is honoured.
>
> (1996: 237)

Fanon's vision of liberation had a profound influence on Edward Said (see Ashcroft and Ahluwalia 1999). Said undertook a contrapuntal rereading of Fanon in order to carry forward Fanon's project of liberation, pointing out that his work was aimed at forcing the metropole to rethink its history in light of the decolonisation process.

Edward Said's emphasis on the impact of the colonial experience on both the colonised and the colonisers borrows directly from Fanon's discussion of the 'pitfalls of nationalist consciousness'. And it is here that Said's reading of Fanon is crucial, because 'he expresses the immense cultural shift from the terrain of nationalist independence to the theoretical domain of liberation' (1993: 323–24). For Fanon, it was important not only to recreate national identity and consciousness in the process of decolonisation but also to go beyond and create a social consciousness at the moment of liberation. Social consciousness became all the more important because, without it, decolonisation merely became the replacement of one form of domination by another.

In *Culture and Imperialism*, Said speculated that Fanon had been influenced by Lukács in reading his *History and Class Consciousness*. This conjecture allowed Said to read violence in Fanon as 'the synthesis that overcomes the reification of White man as subject, Black man as object' (1993: 326). Violence, for Fanon, Said argued, is the 'cleansing force' that allows for 'epistemological revolution' which is like a Lukácsian act of mental will that overcomes the fragmentation and reification of the self and the other. The need for such violence arises when the native decides that 'colonization must end'. For Fanon:

> The violence of the colonial regime and the counter-violence of the native balance each other and respond to each other in an extraordinary reciprocal homogeneity ... The settler's work is to make dreams of liberty impossible for the native. The native's work is to imagine all possible methods for destroying the settler. On the logical plane, the Manicheanism of the settler produces a Manicheanism of the natives, to the theory of the 'absolute evil of the native' the theory of the 'absolute evil of the settler' replies.
>
> (cited in Said 1993: 327)

This quotation has two important implications for Said's hypothesis of Lukács' influence on Fanon. First, this influence meant that Fanon reified the subject and the object. Second, Fanon came to see violence as an act of mental will that overcomes this reification. Said argued that Fanon's was not a simplistic nationalism that arose out of the cleansing force of violence. Rather, Fanon recognised that 'orthodox nationalism followed along the same track hewn out by imperialism, which while it appeared to be conceding authority to the nationalist bourgeoisie was really extending its hegemony'. This allows Said to argue that, in Fanon, the emphasis on armed struggle was tactical and that he wanted 'somehow to bind the European as well as the native together in a new non-adversarial community of awareness and anti-imperialism' (1993: 330–31). For Fanon, all colonial revolutions were to free blacks as well as whites and therefore 'show the white man that he is at once the perpetrator and the victim of a delusion' (1967: 225).

Conclusion

Jean-Paul Sartre, Albert Camus and Frantz Fanon are names that are inextricably linked with Algeria. For all three, Algeria, the French colony, represented an excessive land that was indelibly marked by colossal violence. Each of them was an important axis in both Algeria and France, taking positions that were to divide both nations. The juxtaposition of Camus and Sartre and Fanon illustrates the manner in which the Algerian question polarised a whole generation. For Fanon and Sartre the response to the colonial carnage was not a reaffirmation of the Enlightenment ideals of universal brotherhood, fraternity, justice and equality, ideals that Camus cherished to the very end. Rather, they were committed to destroying the very system that had produced these same inequalities. Above all, it was Fanon who 'lived, fought, and died Algerian' (Macey 2000: 30).

Robyn Dane argues that, because Fanon defies easy classification and in light of the theoretical inconsistencies in his work, he should be viewed as a cultural visionary, 'one of those vexing thinkers for whom we have no label, a philosopher of language, a poetic epistemologist, that person who points to the symbolic, drags us to the event, because we have lost sight of something precious – usually our humanity' (Dane 1994: 75). Dane has argued that Fanon's 'mightiest act was not advocating violent "catharsis", it was legitimizing native rage against the absolute power of imperialism' (79). Fanon sought a way out of the Manichean structure of colonialism, where the black person has two choices: either to turn white so that his or her blackness can no longer be detected or to reverse the colonial order. As Edward Said pointed out, 'One ought to be able to make more precise the interpretations of various political and intellectual communities where the issue is not independence but liberation, a completely different thing. What Fanon calls the conversion, the transformation, of national consciousness, hasn't yet taken place'. (Sprinker 1992: 236)

Chapter 4

Derrida

> I was born in Algeria, but already my family, which had been in Algeria for a long time, before the French colonization, was not simply Algerian. The French language was not the language of its ancestors. I lived in the pre-independent Algeria, but not all that long before Independence. All of this makes for a landscape that is very, very … full of contracts, mistures, crossings. The least statement on this subject seems to me to be a mutilation in advance.
>
> (Jacques Derrida)

> The home of the Jews and the poet is the text; they are the wanderers, born only of the book. But the freedom of the poet depends, in Derrida's interpretation, on the breaking of the tablets of law (slaying Moses again). … Both the poet and the Jew must write and must comment, because both poetry and commentary are forms of exiled speech, but the poet need not be faithful nor bound to any original text.
>
> (Susan Handelman)

The place of Algeria in Derrida's work is the place of origins, and consequently it is the place of the scandalous, the erased, the deferred. There can be no more contentious issue in the philosopher's oeuvre, no more deconstructed concept, than origins: the origin of writing, of meaning, of the text. The rejection of origin itself as an ultimate locus, a beginning, a final arbiter of meaning, lies at the 'centre' of the philosophy and practice of deconstruction. It is no surprise, therefore, that the historical facts of Derrida's upbringing in colonial Algeria have not been widely known; indeed, that the events of his own origin have been systematically elided, excluded and glossed over. Christopher Norris has argued that Derrida's biographical details and his formative experiences are not relevant to an understanding of his work. They only become relevant 'to his *writing* insofar as they take the form of a relentless interrogation of philosophy by one who – for whatever reason – shares rather few of philosophy's traditional beliefs'. This explains 'Derrida's reluctance to supply that familiar kind of background information which relates "life" to "work" through a presupposed logic of one-way causal influence' (Norris 1987: 12).

The location of Derrida the person, however, like the location of other settler Algerians, specifically focuses the 'location' of Derrida's theory. Perhaps no other writer so comprehensively brings into view the question of the status of origins in intellectual work. Do we need to be bound to an understanding of origins as transcendent, or fixed, an immutable beginning? Why should Algeria matter? How do we negotiate the difficult terrain between essentialist notions of influence and presumptions of the text's disassociation from the world?

The fact that Derrida is Algerian raises a number of questions that circulate around the heresy of origin. How different would his work have been had he not been born in Algeria? For example, it is possible simply to read Derrida's work without acknowledging his colonial roots. As Derrida himself has noted, 'I do not believe that anyone can detect *by reading*, if I do not declare it, that I am a "French Algerian" ' (1998: 46). What happens when his Algerian locatedness is taken into account? What impact did his formative years have on his later work? What of deconstructive theory or Derridean logocentrism? Does his overall project reflect his colonial roots and the tensions that arise out of being relocated within a new culture? Is the fate of Derrida of belonging and not belonging in both French and Algerian culture, of occupying that in-between space, part of his own alterity that inevitably makes its way into his writings, relevant to understanding his work? Does his profound influence on contemporary thought need to be contextualised against the backdrop of Algeria and the experience of colonisation? Is it the sense of exile, of being on the margins that allows him to challenge Western theory? Is there a different way of reading and enjoying Derrida's oeuvre whilst taking into account his own Algerian subjectivity? Does his work reflect its postcolonial source, or the tension arising from his experience of displacement? This chapter seeks to understand the effects of Derrida's colonial origin upon his theory and considers the implications for his theory of the suppression of that origin. These are not questions that need to be bound to egregious notions of influence; rather, they approach Derrida's own *texts* in their cultural location, their worldliness. In this respect, these questions are not so much about Derrida's theory as about the locatedness of theory itself.

Origins

Jacques Derrida's Algerian heritage is of long standing. He was born on July 15, 1930, the third son of Aime Derrida and Georgette (Safar) Derrida in El-Biar, Algeria, into a prosperous Sephardic Jewish family whose roots could be traced to those who had fled the Spanish Inquisition.[1] The Derrida family initially lived in a house in La Rue Saint-Augustin but in 1934 moved to a house that was named 'Pardes', 13, Rue d'Aurelle-de-Paladines also in El-Biar (Bennington and Derrida 1993: 325; Powell 2006). It was from this location that he attended school. However, the outbreak of the Second World War was to have a profound impact on the young Derrida, as Algerian Jews were subjected to persecutions despite the absence of any German occupation. It was as a young child that Derrida experienced anti-Semitism when the head teacher at school during roll call declared, 'French culture is not made for little Jews' (Bennington and Derrida 1993: 326). Considering his origins, whether in a literal or metaphoric sense, it is not possible to escape the profound and formative experience of his Jewishness. It has been suggested that Derrida's identity as a Sephardic Jew underlies 'the depth, rigor, and passion of the attack that he launches on the Western tradition' (Megill 1985: 276). Yet, Gideon Ofrat has pointed out recently that, 'beyond a few fitful glimmers, the decisive sway Derrida's philosophy has exercised over Western creativity and critical ideas these past twenty years, called for no illumination of its Jewish aspect' (2001: 1). Nevertheless, it is important to add to this: to recognise that in Derrida's case this very 'Jewishness' has been energised and directed by the pressure of a continually suppressed colonial background. It is a suppression that Derrida himself engaged in, living up to his own pronouncement that 'there is nothing outside the text' by not wanting anything personal to appear in print and, from 1962 to 1979, he went so far as not even to allow himself to be photographed for a publication (Stephens 1991). It is the scars of a colonial background that alert us to the return of the colonial into European thought. It is this colonial background that locates and energises the disruption of European modernity.

In 1941, Derrida joined Lycee Ben Aknoun where at the very beginning of the next school year he was to experience anti-Semitism on a personal level when he was expelled because of his religion. This experience, no doubt, left an indelible mark:

> It's an experience which leaves nothing intact, something you can never again cease to feel. The Jewish children were expelled from school. In the principal's office: 'Go back home, your parents will explain.' Then the Allies land, and it's the period of what was called the two-headed government (de Gaulle-Giraud): racial laws were maintained for a period of almost six months, under a 'free' French government, friends who no longer knew you, the insults, the Jewish lycée with teachers expelled without a murmur of protest from the colleagues. I was enrolled there, but I skipped classes for a year.
>
> (cited in David 1988: 74)

Although Derrida never forgot that moment of double marginalisation, the moment became more embedded in his theory than in his speech, for Algeria itself remains the repressed, the silent, the forgotten origin of his autobiography.

In 1943, Derrida enrolled at Lycee Emile-Maupas, a Jewish school run by teachers who had been excluded from the public school system. It was later in that year that he was allowed to return to Lycee Ben Aknoun but the experience of expulsion, anti-Semitism as well as a desire to play professional soccer all contributed to his failing the baccalaureate exam in 1947. It was at this time that he attended a philosophy class at Lycee Gautier in Algiers and considered a career as a teacher. Nevertheless, he passed the baccalaureate in June 1948 and signed up in the advanced literature class at Lycee Bugeaud in Algiers. In 1950, he went to France for the very first time but it was not until 1952 that he was admitted finally to the Ecole Normale Supèrieure where he met Louis Althusser. The next year he met Foucault and attended his lectures. In 1957, he returned to Algeria to do his military service and was seconded to a school in Kolea, where he taught French and English. In addition, he translated press articles and often met Pierre Bourdieu in Algiers.

Derrida's Algerian origins and his Jewish background are testimony to the importance of his identity, to his feelings of nonbelonging and otherness. It is here that the personal becomes political and inevitably part of Derrida's overall project. The issues of the other, the excluded, the margins, boundaries are all personal in his case. As Derrida himself writes,

> The phenomena which interest me are precisely those that blur the boundaries, cross them, and make their historical artifice appear, also their violence, meaning the relations that are concentrated there and actually capitalize themselves there interminably. Those who are sensitive to all stakes of 'creolization' … assess this better than others.
>
> (Derrida 1998: 9)

The powerful symbolism evoked by the frontier as a site where memory is sanctified is important for rethinking and re-examining the impact of the colonial experience on the imaginary of identity. The following excerpt from an interview with Catherine David of *Le Nouvel Observateur* (N.O.), nevertheless, illustrates the difficulties that Derrida had in contending with Algeria.

N.O.: Just now you spoke about Algeria, where it all began for you …

JD: Ah, you want me to tell you things like "I-was-born-in-El-Biar-in-the-suburbs-of-Algiers-in-a-petit-bourgeois-Jewish-family-which-was-assimilated-but …" Is this really necessary?

N.O.: How old were you when you left Algeria?

JD: Please, now … I came to France when I was nineteen. Before then, I had never been much past El-Biar. The war came to Algeria in 1940, and with it, already then, the first concealed rumblings of the Algerian War. As a child, I had the instinctive feeling that the end of the world was at hand, a feeling which at the same time was most natural, and, in any case, the only one I ever knew. Even for a child incapable of analyzing things, it was clear that all this would end in fire and blood. No one could escape that violence and fear, even if around it …

N.O.: You have quite precise memories of that fear?

JD: Yes ... in 1940, the singular experience of the Algerian Jews. Incomparable to that of European Jews, the persecutions were nonetheless unleashed in the absence of any German occupier.

N.O.: You suffered personally?

JD: It's an experience which leaves nothing intact ... The Jewish children were expelled from school. In the principal's office: 'Go home, your parents will explain'. Then the Allies land, and ... racial laws were maintained for a period of almost six months, under a 'free' French government. Friends who no longer knew you, the insults, the Jewish lycée with teachers expelled without a murmur of protest from their colleagues. I was enrolled there, but I skipped classes for a year.

N.O.: Why?

JD: From that moment – how can I say it – I felt displaced in a Jewish community, closed unto itself, as I would in the other (which they used to call 'the Catholics') ... A paradoxical effect, perhaps of this bludgeoning was the desire to be integrated into the non-Jewish community, a fascinated but painful and distrustful desire, one with a nervous vigilance, a painstaking attitude to discern signs of racism in its most discreet formations or in its loudest denials. Symmetrically, oftentimes I felt an impatient distance with regard to various Jewish communities, when I have the impression that they close in upon themselves, when they pose themselves as such. From all of which comes a feeling of non-belonging that I have doubtless transposed ...

N.O.: In philosophy?

JD: Everywhere.

(David 1988: 74–75).

The autobiographical details that can be gleaned from this exchange, and often recalled by Derrida in several of his later writings and interviews, reveal the complexities faced by the Jewish community in Algeria. The Algerian Jews were essentially nonindigenous 'natives' much like the Indians of Southern and Eastern Africa (Ahluwalia 1995; Ahluwalia and Zegeye 2001). These nonindigenous 'natives' occupied a particularly ambivalent space between the coloniser and the colonised.[2] These subject races were 'virtual citizens' who received preferential treatment under the law. As Mahmood Mamdani points out, they were

> deprived of rights of citizenship, yet considered to have the potential of becoming full citizens. Though colonized, they came to function as junior clerks in the juggernaut that was the civilizing mission. Without being part of colonial rulers, they came to be integrated into the machinery of colonial rule as agents, whether in the state apparatus or in the marketplace. As such, they came to be seen as both instruments and beneficiaries of colonialism, however coerced the instrumentality and petty the benefits.
>
> (2001: 27)

For Derrida, coming from this community has contributed to concerns with identity that are best reflected in his self-designation as a Jewish 'Franco-Maghrebin'. This hyphenated designation, he reminds us, 'does not pacify or appease anything, not a single torment, not a single torture' (Derrida 1998: 11). The anti-Semitism that he describes in the foregoing interview revolves around the question of citizenship, which for these 'virtual citizens' is at the behest of the colonial power. In a recent interview, Derrida spoke about this explicitly:

> The Jewish community in Algeria was there long before the French colonizers. So on the one hand, Algerian Jews belonged to the colonized people, and on the other they assimilated with the French. During the Nazi occupation, there were no German soldiers in Algeria. There was only the French and the Vichy regime, which produced and enforced laws that were terribly repressive. I was expelled from school. My family lost its citizenship. When you're in such a marginal, and unsafe and shaky situation, you are more attentive to the question of your legal authorization. You are a subject whose identity is threatened, as are your rights.
>
> (Rosenfeld 1998)

The question of citizenship dates back to the latter part of the nineteenth century when, as France's control appeared precarious, the French exploited their relationship with the Jewish population in order to ensure their continued rule. In 1870, they were granted full French citizenship by the Crémieux decree and from that time, they identified themselves with the European French (Wood 1998). The effect of granting citizenship was that the *colons* now had an ally community. Relations between the French and the Jewish Algerians, however, were complex, accommodating when the need arose, but generally marked by a great deal of anti-Semitism.[3] The precarious position of the Algerian Jews was made clear in 1940 under the Vichy regime when their citizenship was revoked. It is clearly an experience that has left an indelible mark on Derrida, a mark that makes him highly conscious of what it means to be a French citizen. It is not surprising that in his deliberations on hospitality and citizenship he noted:

> Usually, the foreigner the foreign citizen, the foreigner to the family or the nation, is defined on the basis of birth: whether the citizenship is given or refused on the basis of territorial law or the law of blood relationship, the foreigner is a foreigner by birth, is a born foreigner.
>
> (Dufourmantelle and Derrida 2000: 87)

The link between the Sephardim and postcolonial identity is uncannily deep. In 1492, the very year that Columbus sailed uninvited for American shores, Ferdinand and Isabella expelled the Jews from Spain. Just days after the last ship of Jewish exiles set sail southward, Columbus sailed westward.

The Sephardic Jews expelled by Spain were those Oriental Jews who had spread through North Africa and Spain from the beginning of the dispersion. For several generations the Derrida family were considered indigenous Algerian Jews, revealing that Derrida's African roots were indeed very deep. The link between the discovery of America and the expulsion of the Sephardic Jews is a potent symbol in Derrida's own cultural history. More intriguing, it seems symbolic in the origin of Derrida's philosophy, an overdetermination that would be hard to invent. However, the connection returns with material force in Derrida's own life. This historical experience of the Algerian Jews who occupied such a unique place within colonial Algeria had a profound impact on Derrida's views about citizenship and belonging. In an interview, when he was asked a question about his identity, he responded: 'Each time this identity announces itself, each time a belonging circumscribes me, if I may put it this way, someone or something cries: Look out for the trap, you're caught, take off, get free, disengage yourself. Your engagement is elsewhere' (Weber 1995: 340).

Derrida's relationship with Algeria, or his 'nostalgeria' as he calls it, has at best remained ambivalent.

> No doubt these are the years during which the singular character of J.D.'s 'belonging' to Judaism is imprinted on him: wound, certainly, painful and practiced sensitivity to antisemitism and any racism, 'raw' response to xenophobia, but also impatience with gregarious identification, with the militancy of belonging in general, even if it is Jewish. In short, a double rejection – of which there are many signs, well before *Circumfession*.
>
> (Bennington and Derrida 1993: 326–27)

While condemning France's colonial policy in Algeria he hoped, until the last moment, for a compromise that would induce indigenous Algerians and the *pieds-noirs* to live together peacefully. He even tried to prevent his parents from leaving Algiers in 1962, but soon realised that history had outrun such hopes for a transformed postcolonial state (Bennington and Derrida 1993: 330). In this tendency, we find a desperate desire for the stability of home that seems so at odds with his theory. For him, as we shall see, home, the beginning-point, became 'where you are'. Derrida would go back twice: in 1971, to lecture at the University of Algiers and in 1984, to visit his old home, but effectively Algeria disappeared from his life. It remains, however, the origin of origins, the ultimately deferred, unarticulated, palimpsestic and avoidable site of marginality and displacement.

Origin and displacement

For Derrida, there are no ontological origins. It is from this perspective that the very origins of writing need to be considered. How does it actually appear?

Clearly, this is a question about origins. However, Derrida argues, 'But a meditation upon the trace should undoubtedly teach us that there is no origin, that is to say, simple origin; that the questions of origin carry with them a metaphysics of presence' (1976: 74). The corollary of the anxiety of origin in Derrida's work is the predominance of displacement, a concept that is usually associated with Freud's interpretation of dreams, but which has expanded from a technical psychoanalytic term to a process encompassing a wide range of deconstructive strategies in post-structuralist theory. As Krupnick points out, displacement is not theoretically articulated by Derrida, but deconstruction itself proceeds by way of displacement, first reversing a binary opposition and then displacing it (1983: 1). For Derrida, it is not simply the case that the binary oppositions of metaphysics should be neutralised. Rather, deconstruction entails a reversal and displacement, because within familiar philosophical binaries there is always a violent hierarchy. One term of the binary is always superior to the other. It is the task of deconstruction to disrupt that hierarchy, to place the superior term under erasure. As Spivak points out, the task for deconstruction is:

> To locate the promising marginal text, to disclose the undecidable moment, to pry it loose with the positive lever of the signifier, to reverse the resident hierarchy, only to displace it; to dismantle in order to reconstitute what is always already inscribed.
>
> (1976: lxxvi)

The hierarchical opposition between speech and writing is not eliminated; rather it is *displaced*, cut loose from its metaphysical grounding. Post-structuralism itself is a 'displacement' of structuralism, which does not mean a 'replacement' or unfolding through time: 'It is more a question of an interrogation of structuralism's methods and assumptions' a transformation (Krupnick 1983: 4). In this respect, the term, used in this way, also provides a succinct account of the relationship between colonialism and postcolonialism: displacement as interrogation, engagement, transformation rather than a chronological development from its hegemonic precursor. The binary opposition so prevalent within postcolonial studies, that of the coloniser and colonised, is one that Derrida was all too familiar with. The Algerian War of Independence was testimony of how the superior term could be disrupted, placed under erasure and yet never erased.

Nevertheless, there is another way, a more historical, social and cultural way, in which the term 'displacement' forms a link between Derrida's post-structuralist project and his colonial origins. This is the sense of displacement as an *experience*: the experience of being out of place, *unheimlich*. The word itself thus comes to embody in its different uses both the concept of interrogation central to deconstruction, and the concept of cultural disarticulation that emerges as a fundamental feature of postcolonial experience in language, place and culture. As Ofrat argues, 'Derrida identifies this consciousness of estrangement from roots and tradition, of amnesia, with deconstruction. The eternal estrangement between writing and origin is a person's sentence of estrangement between his culture and its sources' (2001: 17–18).

This connection is itself a 'displacement' rather than a history, an etymology. In this displacement, we find the political paradox of deconstruction. For if, as Krupnick claims, deconstruction as Derrida 'practices it allies itself with the voiceless, the marginal, the repressed' (1983: 2), then it would seem that the occlusion of origins, the elision of the material location that Algeria metonymises, disables the political efficacy of that alliance, for it has 'no conviction that the old … order can be transcended' (2). It is in this aporia in Derrida's deconstructive strategy, the gap between the alliance with the marginalised and emancipatory potential of that alliance, that we find the repression of his own colonial origin – Algeria.

In Derrida's Algeria, we find a double cultural displacement. No matter how long-standing his family's residence in Algeria, a sense of cultural displacement was impossible to avoid. The very character of French colonialism – with its prodigious propulsion towards assimilation, its legislation of colonies as departments of France, its overwhelming linguistic and cultural centralisation – far from giving colonies a sense of cultural integrity, installed a spiritual and cultural displacement (in *all* cultural groups) even more strongly than in British colonies. This displacement was all the more disabling in those *pieds-noirs* and Jewish Algerians whose link to the soil of that country seemed to weaken their links with a France that most never visited. For the cultural and political hegemony of French colonialism allowed little room for the kind of postcolonial identity construction that occurred in British colonies. The lingering 'nostalgia for a different Algeria', which characterises the refusal of *pieds-noirs* to accept the changing political status of Algeria, is a poignant demonstration of the manner in which French colonialism kept Algerian culture in a permanent state of displacement. The radical strategy of *négritude* that arose in Francophone rather than the Anglophone colonies was a resounding testament to the incorrigible nature of Francophone cultural hegemony.[4]

When we consider Derrida's location in this hegemony, the displacement that he shared with other French Algerians was intensified, layered by the marginality of his own Jewishness. We cannot talk about Derrida's roots without talking about his Jewishness. However, by the same token, we cannot talk about his Jewishness without talking about his colonial roots, his Algerian origins. The experience of exclusion, of being sent home on his first day of school at Lycee Ben Akoun in 1942, even though the Germans did not occupy the country, was an experience that affected him for the rest of his life. Derrida remembers this as a formative moment, when the radical instability of his own identity was forced upon him. After the Allied landing in France racial laws were nevertheless maintained for a period of almost six months in Algeria, 'under a "free" French government, friends who no longer knew you, the insults, the Jewish lycee with teachers expelled without a murmur of protest from the colleagues' (David 1988: 74). Even in the case of his Jewishness, the sense of displacement was exacerbated by his Algerian location.

The colonial and the diasporic are thus deeply embedded in Derrida's work, not as causes but as displacements, for arguably the strategy of displacement that pervades his work is itself a displacement of the dis-location, the displacement, of his colonial and cultural origin. In *Glas* Derrida speaks of a formative moment of dislocation:

> In Algeria, in the middle of a mosque that the colonialists had changed into a synagogue, the *Torah* once out from *derrière les rideaux*, is carried about in the arms of a man or child. … Children who have watched the pomp of this celebration, especially those who were able to give a hand, perhaps dream of it long after, of arranging there all the bits of their life.
>
> What am I doing here? Let us say that I work at the origin of literature by miming it. Between the two.
>
> (Derrida 1974: 268–69)

Here, we find the young Derrida, and Algeria itself, disappearing into the third person, displaced into the region 'between the two' worlds, a displacement into which his own deconstruction of European modernity plunges. Spivak interprets this passage as 'the Jewish child's inspiration of the absence of the father or Truth behind the veil, an inspiration that allows him to place his autobiography in that place producing the "origin of literature" ' (Handelman 1983: 98).

By placing his autobiography in the place of the Father his 'story' takes on the patriarchal power of the Father as it elides the disturbing biographical history of his Algerian identity. What Derrida is 'miming' is the centrality of the *Torah*. Writing this many years later, he recreates, re-reads, reinterprets, reinscribes a reality that is deeply inflected with Algeria. That a mosque has been taken over by colonial authorities to be made into a synagogue encapsulates the ambivalent location of Algerian identity that Jewishness works to suppress. This form of displacement was a common feature of colonial authority and in ethnic oppositions of various kinds. One could say that Derrida's displacement of the *Torah* is paradoxically a displacement of the colonial marginality that resists incorporation into the universalist space 'between the two'. Miming the *Torah*, he reinscribes its patriarchal dominance. The key point about this is that Algeria, the place of identity, is outside, permanently displaced by the Word.

What becomes most resonant in this passage is the deep anxiety of origin that permeates Derrida's thinking. Susan Handelman uses this autobiographical passage from *Glas* to launch into a compelling exposition of Derrida's debt to the tradition of heretic hermeneutics that characterises rabbinical interpretation of the *Torah*. 'To place his own autobiography in place of the *Torah* is, first of all, to displace the most primary and authoritative Jewish text – and yet, at the same time, paradoxically to continue it' (Handelman 1983: 98). Displacement may be taken, as Handelman explains, as a key term for Jewish hermeneutics in general.

While most readers of Derrida interpret his deconstruction of European logocentrism as an extension of a Nietzchean tradition of deconstruction, Handelman sees this as an extension of that displacement which is the very mode of Rabbinical interpretation.

> To be both master and servant of the Book is itself a paradoxical condition; it defines the creative tension of the Rabbinic relation to the text. For the Jews as the 'People of the Book,' the central issue is how to deal with a canonical, divine Text that claims to be the essence of reality. In other words, the central problem is that of interpretation … As a solution, the Rabbis created a system of interpretation that *itself* became another equally authoritative canon, another Scripture.
>
> (Handelman 1983: 99)

The palimpsestic 'text' of interpretation becomes as authoritative as the original text. This is a strong foretaste of the displacement and deferral that characterises Derrida's work. For what is remarkable about this heretic tradition is that the Rabbis 'accomplished in their "canonical" hermeneutic … a "revolution from within," freely reshaping and re-creating the Scriptures that had been handed down to them' (1983: 100). This question raised by the Rabbinical text is surely one source of the dissolution of boundaries in Derrida: the boundary between literature and philosophy, the boundary between the text and context, the boundary between the signifier and signified. It is this question that perhaps underlies his most notorious statement: 'there is nothing outside the text'. The interpretation of this statement, Benson argues, is that 'Derrida wants to insist both that understanding is contextual and that texts (or the world) have a meaning which cannot be simply constructed however we like' (2000: 40).

Derrida is not so much the disrupter of tradition, but one who subscribes to a different tradition. According to Handelman, the great problem of Jewish thought, especially for those thinkers who absorbed Western philosophy yet still retain their affiliations to the *Torah*, was the desire on one hand for 'an all-encompassing Scripture, a Writing that weaves together the fragments of reality', yet, on the other hand, the reality of a text that 'simultaneously disseminates endless new meanings' through its interpreters (1983: 102). It is because of this, she argues, that:

> Derrida, as part of this heretic hermeneutic, is obsessed (like Freud and Bloom) with the question of origins, and with the need to undo, re-write, or usurp origin – above all, through acts of revisionary interpretation. This is, of course, also a displacement of the 'father' – the authoritative originating principle. Derrida's target is all the fathers of philosophy.

> His project: to deconstruct the entire Western tradition of 'onto-theology', to undo 'logocentrism', to send the Word into the exile of writing.
>
> (1983: 102)

Although Handelman puts up a convincing case, it is important to remember that Derrida is often read as belonging either to a Jewish or Greek tradition. However, Geoffrey Bennington, suggests that such a reading can be problematic, and offers a 'non-dialectical way out', arguing that he is 'neither Jew nor Greek, but "Egyptian", in a non-biographical sense' (Bennington and Derrida 1993: 99). Bennington's sentiment is one that Derrida articulates in an interview:

> I consider my own thought paradoxically, as neither Greek nor Jewish. I often feel that the questions I attempt to formulate on the outskirts of the Greek philosophical tradition have as their "other" the model of the Jew, that is, the Jew-as-other. And yet the paradox is that I have never actually invoked the Jewish tradition in any "rooted" or direct manner. Though I was born a Jew, I do not work or think within a living Jewish tradition. So that if there is a Judaic dimension in my thinking which may from time to time have spoken in or through me, this has never assumed the form of an expert fidelity or debt to that culture. In short, the ultimate site (*lieu*) of my questioning would be neither Hellenic nor Herbaic if such were possible. It would be a non-site beyond both the Jewish influence of my youth and the Greek philosophic heritage which I received during my academic education in French universities.
>
> (Kearney 1984: 107)

This is a major concern given Derrida's obsession with origins. A crucial part of Derrida's hermeneutic is to usurp origin. Nevertheless, this neglects Derrida's own origin. For his origin – not filiative, but geographical, cultural – is the place of displacement. Derrida's *place* of origin – Algeria – is already the displacement of the Father – France – a displacement that is the source and scene of actual violence. Algeria as origin is not merely usurped and displaced in Derrida's work. It is also, paradoxically, the origin of displacement, the origin of disruption. The binary of Algeria/France is not so much reversed as erased in Derrida's thinking, an erasure that, while usurping origins and giving free reign to the play of signifiers, underlies the great problems deconstruction has in placing itself in the world. 'If psychoanalysis might be seen as one attempt to cure the neurosis of the Jew-in-exile', says Handelman, 'deconstructionism could be thought of as another' (1983: 123). Displacement, as it appears in deconstruction 'is both the *condition* and *answer* to exile' (127).

This erasure of location, of the place of 'origin', is linked in Derrida to the deconstruction of history, the narrative of the past. The end of history for Derrida is, in an important sense, the end of identity, a deconstruction of origin, which, for the historical subject Jacques Derrida, is the end of Algeria and the beginning of indeterminacy.

However, for Derrida, by its very provisionality, its anxious politicalf cultural and historical nature, Algeria becomes the source deferred, the origin beyond history and hence confirms the provisionality of all sources. Algeria thus is located in Derrida's thinking as the paradoxical place of displacement. Despite Derrida's difficulty with Algeria as his own place of origin, it seems too easy, too facile, to equate Derrida's sense of non-belonging with the principles of displacement, difference and deconstruction that characterise his work. Nevertheless, it is impossible, or at least problematic to ignore Derrida's Jewishness and Algerianess with his suspicion of origin. Even more poignantly, the absence of the originary is the absence of a discourse from which and within which it may be spoken. If one day 'I had to tell my story', says Derrida,

> … nothing in this narrative would start to speak of the things itself if I did not come up against the fact: for lack of capacity, competence, or self-authorization, I have never yet been able to speak of what my birth, as one says, should have made closest to me: the Jew, the Arab.
>
> (1989: 31)

The trope of displacement in deconstruction continually rehearses the refrain of loss and displacement in Derrida's life.

> Older forms of thinking and feeling *must* change with such a displacement. Displacement itself takes on a new sense. It refers not to an essentially conservative 'reformulation' that has the effect of keeping the best of the old while adapting to new circumstances. Instead, displacement now refers to a violent intervention intended to shake and demoralize the old order.
>
> (Krupnik 1983: 12)

The confluence of Jewish and Algerian displacement occurs in the complex phenomenon of 'diaspora'. In diaspora, the concurrently desolating and empowering impetus of exile drives the intellectual's propensity to break new conceptual ground. In some cases, as Said points out, this propensity leads (in the case of Auerbach and Adorno for instance) to the exile's prominent place in the advancement of Western culture (Said 1984). However, more often, by loosening the intellectual's ties with tradition, by making ambivalent that connection with 'home', it leads to a critical and disruptive questioning of that tradition. It is not surprising then that the most vigorous dismantling of the assumptions of Western intellectual orthodoxy comes from its margins.

The link between Derrida's sense of 'non-belonging' and the centrality of displacement in his theory is not a simple causal definition of origins.

Rather, it illustrates the true importance of Said's term 'worldliness'. For the 'worldliness' of Derrida's texts may be located as a structure of attitude and reference rather than a controlling influence. The world of this worldliness is a colonial world, the colonial world of French Algeria, the filiative world of the 'not quite French'. This introduces into his work the ambivalence of colonial identity itself, a marginality from which Derrida could launch his disruption of the dominance and logocentric integrity of Western philosophy. The very lesson of grammatology, David Keller points out, 'is that meaning is the result of différance, and différance is social/cultural/political/historical. Meaning does not have a specific Origin' (2001: 71).

Politics, identity and différance

The erasure of location in this concern with alterity underlies post-structuralism's erasure of the notion of identity itself and of that ordered line of history that would seem to confirm it. Derrida's own displaced and ambiguous identity (an ambiguity in which he seems to take delight) forces us to face the interrelationship between politics and identity in the postcolonial world. In *The Other Heading*, he says:

> To begin, I will confide in you a feeling. Already on the subject of headings [caps] – and of the shores on which I intend to remain. It is the somewhat weary feeling of an old European. More precisely, of someone who, not quite European by birth, since I come from the southern coast of the Mediterranean, considers himself, and more and more so with age, to be a sort of over-acculturated, over-colonised European hybrid. (The Latin words culture and colonisation have a common root, there where it is precisely a question of what happens to roots). In short, it is, perhaps, the feeling of someone who, as early as grade school in French Algeria, must have tried to capitalize, and capitalize upon, the old age of Europe, while at the same time keeping a little of the indifferent and impassive youth of the other shore. Keeping, in truth, all the marks of an ingenuity still incapable of this other old age from which French culture had, from very early on, separated him.
>
> (1992: 67)

This feeling of being an 'old' European is for Derrida much like Europe itself, which exhibits a certain air of age and exhaustion. At the same time, Derrida sees the possibility of a 'younger' Europe because 'a certain Europe does not as yet exist'. It is precisely out of this that the possibility of new Europe arises. Derrida sets himself the task of responding to Paul Valéry's question 'What are you going to do today?', in his discussion of European identity. The dilemma is a choice between a traditional European identity and the celebration of difference or to work to protect an older notion of European identity. For Derrida this binary opposition is unacceptable and he 'maintains that radical responsibility lies in negotiating the tension between the two responsibilities and renouncing neither of these imperatives' (Calarco 2000: 56). His response is that Europe is located in a singular unprecedented time and position that means that Europe does not have to become aligned with either the traditional or new idea of Europe. He insists that,

> the question of the heading of Europe left to us is not a singular question. It involves a call to be responsible both to Europe's heading and to the other of its heading. Derrida calls this an *aporia*, a double bind, or a double obligation. Yet how might we begin to assume such an aporetic responsibility, one that is contradictory and double? How can we make ourselves both the guardian of European identity as well as—and at the same time—guardians of an idea of Europe that consists in not closing off its identity, in not closing itself off to the other of the heading.
>
> (Calarco 2000: 56)

Derrida links the question of his identity to the question of Europe as an example of domination. What, he asks, is Europe? How has Europe traditionally been defined and how is the current world situation changing that definition? He retains some element of his own hybrid identity in the phrase 'the indifferent and impassive youth of the other shore', but one might imagine that any African – and Derrida is Algerian by birth – who contemplates the Europe of which Derrida speaks so eloquently must naturally enquire how it has affected Africa. That he does not, testifies to an absence in the European imagination as much as an absence in his own.

> I am European, I am no doubt a European intellectual, and like to recall this, I like to recall this to myself, and why would I deny it? In the name of what? But I am not, nor do I feel, European in every part, that is, European through and through. By which I mean, by which I wish to say, or must say: I do not want to be and must not be European through and through, European in every part. Being a part, belonging, as 'fully a part,' should be incompatible with belonging 'in every part.' My cultural identity, that in the name of which I speak, is not only European, it is not identical to itself, and I am not 'cultural' through and through, 'cultural' in every part. If, to conclude, I declared that I feel European among other things, would this be, in this very declaration, to be more or less European? Both, no doubt. Let the consequences be drawn from this. It is up to the others, in any case, and up to me among them, to decide.
>
> (1992: 82–83)

Derrida's deep indebtedness to the history of European philosophy seems to conflict with the deconstruction of his own philosophical origin. According to Derrida, Western metaphysics is

> the white mythology which reassembles and reflects the culture of the West: the white man takes his own mythology, Indo-European

> mythology, his own *logos*, that is the *mythos* of his idiom, for the universal form of that he must still wish to call Reason. Which does not go uncontested.
>
> (1982: 213)

Here we see perhaps one of the most ambiguous consequences of the rise of post-structuralism. Robert Young says of deconstruction, 'If one had to answer … the general question of what is deconstruction a deconstruction of, the answer would be, of the concept, the authority, and assumed primacy of, the category of "the West" ' (1990: 19; Syrotinski 2007; Hiddleston 2005). Paradoxically, this deconstruction of the primacy of the West has itself become, since the 1960s, a pre-eminent sign of Western intellectual domination.

The political implications of this paradox are extensive, and greatly exacerbated by the disappearance of subjectivity in Derrida's work. For it is in the area of the political that questions of Derrida's own identity and of his agency as a subject become particularly problematic for deconstruction. Cornell West, in his presentation of the project of the 'new cultural politics of difference' draws attention to the contradictory political efficacy of deconstruction. 'Most of the controversy about Derrida's project', says West, 'revolves around this austere epistemic doubt that unsettles binary oppositions while undermining any determinate meaning in the text' (1990: 30).

> The major shortcoming of Derrida's deconstructive project is that it puts a premium on a sophisticated ironic consciousness that tends to preclude and foreclose analyses that guide action with purpose. And given Derrida's own status as an Algerian-born, Jewish leftist marginalised by a hostile French academic establishment (quite different from his reception by the youth in the American academic establishment), the sense of political impotence and hesitation regarding the efficacy of moral action is understandable – but not justifiable. His works and those of his followers too often become rather monotonous, Johnny-one-note rhetorical readings that disassemble texts with little attention to the effects and consequences these dismantlings have in relation to the operations of military, economic and social powers.
>
> (1990: 30)

This is a vigorous and representative critique that demonstrates a widespread difficulty with Derrida's position and more particularly with the political consequences of the academic adoption of deconstructive practice. West's argument makes a good case not only for recovering Derrida's bracketed Algerian origins, but also for restoring the postcolonial dimension to deconstruction. 'But if Derrida insists that Deconstruction is "not neutral" ', says Mustapha Marrouchi, 'that "it intervenes in the world," … then we have reason to demand that he tell us about his ideological ties and personal identity and postcolonial background in order to think and read Derrida differently and in novel ways, too. Otherwise, by denying his Algerian source, Derrida rejects marginality and the marginalised, thus forcing Deconstruction to remain an impotent hermeneutics stemming from the center' (Marrouchi 1997: 22). For both West and Marrouchi, the retreat of deconstruction from the world, as potently demonstrated in its retreat from its colonial origins, undermines its claims to an ethical and political function. For this retreat is a retreat from its own worldliness, from those very affiliations that sustain its potential agency.

West might reach different conclusions if he were to distinguish between deconstruction as a *strategy* and deconstruction as a *philosophy*. As David Keller points out,

> Upon close scrutiny, deconstruction turns out to be a rigorously and carefully constructed philosophical theory which asserts that any text's meaning is overlaid with a complex constellation of social innuendo, explicit or not.
>
> (2001: 73)

Deconstructive philosophy, by revealing what Derrida claims to be a western obsession with presence, by attenuating meaning through *différance*, by attempting to dismantle notions of subjectivity and representation, actually undermines its political effectiveness as a strategy. For, as a technique for demonstrating how a text, any kind of text, contradicts its underlying assumptions, deconstruction may be of great use to 'analyses that guide action with a purpose', as West puts it. While many deconstructive readings may well be 'monotonous, Johnny-one-note' repetitions of a trademark self-consciousness, there is no inherent reason why the strategy of deconstructive reading cannot serve a social purpose. Its fundamental combativeness in its approach to texts supports this possibility.

Nevertheless, the efficacy of deconstruction as a technique raises questions about the subject performing the deconstruction, questions that pose unresolvable problems. As Paul Smith puts it, the supposed agent of deconstructive practice 'is paradoxical insofar as it acts, has effects, produces texts and so on; but still its role is passively to encounter forces which do not depend on it' (1988: 50). Derrida's own political commentary demonstrates a subjective agency that, according to deconstruction, cannot exist. The disappearance of subjective agency in Derrida's theory, and reappearance in his actions, offers itself as a model for the paradoxical absence and continued presence of Algeria. The retreat from its own worldliness becomes a critical problem for deconstruction for this reason. For if the signifier is nothing but a confluence of traces, yet statements about the real world can be made, then such a contradiction throws into question either the theory of signification or the statements about the world.

Derrida's definitive phrase 'there is no "outside" to the text' may be interpreted to mean that there is no unitary context beyond the text. 'Every element of a context is itself a text with its context which in its turn ... etc. Or else every text is only part of a context. There are only contexts and one cannot proceed to make the usual text/context distinctions unless one has already taken the text in itself, out of "its" context, before demanding that it be placed back in that context' (Bennington and Derrida 1993: 90). Yet, Derrida's own comments on social reality from South Africa to Israel suggest that such a doctrine, persuasive though it may be, does not help us to make statements about the world, but merely to read them. 'There is no "outside" to the text' may conversely be seen to advocate an isolated, apolitical reading of reality, which stands as an adversary to 'context' and, in its most extreme form, suggests that it is impossible to escape from the isolated literary text. This prevarication over textuality is precisely the situation Said contests in his proposition of the worldliness of the text. Every text is a text in the world, and it is this very worldliness that brings Derrida's Algerian identity to prominence. No doubt, the text in Derrida's remark, as he himself has claimed, also means the larger cultural text. Indeed there can be no escape from culture, history, destiny in social and political terms. As Derrida writes about on apartheid:

> [T]here is no racism without a language. The point is not that acts of racial violence are only words but rather that they have to have a word. Even though it offers the excuse of blood, colour, birth – or rather, because it uses naturalist and sometimes creationist discourse – racism always betrays the perversion of a man, 'the talking animal.' It institutes, declares, writes, inscribes, prescribes. A system of marks it outlines in order to assign forced residence or to close off borders. It does not discern, it discriminates.
>
> (Derrida 1986: 331)

What happens when we deconstruct this statement? Not only does it have nothing to do with South Africa but also it has nothing to do with deconstruction. What, for instance, is the significatory weight of a 'perversion' in a scheme in which all meaning is a 'perversion', a displacement, a deferral of the signifier? Where is 'racism' signified? Could it be that racism cannot exist in deconstruction, but only in the experience of 'acts of racial violence', that situation of colonial othering on which Derrida has turned his back in order to reinscribe the '*Torah*' of writing? Whether Derrida's own interventions have been characterised by 'a sense of political impotence and hesitation' (West 1990: 30), as Cornell West claims, his political comments demonstrate contradictions that seem inevitable to his theory. Whether he talks about South Africa or Israel, Derrida gives voice to that which deconstructive philosophy persistently denies – his ability to speak as a free subject.

We might say that this contradiction is located in his identity itself. Identity is not something one possesses, but something that must be continually negotiated, and the Algeria of his childhood represented a formative contradiction in Derrida's self-negotiation: to the Algerians he must have been undeniably French, but to the French he was a Jew, and expelled from school at the beginning of the war. The contradictoriness of Derrida's theory lies in the status of the 'text' of his identity. Might this be the reason 'identity' is continually deconstructed in his theory? For, just as the self is located in the other, so it is the *différance* of the postcolonial that becomes important. It is *différance* that resists the certainty of origin in Derrida's work. However, the provisionality and constructedness of origins does not obviate their necessity and power. One reason for Derrida's silence about Algeria is that Algeria itself had become, by the time of his entering university, a text being rewritten in the French imagination. Derrida cannot enter his postcolonial origin, so to speak, until he can enter a discourse with which to construct such an origin. Post-structuralism cannot, by its very nature, provide that discourse.

There is probably no clearer place for Derrida's Algerian identity than in his best-known neologism – *différance*. While *différance* is the strategy that most problematises notions of origin, particularly notions of identity, it is *différance* and its relevance to the issue of identity that most implicates Derrida, the historical being, in his theory. This becomes illuminated in the use Stuart Hall makes of the concept. Hall proposes that there are two ways of thinking about cultural identity. The first position defines 'cultural identity' in terms of 'one shared culture, a sort of collective "one true self," hiding inside the many other, more superficial or artificially imposed "selves," which people with a shared history and ancestry hold in common' (1990: 223). This centripetal view of identity leads to notions of *négritude* or to ideas of the coherence of the African heritage, the underlying unity of black people. 'Crucially', says Hall, 'such images offer a way of imposing an imaginary coherence on the experience of dispersal and fragmentation … by representing or "figuring" Africa as the mother of all these different civilisations' (224), a triangle, for instance, of the Caribbean, the USA and the UK that is 'centred' in Africa.

There is another view of cultural identity, however, that recognises the critical points of difference that constitute 'what we really are'; or rather 'what we have become'. 'Cultural identity, in this second sense, is a matter of "becoming" as well as "being" ' (Hall 1990: 225). Hall recognises that difference exists alongside continuity and, of course, the perfect concept for this is Derrida's notion of *différance*, which incorporates both difference and deferral, identity and becoming. The difference by which identity is constituted is a difference that changes, not only in relation to its others but also, so to speak, in relation to its own origin. *Différance* is chiefly deployed for the purposes of signification and 'challenges the fixed binaries which stabilise meaning and representation and show how meaning is never finished or completed' (229). In every statement of meaning, there is always a trace of other meanings, other statements we might make. Nevertheless, all these approaches to meaning are relevant to identity, for identity is, perhaps, the ultimate 'signified'. If identity is located by difference, these differences are always deferred.

As is the identity of 'Jacques Derrida'. This name locates an identity: writer of over forty books, celebrated French intellectual, driving force of the post-structuralist domination of theory in the anglophone world. Yet, the differences that 'locate' Jacques Derrida are also located in *différance*. The very inconclusiveness of his deferred identity has roots in a material history: the marginal and indeterminate cultural identity of the Algerian Sephardic Jew. To what extent, we might ask, is this material history implicated in the very strategy – *différance* – that is designed to problematise historical meaning? When we consider the marginal, problematic, interstitial space of Derrida's childhood, we enter the very ground of *différance*, because his origin is not *there*, indeed it is too powerful an influence for that. Rather, the colonial origin is the continual inflection of a theory and a range of strategies that continually problematise and undermine the centrality of European modernity. Here, perhaps, is the ultimate paradox, for the most prominent contemporary attack on Western logocentrism, the post-structuralist philosophy of Jacques Derrida, appears as yet another sign of the global dominance, the 'centrality', of Europe.

Structure, sign and play

Robert Young notes that, four years after the French left Algeria, Derrida through the notion of *écriture* proposed the idea of a structure without a centre,

> or, if that was unthinkable, the problematic way in which in the human sciences, structures are always organized around centres, origins, points of presence and power, while their boundaries remain impermeable and open. Open to people like him. To those who cross borders – gypsies, nomads, tribals who dissolve the sedentary strictures enforced by the state.
> (Young 2001a: 417)

Young's astute observation is an important one if we are to ask the question, What happens when we begin to read the influence of Derrida's childhood, the influence of his Algerian roots?

It is very much in this spirit that Lee Morrissey challenges the commonly held notion that Derrida's project lacks a relationship with either history or politics. Morrissey re-examines 'Structure, Sign, and Play' through the lens of the liberation of Algeria in 1962 and suggests that what emerges is a 'Derridean argument much more politically and historically aware than his work is generally thought to be, especially in the earlier essays' (Morrissey 1999: 1).

Derrida begins the essay 'Structure, Sign, and Play' writing: 'perhaps something has occurred in the history of the concept of structure that could be called an "event" '. He questions what such an event would be and suggests 'its exterior form would be that of a rupture' (Derrida 1978: 278). This rupture needs to be seen as the very rupture of Algeria from France, as the liberation of Algeria. A reason for this essay not being read in this particular way is probably a result of the American ignorance of Francophone Africa as well as the particular appropriation of Derrida within American literary circles.

It is the discussion of 'the centre' that provides insights into how to read this essay from a different register. This is Derrida's argument about the centre:

> it has always been thought that the center, which is by definition unique, constituted that very thing within a structure which while governing the structure, escapes structurality. This is why classical thought concerning structure could say that the center is, paradoxically, *within* the structure and *outside* it. The center is at the center of the totality, and yet, since the center does not belong to the totality (is not part of the totality), the totality *has its center elsewhere*. The center is not the center.
>
> (Derrida 1978: 279)

The centre in this context is one that is always elsewhere, always deferred. Morrissey gives the example of South Africa's National Party's response to the Truth and Reconciliation Commission when it argued that it was not aware of what the army was doing to black South Africans, thereby suggesting that power did not reside at the centre. The concept of the centre as always being deferred was vital to the Algerian War where it was never clear whether the centre was in Algeria or indeed in France. As Morrissey explains,

> Algeria had undergone a substitution of center for center, and in 1942, this new center neutralized a possibility for freeplay, mastering a certain anxiety; but the center, the structure, had repositioned … From the viewpoint of Algeria … it could be said that Paris governs while escaping what is applied to the rest of the structure, the governed.
>
> (1999: 3)

It is precisely in this recognition of how structures structure people that an event can be seen as a rupture as in the case of Algeria. What is interesting about the discussion of metaphors and metonymies in this text is that the text can be read on several different registers. It is possible to see how Derrida described his work as not belonging strictly to either literature or philosophy but that perhaps ' "autobiography" is perhaps the least inadequate name' (Derrida and Attridge 1991: 34). What is being suggested is that of course there is much more in the text then simply Derrida's biography. As Morrissey points out, this text 'could describe a decolonising experience in Algeria, that word, "Algeria", is but a metonymy for a confluence of factors, larger than, and also visible elsewhere besides, Algeria' (1999: 8).

Circumcision

In his 'Circumfession' Derrida makes a remarkable claim: 'Circumcision, that's all I've ever talked about' (Bennington and Derrida 1993: 70). The language of alterity Derrida chooses comes to circulate entirely around the 'real' fact of his circumcision. This 'immemorial' (because unremembered), incontrovertible and final inscription on the body becomes in Derrida the very discourse within which his writing is conceived, the one access he has to the embodiment of his own Jewishness, and, in his excessive and fetishised commentary, the key to his writing.

> Circumcision, that's all I've ever talked about, consider the discourse on the limit, margins, marks, marches, etc., the closure, the ring (alliance and gift), the sacrifice, the writing of the body, the *pharmakos* excluded or cut off, the cutting/sewing of *Glas*, the blow and the sewing back up, whence the hypothesis according to which it's that, circumcision, that, without knowing it, never talking about it or talking about it in passing, as though it were an example, that I was always speaking or having spoken, unless, another hypothesis, circumcision itself were merely an example of the thing I was talking about, yes but I have been, I am and always will be, me and not another, circumcised, and there's a region that's no longer that of an example. … [I]n my family and among the Algerian Jews, one scarcely ever said 'circumcision' but 'baptism,' not *Bar Mitzvah* but 'communion,' with the consequences of softening, dulling, through fearful acculturation, that I've always suffered from more or less consciously, of unavowable events, felt as such, not 'Catholic,' violent, barbarous, hard, '*Arab*,' circumcised circumcision, interiorized secretly assumed accusation of ritual murder.
>
> (Bennington and Derrida 1993: 70–73)

Derrida refers to himself as a Marrano, a pig, the name given to Spanish Jews who, although they were forced during the inquisition to convert and eat pork, continued to practise their faith in secret. As Derrida writes, 'I am one of those marranes who no longer say they are Jews even in the secret of their own hearts, not so as to be authenticated marranes on both sides of the public frontier, but because they doubt everything' (Bennington and Derrida 1993: 170–71). It is clear that for the Marrano Jews, the hiding of Jewish rituals was a strategy of survival, the very strategy that Derrida appropriates in being able to survive as an Algerian Jew at the centre. Nevertheless, he is always conscious of not-belonging, of being on the margins: 'isn't this the reason that I always adopted a stance to provoke them and give them the greatest desire, always on the verge, to expel me again' (Orfat 2001: 7).

Jill Robbins argues that Derrida's text 'Circumfession' is the first text where he 'writes something *like* a Jewish autobiography' (1995: 24). This text is about Derrida's childhood in Algeria, the death of his mother and a meditation on the Jewish ritual of circumcision. However, 'of himself, of his

Jewish and Algerian background, Derrida says nothing' (29). There is a constant reference to Augustine who also came from Algeria. As Robbins points out, 'When he interpolates Augustine into his text, he puts Augustine in the place of scripture, that is, Augustine's is the text that overwhelms his own' (25).

Derrida addresses the question of language and the question of Latin that is also the language of philosophy and theology. It is a language that he was forced to learn 'when Vichy had made it, I believe, obligatory in the first form just before booting me out of school in the Latin name of the *numerus clausus* by withdrawing our French citizenship' (Derrida and Bennington 1993: 211). This event was for Derrida his 'expulson from Frenchness' (248). Derrida's reflection of the question of language and the language of origins can be seen in the following:

> I still do not know, today [12-23-76] how you say 'circumcision' in pretty much any language other than French, scarcely, obviously, in Hebrew.
>
> I'm reaching the end without ever having read Hebrew, see someone who multiplies dancing and learned circumvolutions in a foreign language for the simple reason that he must turn around his own unknown grammar, Hebrew, the unreadability he knows comes from, like his own home.
>
> (Bennington and Derrida 1993: 286–87)

> I must have pretended to learn Hebrew so as to read it without understanding it, just before the *bar-mitzvah*, which they also called the 'communion' ... and I did my 'communion' by fleeing the prison of all languages, the sacred one they tried to lock me up in without opening me to it, the secular they made clear would never be mine.
>
> (Bennington and Derrida 1993: 288–89)

The question of language is intimately tied to Derrida's origins. While his circumcision inextricably marked his body and rendered him Jewish, his particular circumstances of growing up in Algeria meant that he never really learnt Hebrew, but only French, with all the promise of what French meant to the Algerian Jews: democracy, secularity and universalist ideals. However, the stripping of French citizenship made these notions alien. His circumcision then becomes an immemorial event that marks him. Derrida connects writing to circumcision and explains his lifelong preoccupation with writing, the sense of guilt that he can never separate from writing: Does one ask for pardon in writing, or does one ask for pardon for the crime of writing? It anticipates Derrida's desire for self-surgery, to mark himself: 'I am also the mohel my sacrificer. I write with a sharpened blade. If the book doesn't bleed, it will be a failure' (Robbins 1995: 28). It is because of this that Derrida proclaims: 'circumcision, that's *all* I've ever talked about' (Bennington and Derrida 1993: 70). Robbins argues that for Derrida the very experience of circumcision is Judaism, which as a mark of the covenant becomes inseparable from Derrida's notion of the mark, trace and writing. Circumcision makes an extremely evocative sign of deconstruction. The constant reminder of origin, of belonging, of identity is itself a trace, a sign of the absent. Nevertheless, can we trace Derrida's postcolonial itinerary, marks, signs that tell of his footprints to the source (Algeria)?

Is this the reason Algeria remains such an absence in Derrida's work? Circumcision, the permanently absent trace, is Derrida's constantly reiterated, constantly reinvented discourse of origin. It is in this that the philosophic obsession with being finds its fullest expression: the trace, the surplus, the absence that comes to define him. Algeria appears to have no obvious place in Derrida's circumfession because it is everywhere in his ouevre.

Monolingualism

It is perhaps in *Monolingualism of the Other* that Derrida is most candid about his own self-designated identity as a Franco-Maghrebin. It is an autobiographical book in which Derrida recognises that one's origins are multiple, varied and wounded. It is 'about the illusions of authenticity, the anxiety of influence, and the haunting effects of hybridity' (Maley 2001: 123). This is a complex book in which Derrida intertwines philosophical and personal reflections on questions of language, identity and memory. The text reveals a Jewish French Algerian 'tattered of identity and rootless, neither here nor there, within the culture and beyond it, within his Judaism and without it, formulates his dissociation, cultural, and autobiographical, as universal truth of culture and language' (Ofrat 2001: 15). Although Derrida is careful to point out that this book is not simply about his experience, he admits that he could not deal with the issues without examining his own genealogy. In this moment of self-reflection, it becomes evident that Derrida was experiencing a crisis of identity. However, this reflection is not aimed at reclaiming a past but rather at recognising the wounds that scar him. As Geoffrey Bennington points out, this gives rise to 'impatience with gregarious identification, with the militancy of belonging in general' (Bennington and Derrida 1993: 327). For Derrida, identity is never given, received or attained, rather 'only the interminable and indefinitely phantasmatic processes of identification endures' (Derrida 1998: 28).

Nevertheless, we can see that this sense of estrangement from roots, this amnesia, is associated with deconstruction. As Ofrat points out, 'the eternal estrangement between writing and origin is a person's sentence of estrangement between his culture and its sources' (2001: 18). Central to these cultural processes is the question of language. Arabic and Berber languages were suppressed by the colonial authorities as legitimate languages that could be studied at school. Although French was the official language of the colonies, Derrida points out that it was effectively forbidden (through an 'interdict'), it was beyond the reach of the colonial subjects, the *pieds-noirs* or the *indegènes*.

Derrida makes the point that he is a monolingual individual, that French, his only language, is not even his own. He ponders what this means by reflecting on source languages and arrival languages, both of which are always deferred, always out of reach. For Derrida, this situation is originary as these multiple languages are related in some sense through translation but not translating any one source of language. As Bennington points out, 'this situation is originary, and that anything like a subject arises from it, secondarily. The "subject", on this account, is born in this zone of arrival without arrivals, and is born as the desire to reconstitute the missing source language or departure language' (Bennington 2000: 1). In this way, Derrida reiterates his deconstructive thought that what is original is always complicated or multiple and that 'attempts to assign a simple origin to this multiplicity emerge as a secondary formation from and against that originary complexity' (Bennington 2000: 1). Bennington points out that this text is an attempt by Derrida to reflect on postcoloniality and in particular the question of language.

> The elementarily uncomfortable upshot of this is that there is no prospect of an end to 'alienation' or coloniality (if it is true that every one is alienated with respect to the language of the other, and if it is true that all culture is colonial), but that the politics of culture and the colonial consists in the type of repeatedly insecure act of invention for which Derrida calls (and which he also, regularly, appears to bring off, marking the one alienated language-of-the-other he speaks with the event of a signature), and which invents in the affirmed risk of compromise with a new language of mastery or of the master.
>
> (Bennington 2000: 11)

While Bennington's reflections on colonialism are interesting, he does not seem to capture the importance of language in French colonialism. In his own case, Derrida confesses how he has been deeply affected by this linguistic hatred and dispossession by being intolerant of accented French: 'I concede that I have contracted a shameful but intractable intolerance: at least in French, insofar as the language is concerned, I cannot bear or admire anything other than pure French' (1998: 46).[5]

This remarkable confession is reminiscent of Fanon's discussion in *Black Skin, White Masks* (1986) of the importance of the French language in Martinique. The mastering of the colonisers' language, Fanon argued, was the 'key capable of opening doors that were barred' (1986: 38). The person who possesses a language 'consequently possesses the world expressed and implied by that language. What we are getting at becomes plain: Mastery of language affords remarkable power' (18). It is all the more remarkable when this is juxtaposed to Derrida's recent reflections on the foreigner. He asks:

> must we ask the foreigner to understand us, to speak our language, in all senses of this term, in all its possible extensions, before being able and so

> as to be able to welcome him into our country? If he was already speaking our language, would the foreigner still be a foreigner and could we speak of asylum or hospitality in regard to him? This is the paradox.
>
> (Dufourmantelle and Derrida 2000: 17)

This is indeed the paradox of Derrida's Algerian roots. The inability to admire anything but pure French raises the issue about his own foreignness. Is this desire for pure French, an attempt to ensure that his own foreignness is not detected?

Hélène Cixous provides an interesting insight into the relationship that both she and Derrida have to the French language. This relationship is based on their foreignness, on being outsiders and can be likened to the relationship that Conrad has with English:

> He [Derrida] has a way of listening to the French language that is meticulous, vibratile, virgin: new, young. He hears as quickly as it speaks. Like a second language: as one reads languages by the roots. Talking is a marvellous act that escapes us: it is to hear Language speaking its languages in language. To hear oneself, to overhear oneself, to catch one's own hints. To accept this surprising phenomenon: when we swim it, when we gallop it, language always tells us volumes more than we think we are saying. I recognise his foreign relationship to the French language. I also have a foreign relationship to the French language. Not for the same reasons but from the start it was there. He has himself made the portrait of his own foreignness.
>
> (Cixous and Calle-Gruber 1997: 84)

The contradictions of striving for 'purity', for searching for the central essence of the French language are not lost on Derrida, who reminds us that he has never ceased questioning the motif of 'purity' in all its forms: 'the first impulse of what is called "deconstruction" carries it toward this "critique" of the phantasm or the axiom of purity, or toward the analytical decomposition of a purification that would lead back to the indecomposable simplicity of the origin' (1998: 46). He nevertheless has a compulsive demand for it, a demand that arises from being located in Algeria.

If Derrida is reluctant to be identified as French but instead prefers the postcolonial designation of Franco-Maghrebin, Mustapha Marrouchi suggests that it is something to which he should 'own up' so that we might read deconstruction differently.

> [I]f Derrida 'insist[s] that Deconstruction is not neutral'; that 'it intervenes in the world', … then we have reason to demand that he tell us about his ideological ties and personal identity and postcolonial background in order to think and read Derrida differently and in novel ways, too.

> Otherwise, by denying his Algerian source, Derrida rejects marginality and the marginalized, thus forcing Deconstruction to remain an impotent hermeneutics stemming from the center.
>
> (1997: 22)

In *Monolingualism of the Other*, Derrida finally comes out and succumbs to that demand, aligning deconstruction to his Franco-Maghrebian genealogy. He writes:

> Certainly, everything that has, say, interested me for a long time – on account of writing, the trace, the deconstruction of phallogocentrism and 'the' Western metaphysics ... all of that could *not* not proceed from the strange reference to an 'elsewhere' of which place and the language were unknown and prohibited even to myself, as if I were trying to *translate* into the only language and the only French Western culture that I have at my disposal, the culture into which I was thrown at birth, a possibility that is inaccessible to myself.
>
> (1998: 70)

This alignment of deconstruction with his own genealogy is all the more remarkable when considered in light of his earlier proclamation: 'circumcision, that's all I've ever talked about'. At a conference in April 2003 at the Humanities Research Center at Irvine, Derrida argued that it was race that he was concerned about from the very beginning. Is this the very playfulness that Derrida has come to be associated with? Is this part of the accusations levelled at him for not having any political commitment? On the other hand, is it that Derrida steadfastly conforms to his own methodology? In the three issues, circumcision, his Franco-Maghrebian identity and race, there is a common thread that links all these seemingly disparate concerns – the spectre of Algeria.

Derrida's Algerianness was certainly not lost on Richard Stern, who described him as 'an upper-level, not absolutely top-grade French bureaucrat, an administrator in a colonial territory (such as the Algeria) in which he spent his early life' (1991: 20). Yet, what is remarkable is that despite having resided in Algeria for most of his formative years he remained monolingual. This is indeed amazing given that even the colonial administrators that Stern alludes to were particularly apt at acquiring the language of the country in which they resided. For Derrida, his monolingualism is all the more puzzling given that his family had resided in the country for centuries. It is here that one begins to discern how the affiliation with France is far greater than any relationship to Algeria. Arabic, the indigenous language, was rejected for French not only because of the obvious power connotations attached to it as Fanon has described but also because it, Arabic, was despised by the French settler population.

Death and spectres

Death remained a topic that Derrida was incessantly concerned with since his earliest works. As Roger Starling so accurately captures,

> Death, for Derrida, is not *simply* the mark of absence or finitude, but is also both inscribed and exceeded by the trace, iterability, *sur-vivance*, and so on. It is a figure, in other words, not only of limit or necessity, but also of hope, possibility, and *affirmation.*
>
> (2002: 107)

So strong is this theme, Starling argues, that 'Culture, for Derrida, even "culture in general", is irreducibly a culture *of mourning*' (110). Such a culture originates in the very topology of mourning. Derrida's use of the term mourning can be found in *Specters of Marx*, where he argues that it 'consists always in attempting to ontologize remains, to make them present, in the first place by *identifying* the bodily remains and by *localizing* the dead (all ontologization, all semanticization – philosophical, hermeneutical, or psychoanalytical – finds itself caught up in this work but, as such, it does not yet think it …)' (Derrida 1994: 9).

Indeed, for Derrida a subject is constituted through a recognition that it is inextricably bound to mourning. As he explains,

> I speak of mourning as the attempt, always doomed to fail (thus a constitutive failure, precisely) to incorporate, interiorize, introject, subjectivize the other in me. Even before the death of the other, the inscription in me of his or her mortality constitutes me. I mourn therefore I am, I am – dead with the death of the other, my relation to myself is first of all plunged into mourning, a mourning that is moreover impossible. This is also what I call ex-appropriation, appropriation caught in a double bind; I must and I must not take the other into myself; mourning is an unfaithful fidelity if it succeeds in interiorizing the other ideally in me, that is, not respecting his or her infinite exteriority.
>
> (1995: 321)

The term 'hostipitality' was coined by Derrida to capture the risk and complexity that is entailed in the concept of hospitality. As Derrida argues 'it is to death that hospitality destines itself – death thus also bearing the figure of visitation without invitation, or haunting well- or ill-come, coming for good or ill' (2002: 360).

Throughout his work on death and mourning, Derrida notes that it is death's radical unknowability that makes it a site for ethics to take place. One cannot know death. As Jean-Luc Nancy puts it, 'I recognize that in the death of the other there is nothing recognizable. And this is how sharing – and finitude – can be inscribed' (Nancy 1991: 33). It is death that binds us together with that which can never be bound. As Watkin points out,

> Death is always in the negative, which is not to say that it is tantamount to Hegelian theories of negation and subjectivity. Rather we must take this negativity more as a simple speech act of refusal. One cannot vote for death; it has no policies. It is death's job to say no to everything.
>
> (2002: 221)

For Derrida, the great meditations about friendship are ultimately meditations on loss (Derrida 2001; Deutscher 1998: 159). Derrida's *Politics of Friendship* is essentially a long consideration of the implications of one phrase attributed to Aristotle: 'O my friends, there is no friend'. *Memoires for Paul de Man* deals with the issue of mourning a lost friend head on. When a friend dies, they live on in the mourner, which is one of the awesome responsibilities of mourning. As Derrida explains,

> the being 'in us' of the other, in bereaved memory, can be neither the so-called resurrection of the other *himself* (the other is dead and nothing can save him from this death, nor can anyone save us from it), nor the simple inclusion of a narcissistic fantasy in a subjectivity that is closed upon itself or even identical to itself ... Already installed in the narcissistic structure, the other so marks the self of the relationship to self, so conditions it that the being 'in us' of bereaved memory becomes the *coming* of the other, a coming of the other. And even, however terrifying this thought may be, the first coming of the other.
>
> (1986: 21–22)

Although Derrida has frequently indicated that he does not have any explicit affiliation with Judaism as a religion, Christopher Wise argues, 'Derrida's disavowal is implausible if not altogether disingenuous' (Wise 2001: 56). While he rejects religion, his use of the concept of 'messianicity' is based on the notion that, 'You cannot address the other, speak to the other, without an act of faith ... a faith that cannot be reduced to a theoretical statement' (Derrida 1994: 22; 2002).

It is not surprising then to find Warren Montag arguing that, 'what Derrida once denounced as logocentrism ... might more accurately be called a "pneumacentrism" ' (1999: 73). The idea of faith that Derrida appropriates, Susan Handelman argues, is inspired by the Jewish idea of an invisible God that 'is manifested through sound and the divine word does not become "fulfilled" or hypostatized into a present being. Revelation is not appearance' (Handelman 1982: 34).

In his analysis of *Specters of Marx*, Wise argues that what Derrida considers to be a rethinking of the ideological, as a

> ... 'universal messianicity', actually imposes a concept of the universal that is saturated with historical particularity and a specific political bias. Derrida's messianic structure militates for a Jewish concept of messianic

> truth as absence that in fact subordinates non-Jewish peoples, especially Palestinian Christians and Muslims, to its own idiosyncratic logic. For Derrida, then, it may not be Marx's latent metaphysics that provides the biggest obstacle for those who continue to insist upon the viability of Marxist theory (although this too must be taken into account), but the possible refusal of leftist theorists to adhere to a Zionist-friendly concept of ideology.
>
> (Wise 2001: 71)

The revolutionary energies of Marxism, Derrida argues, are all the more important at this particular juncture when there is such theoretical transformation underway. The task for Marxism is to renew itself in light of new conditions of the political despite the fact that the very space of the political is being displaced. In short, what he is arguing is that a new politics is necessary for a new political space. This new politics has to be attuned to deal with spectres, because the new conditions of the politics introduced as a result of tele-techno-media apparatuses are themselves spectral.

While the end of communism signals a major blow to the Marxist project, Derrida argues that the end of the Soviet era raises new spectres for the West, a 'haunting that belongs to every hegemony' (1994: 37). The proclamation of the end of history raises a new possibility for Derrida, a possibility of forging a New International, an International that recognises the power of spectres to challenge every hegemony. This would be an alliance of a 'kind of counter-conjuration, in the theoretical and practical critique of the state of international law, the concepts of State and nation, and so forth' (Derrida 1994: 86). Szeman argues that the aim of Derrida's book is to 'prompt us to remember spectres, to see them as something to be kept close instead of conjured away, to think them in all their guises and, in so doing, to be heirs to Marx's spirit at this most difficult time' (2000: 109).

In both his writings on death and spectres, Derrida is remarkably consistent and faithful to his overall project of deconstruction. Here, as elsewhere, we can link up these writings with his own biography, his own roots, his mourning from being removed from Algeria. It is that (be)longing that Derrida is mourning. The very notion of spectres and the spectres of Marx need also to be contextualised against his reservations, his suspicions about the role of the French Communist Party in supporting the Algerian War. His *Specters of Marx* needs to be seen as an effort to exorcise Marx and Marxism from that particular history.

Conclusion

The fact that Jacques Derrida's origins, his traces, are being read in such different ways, Greek, Hellenic, Jewish, French and Algerian, is testimony to his capacity to elude the very question of origins. It is a testimony that cannot simply be pinned down. In all this, Derrida is clearly true to his own method of deconstruction. It appears that Derrida embodies the very theory that he expounds. As Gideon Ofrat notes,

> ... the story of Derrida's past (i.e., his identity) is doomed to fracturing and internal antagonisms. It is not fortuitous that he seizes upon the texts of 'others' (it is beyond Derrida to tell his own story without resort to reading and interpretation of philosophical and literary texts).
>
> (Ofrat 2001: 5)

His identity is certainly fragmented, tattered and rootless. It is perhaps not coincidental then that, for someone whose oeuvre is so colossal, he is generally consumed through a growing number of anthologies that take up some fragment of his writing. As Simon Wortham points out, ' "Derrida" is anthologized to a wider extent and in a greater number of ways than almost any contemporary thinker' (2000: 152). This very fragmentation of Derrida's work may well be an important way to think about his own identity as fragments that are difficult to assemble together into a coherent whole.

This excavation of Derrida's postcolonial roots is neither meant to force him to face up to his origins nor to rescue desconstruction. The postcolonial origin of deconstruction demonstrates the ambivalence of deconstruction, an ambivalence that hinges on a crucial contradiction: the contradiction between the marginality (and indeed, provisionality) of the Algerian experience that seeks to dismantle the master discourse of the West, and the simultaneous disavowal of that marginality that puts deconstruction at the centre of European thought. The focus on identity and the Algerian question is clearly not in the spirit of Derrida's deconstruction project, a project that has steadfastly sought to challenge Western metaphysics and the notion of an essential centre. As Derrida the foreigner explains,

> The Foreigner shakes up the threatening dogmatism of the paternal logos: the being that is, and the non-being that is not. As though the Foreigner had to begin by contesting the authority of the chief, the father, the master of the family.
>
> (Dufourmantelle and Derrida 2000: 5)

The idea of origins is one that has been problematised by post-structuralism and yet Algeria remains like a ghost, as part of the culture in which Derrida was deeply imbued, a culture that continues to shadow him. It is Derrida himself who has pointed out that taking leave of something forces us to consider its significance. It is that departure from Algeria that needs to be taken into account, to be foregrounded, in order to consider its full significance. Derrida's biography, replete with cultural estrangement not only in Algeria but also France, forces us to question whether his writing is 'perforce philosophical therapy, conveying the message that there is no cure?' (Orfat 2001: 3).

Chapter 5

Cixous

> Everyone knows that a place exists which is not economically or politically indebted to all the vileness and compromise. That is not obliged to reproduce the system. That is writing. If there is a somewhere else that can escape the infernal repetition, it lies in that direction, where *it* writes itself, where *it* dreams, where *it* invents, new worlds.
>
> (Hélène Cixous)

> I learned from the newspapers that in the Algiers Casbah a leader of the FLN [Yacef Saâdi] and his young woman companion [Zohra Drif] were holding out against the assaults of the French army. I read the instantaneous legend. In the Casbah, the oldest of Algeria's cities, the most folded up, the convoluted one, the cascade of alleyways with the odors of urine and spices, the secret of Algiers, and, if I had been able to name it then by its hidden name, I would have called it the savage genitals, the antique femininity. Yes the Casbah with its folds and its powerful and poor people, its hunger, its desires, its vaginality, for me it was always the clandestine and venerated genitals of the City of Algiers.
>
> (Hélène Cixous)

Hélène Cixous is a specular border intellectual whose work is widely acclaimed and ensconced firmly in the interstitial space between theory and fiction. Her work is often described as écriture feminine, feminine writing, not only because of its rather poetic style but also because of the way it captures the position of women who have been 'silenced in and alienated from culture' (Rye 2002: 166). Cixous herself informs the reader of the different forms of writing that she is engaged in as well as the different ways in which her audience, depending upon their location, 'know' her: as a playwright, novelist, or theoretician. In the United States, which Cixous has often visited since the 1960s, she has been known, until recently, principally as a theorist. Cixous has recalled her fascination and engagement with New York in her recent work, *Manhattan Letters from Prehistory* (2007). What is interesting is that Cixous herself seems to feed the very separation of her persona, albeit proclaiming that she can only be understood by taking into account all her diverse activities. She informs her audience that 'in fictional texts I work in a poetic form and in philosophical contents on the mysteries of subjectivity' (Sellers 1994: xvi).

As a border intellectual Cixous' life and work is located in the interface between Algeria and France. Cixous was born in Oran, Algeria, on 5 June 1937 to a Jewish French-colonial father who was a doctor and an Austro-German mother and grew up speaking several languages including French, German and Arabic. Her father died when she was eleven and this event has marked all her writing. She has pointed out many times that she considers German to be her mother tongue rather than French. Cixous went to France as a student and in 1959 passed the prestigious agrégation in English. She married and had two children. In 1962, she became an assistant at the Université de Bordeaux. In 1965, she and her husband were divorced and Cixous moved from Bordeaux to Paris. In 1968, she attained the *Docteur ès Lettres* and was appointed *Chargé de Mission* to found the experimental Université de Paris VIII-Vincennes, now at Saint Denis, as a result of the student riots of May 1968. Her focus on fighting personal and institutional repression is aligned with several other French post-structuralists including Derrida, Lyotard, Deluze, Guttari and de Certeau (Conley 1991b: xiii). In the new climate post-1968, Paris VIII was seen as an institution that would emphasise innovation. In the same year, Cixous was appointed professor of English literature at Paris VIII. It was there, in 1974, that she founded the Centre de Recherches en Etudes Féminines and became its Chair, a position she held until recently (Conley 1991a).

Growing up as a Jewish French Algerian Maghrebin, Cixous was able to witness at firsthand the brutality of the colonial system not only for the Algerian population but also for the Jewish population (Cixous 2004a: 118). She captures the impact of this formative experience:

> I learned everything from this first spectacle: I saw how the white (French), superior, plutocratic, civilised world founded its power on the repression of populations who had suddenly become 'invisible', like proletarians, immigrant workers, minorities who are not the right 'color'. Women. Invisible as humans. But, of course, perceived as tools – dirty, stupid, lazy, underhanded, etc. Thanks to some annihilating dialectical magic. I saw that the great, noble, 'advanced' countries establishing themselves by expelling what was 'strange'; excluding it but not dismissing it, enslaving it. A commonplace gesture of history: there have to be *two* races – the masters and the slaves.
>
> (Cixous and Clément 1986: 70)

Cixous has consistently called for a change in attitudes to difference, on the grounds that it needs to 'involve "feminine" acceptance of whatever is recognised as "other" ' (Sellers 1988: 3). The theme of difference constitutes an important part of her writings and has reverberations throughout her project. Difference is a central theme that pervades her work and is inextricably linked to feminist scholarship. Cixous places a great deal of emphasis on sexual, linguistic and other differences that she sees as being central to a feminine approach to research. Feminine research, she argues, must incorporate the study of the differing conceptualisations of the essential conditions of life. Susan Sellers points out that Cixous 'endorses her belief in the value of literature as the site of the inscription of these differences, and describes how "feminine" writing presents radical alternatives to the appropriation and destruction of difference necessitated by phallic law' (1988: 7).

Such a notion of difference allows Cixous to call for an alternative approach to politics, a feminine approach that is based upon respect for the other. Such respect entails changes in virtually all relationships in which individuals engage, including those of a social, political and sexual nature, which inevitably forces changes in the cultural and political order. The centrality of difference and otherness go to the heart of Cixous's identity and can be traced to her Algerian roots. Indeed, like Derrida, she continuously transgresses the lines between the personal and the political. Cixous herself captures the impact of the trace of Algeria:

> I was born at/from the intersection of migrations and memories from the Occident and Orient, from the North and South. I was born a foreigner in 'France' in a said-to-be 'French' Algeria. I was born in not-France calling itself 'France'. To tell the truth we have to trap the appearances with quotation marks. We are not what we are said to be.
>
> (Sellers 1994: xv)

For Cixous, the many challenges that life presents, including the death of a parent, the experiences of exile, war, foreignness and the joy of childbirth, are all opportunities that underpin her writing. She reveals how writing became intertwined with herself and the other, how it became part of her body, her family, her culture, her ethnic identity, her gender, her country and even her town. She writes that her works are part of a constitutive whole that enmeshes her own story with the brutal experiences that she has encountered: 'thus my life's path will have crossed through exile + a world war + a second exile – change of country + colonial – decolonial wars + children brought into the world or lost + joys + bereavements + joys acute as bereavements …' (Sellers 1994: xv).

During the 1970s, Cixous produced a series of works that set out to explore the relations between women, femininity, feminism and the production of texts. The style that she adopted can best be described as metaphorical, poetic and explicitly antitheoretical, making it difficult to subject her work to a systematic analysis. Cixous is full of paradoxes. For example, she argues that she does not believe in theory and analysis albeit that she herself practises both. Despite being recognised as one of the leading feminist theorists, she declared that she is neither a feminist nor does she have to produce theory.

Her refusal to be labelled as a feminist is a reaction to a certain definition of feminism that she sees as 'a bourgeois, egalitarian demand for women to obtain power in the present patriarchal system' (Moi 1985: 103). Instead, she prefers to be considered as part of the broader women's movement.

Algeriance

In her autobiographical text, *My Algeriance*, which was written for her brother Pierre, Cixous writes that she was certain that Algeria belonged to the Arabs and that they 'were the true offspring of this dusty and perfumed soil' and yet she says 'when I walked barefoot with my brother on the hot trails of Oran, I felt the sole of my body caressed by the welcoming palms of the country's ancient dead, and the torment of my soul was assuaged' (1998: 153). However, being French is the thing that she finds puzzling, perhaps even uncomfortable: 'To be French, and not a single French person on the genealogical tree, admittedly it is a fine miracle but it clings to the tree like a leaf menaced by the wind' (154).

Cixous's relationship with France and her position as a French national is disturbing because of the irony of French citizenship and the manner in which it affected her family. Her grandmother was given French citizenship in 1918, which saved her from the German army at the last minute in 1938. However, in Algeria their French citizenship was taken away in 1940. She and her brother were not allowed to go to school and her father, who had until 1939 served as a Lieutenant on the Tunisian front in the French army, was not allowed to practice medicine. It is this experience, Cixous claims, that gives her a certain freedom from being trapped, from being confined by the strictures of nationality. She writes:

> Neither France, nor Germany nor Algeria. No regrets. It is good fortune. Freedom, an inconvenient, intolerable freedom, a freedom that obliges one to let go, to rise above, to beat one's wings. To weave a flying carpet. *I felt perfectly at home, nowhere.*
>
> (1998: 155)

As a child she grew up with two memories which included not only her own childhood but also her mother's: 'The German childhood of my mother came to recount and resuscitate itself in my childhood like an immense North in my South' (Cixous and Calle-Gruber 1997: 181). It is through this connection with her German mother and grandmother that, although Cixous sees herself as 'profoundly Mediterranean of body, of appearance, of *jouissances*, all my imaginary affinities are Nordic' (181). Her paternal family were Jews who were forced out of Spain to Morocco and her father's grandparents were from Tangier and moved to Algeria, to Oran, which is for Cixous 'my native city'. In Oran, she encountered 'a city full of neighbourhoods, of peoples, of languages. There were Spanish, who were Catholic; the Arabs, the Jews.

And the French. There were French French from France. And in the French there were also Jews and the Spanish' (182).

Cixous grew up in Algeria at a time when Europe was in turmoil, when anti-Semitism was at its zenith. She writes that 'I was born in an opposite age: an age of nationalisms, of re-nationalisms. My life begins with graves. They go beyond the individual, the singularity' (1997: 189). She speaks of the pain and horror of her mother's family whose fate was either the concentration camps or being scattered all over the world, separated from home. She says that this 'gives me a sort of world-wide resonance. I have always felt it because the echoes always came from the whole earth' (189). In Oran, she found paradise despite widespread anti-Semitism. Her happiness was, however, clouded by secret fears because 'on earth there cannot be paradise'. Those fears were realised with the death of her father, as she explains:

> Hell began: it is not only because we had lost everything; but also because with great urgency I had to carry out a mutilating mutation of identity. As the eldest of the family, I was obliged in many circumstances to become my father, for reasons of survival, of the honour of my mother or of my family.
>
> (1997: 197)

Cixous points out that the noun 'Algerian' is a recent development and that previously 'Algerian' was an adjective. She captures the colonial brutality that ensured that people were crudely classified:

> We always lived in the episodes of a brutal Algeriad, thrown from birth into one of the camps crudely fashioned by the demon of Coloniality. One said: 'the Arabs', 'the French'. And one was forcibly played in the play, with a false identity. Caricature-camps. The masks hold forth with the archetypal discourses that accompany the determined oppositions like battle drums.
>
> (1998: 156)

She questions the very name 'Cixous'. It is, she points out, not a French name or for that matter an obviously Jewish name (Manners 1999). There were even rumours when she was growing up that it was an Arab name, or the name of a Berber tribe. She almost did not use the name when her first book was to be published, when she considered using a name from her maternal lineage. Nevertheless, she says, 'I caught myself just in time; my name, my nose, too big too aquiline, my prominences. My excessive traits. At the last minute I renounced renouncing my marks. Accept destiny. What I kept away from, in keeping my name and my nose, was the temptation of disavowal' (Cixous 1998: 158).

The effect of Algeria is so profound on Cixous that she notes that the first sentence of her first fictional text, *Inside* (1986), was 'My *house is encircled*' (1998: 159). After the war, her family moved from Oran to Algiers, where they lived in the Clos Salembier, which, under its 'very French name', was a 'very Arab and miserable neighborhood'. Living in this particular area of Algiers was a courageous act, because very few Europeans and French lived there. Yet, despite living there, they were unable to be inhabitants. Just a few metres from their house was the Ravin de la Femme Sauvage where 50,000 indigenous people lived in an area that 'remained impenetrable'. Cixous notes that in 'three meters our poverty was wealth' (160). Her family were not treated as foreigners, because her father was a doctor and her mother a midwife. She recounts that her brother told her that, during the war for independence, French houses in their street were burnt down 'except my mother's house. She was the midwife after all' (160).

French citizenship for Algerian Jews was a vexed issue. The ambivalence of French citizenship, which plagued Derrida, also affects Cixous profoundly:

> And we the Jews, the forever-illegitimate, we were legitimate? unstable but all the same legitimate? Confusion and violence. In the Clos Salembier I lived the horror of those who know and *want* themselves to be illegitimate, who want to affirm their right to illegitimacy and who find themselves by mistake, when one shuffles history's deck of cards, mixed at times with the pack of legitimate.
>
> (1998: 163)

The legitimate were the French from Algeria who were more French than the French themselves. She recalls the relief of being declared non-French in 1941. This was the time when 'we were no longer among the oppressors. I knew the peace of the poor, and the exultation of the outlawed. Without fatherland, without awful inheritance, with a hen on the balcony, we were incredibly happy like savages absolved of sin' (1998: 165–66). Cixous points out that she knew from the beginning that she was destined to leave, she came from a family that was on the move, but she did not consider this to be a form of exile. For her, there was no need for a 'terrestrial, localised country' (167). She never felt the loss of Algeria, because it never belonged to her. Rather, she identified with Algeria's loss because of its colonisation and 'its rage at being wounded, amputated, humiliated. I always lived Algeria with impatience, as being bound to return to its own. France? I did not know it and I knew no one there. My German Jewish family had emigrated to twenty different countries but not France' (167–68).

It was with this sense of not belonging, but also of not being in exile, that Cixous arrived in France. France was for her the chance of genealogy and history, a sort of passing, a sortie. She writes:

> To depart [so as] not to arrive from Algeria is also, incalculably, a way of not having broken with Algeria. I have always rejoiced at having been

> spared all 'arrival'. I want *arrivance*, movement, unfinishing in my life. It is also out of departing that I write …
>
> (1998: 170)

Autobiography and rootprints

It is out of this departure that Cixous came to writing, equating it with her autobiography. Underlying autobiography is the constructed narrative of a biography of a life as lived as the focused embodiment of a story of resistance, struggle and the definition of personal and national identity. The lived experience, reconstructed and re-presented in autobiography, constitutes a narrative of identity formation (Cixous 2006). Cixous writes:

> I come biographically, from a rebellion, from a violent and anguished direct refusal to accept what is happening on the stage on whose edge I find I am placed, as a result of the combined accidents of History. I had this strange 'luck': a couple of rolls of the dice, a meeting between two trajectories of the diaspora, and, at the end of these routes of expulsion and dispersion that mark the functioning of Western History through the displacement of Jews, I fall. – I am born – right in the middle of a scene that is the perfect example, the naked model, the raw idea of this very process: I learned to read, to write, to scream, and to vomit in Algeria.
>
> (Cixous and Clément 1986: 70)

Verena Andermatt Conley notes that Cixous, an Algerian, Jew and woman, has been thrice culturally and historically marked and that it is because of this that she 'vows to fight on all fronts against any form of oppression' (Conley 1984: 4). Her method of fighting is political albeit textual in nature with the objective 'to read and write texts in order to displace the operating concepts of femininity in major discourses governing (Western) society' (5). Cixous presents her childhood in this way: in Algeria she came to write; there her understanding of the 'Other' came into focus and clarity. In her early work, Cixous wrote about the restrictions imposed by family, writing a sortie, a passage out through a representation of her childhood in Algeria. Conley argues that,

> Cixous had written about her position in the family triangle next to her brother, absent (dead) father, and German mother, a practising midwife who introduced Cixous at an early age to alterity and the guttural sounds of another tongue. Cixous's white sandals of childhood and the red hot Algerian sun, contrasted with the mists of northern regions, are motifs which will circulate texts.
>
> (1984: 17)

It is in In *Portrait du Soleil* (1973), an 'overtly autobiographically text whose title mockingly carries echoes of Western heliocentrism', Cixous attempts to represent the unrepresentable. It is about representations of the other. It is a 'feminine story of the eye, not one that beholds its object at a distance in a reappropriating manner but one that reinscribes the structure of the eye differentially' (Conley 1984: 40). The emergence of the third body results in the interstitial space between reading and writing. Cixous begins with the orange as a simulacrum of the sun, which is not unattainable but signifies the very origins of the narrator: 'The-sun-orange-origin: Oran-je, Oran-I, from Oran am I'. Oran, is of course Cixous's city of origin that is 'metamorphosed into the orange'. As Conley points out, it is 'A non-origin, the capital letter is replaced by a letter in lower case, the uniqueness by a proliferation of fruity simulacra. A first separation, a first cut, is but a first disjunction: a word cut and grafted onto other words. "The first time I cut a word, it was it [the orange]" ' (1984: 41). Given these origins, it is not surprising that Cixous's texts are located firmly outside the Occidental tradition. The tempo and 'indeed their lack of style – is in cadence with lacunary moments of grammatical inconsistencies, sentence fragments, image signs, portmanteau words, litanic inscriptions, and jets of letters of infinite regress' (86).

As a child, Cixous experienced and witnessed the excesses of colonialism and the manner in which the other is constructed in opposition to the self, as in the Hegelian dialectic of the master and the slave. She was all too familiar with the manner in which the French enslaved their Algerian subjects. However, she notes that this entailed the paradox of otherness: 'The other is there only to be reappropriated, recaptured, and destroyed as other. Even the exclusion is not an exclusion. Algeria was not France, but it was "French" ' (Cixous and Clément 1986: 71).

This idea that Algeria was 'French' is important to Cixous, because it mirrors her own identity construction. She was born in Algeria, her father 'Sephardic – Spain – Morocco – Algeria – my mother, Ashkenazy – Austria – Hungary – Czechoslovakia (her father) and Spain (her mother)' (131). With such a varied background, Cixous questions her own 'French' identity:

> So where are we in history? I side with those who are injured, trespassed upon, colonised. I am (not) Arab. Who am I? I am 'doing' French history. I am a Jewish woman. In which ghetto was I penned up during your wars and your revolutions. I want to fight. What is my name? I want to change life. Who is this 'I'? Where is my place? I am looking? I search everywhere. I read, I ask. I begin to speak. Which language is mine? French? German? Arabic?
>
> (1986: 71)

Cixous considers herself lucky to have been born in Algeria. Making her Jewish identity prominent, she speculates that had she been born in France or Germany she would have suffered the fate of some of her relatives: she would 'anonymiserate eternally from Auschwitz' (1986: 71). This process of identity formation defined her childhood and left an indelible mark. She lives in a continuous state of rebellion where 'it is impossible for me to live, to breathe, to eat in a world where my people don't breathe, don't eat, are crushed and humiliated. My people: all those that I am, whose same I am. History's condemned, the exiled, colonised, and burned. Yes Algeria is unliveable. Not to mention France. Germany! Europe the accomplice! ...' (72).

Cixous seeks a way out of this quagmire, and the way out for her is writing, for, 'if there is a somewhere else that can escape the infernal repetition, it lies in that direction, where *it* writes itself, where *it* dreams, where *it* invents, new worlds' (1986: 72). Through writing Cixous is able to escape the identity that has been ascribed to her; she can imagine a new world, a world that does not constrain, does not oppress and repress its subjects. Indeed, she searches for a better world:

> ... I leave the real, colonial space; I go away. Often I read in a tree. Far from the ground and the shit. I don't go to read just to read, to forget – No! Not to shut myself up in some imaginary paradise. I am searching: somewhere there must be people who are like me in their rebellion and in their hope ... I don't know who, but when I am big, I'll find them and join them, I don't yet know where. While waiting, I want to have only my true ancestors for company ... my true allies, my true 'race'. Not this comical, repulsive species that exercises power in the place where I was born.
> (1986: 72)

Although Cixous has written a great deal about the influence of the death of her father, it was only much later that she wrote about her mother in her book titled *Osnabrück* (1999). Osnabrück is the name of the German town where her mother Eve grew up and the book is an account of the inspiration that her mother has provided for her in her work. This inspiration is 'both necessary and impossible' (Running-Johnson 2001: 116). Here Cixous points out how her writing is intimately connected to her mother, who is not only her 'other' but also her source, 'the changing being who accompanies her life as well as the one who produced it' (121).

In *Rootprints*, which is as close to an autobiography of Cixous that one can get, there is 'Inter Views', which is a discussion between Cixous and Calle-Gruber. Here Cixous reveals the importance of poetic writing: 'I apply myself to 'seeing' the world nude, that is, almost e-nu-merating the world, with the naked, obstinate, defenceless eye of my nearsightedness. And while looking very very closely, I copy. The world written nude is poetic' (1997: 3).

Reflecting on her theoretical texts, which were overtly political and part of the women's movement, particularly in the 1970s, Cixous points out that her vocation is not political despite recognising that all expression is indirectly always political. She writes:

> The ethical question of politics, or of responsibility has always haunted me ... I am at once always on the alert (this began when I was three years old, in the streets of Oran, I remember clearly), always tormented by the

> injustices, the violences, the real and symbolic murders – and at the same time very menaced, too menaced in truth by the excesses of reality.
>
> (1997: 6)

The ethical question for Cixous is the question of otherness and one that is central to her work. It is a question that she deals with through the notion of '*entredeux'* which is a kind of interstitial space. Cixous explains that we are often thrown into a kind of strangeness a state of being abroad whilst at home. It is this that she has called *entredeux.* She has pointed out that 'wars cause *entredeux* in the histories of countries. But the worst war is the war where the enemy is on the inside; where the enemy is the person I love the most in the world, is myself' (10).

For Cixous, writing is inseparable from reading, from living and from the body. These processes are interconnected. She seeks to write on her insides, on her skin just as Stendhal wrote on his waistband. She tries to write the present even though it is impossible but it is that process which is itself transformative. Writing begins from the unknown, the inexplicable, the mysterious to which she is particularly attuned (Cixous 2004a). She writes:

> It begins to search in me. And this questioning could be philosophical: but for me, right away it takes the poetic path. That is to say that it goes through scenes, moments, illustrations, lived by myself or by others, and like all that belongs to the current of life, it crosses very many zones of our histories. I seize these moments still trembling, moist, creased, disfigured, stammering.
>
> (Cixous and Calle-Gruber 1997: 43)

This quest for knowing where she belongs, what her place is, leads her to imagine herself in different historical times as characters she has read about, to imagine what sort of road she would have taken in that particular time, to imagine a 'better' world. However, reality intervenes:

> Then the day comes – rather late for that matter – when I leave childhood. My anger is unmollified. The Algerian war approaches. Societies falter, I feel – the smell of my blood, too, is changing – a real war is coming, coming to a boil. And I quit being a child who is neuter, an angry bundle of nerves, a me seething with violent dreams, meditating widespread revenge, the overthrow of idols, the triumph of the oppressed.
>
> (Cixous and Clément 1986: 74)

Cixous sees a definitive continuity between her childhood, her children and her writing. In 1955, she left Algeria for France and at the Lycée Lakanal, she 'felt the true torments of exile. Not before. Neither with the Germanys, nor with the Englands, nor with the Africans, I did not have such an absolute feeling of exclusion, of interdiction, of deportation'

(Cixous and Calle-Gruber 1997: 204). Despite her feeling of paradise in Oran, Cixous says:

> In Algeria I never thought I was at home, nor that Algeria was my country, not that I was French. This was part of the exercise of my life: I had to play with the question of French nationality which was aberrant, extravagant. I had French nationality when I was born. But no one ever took themselves for French in my family. Perhaps, on my father's side, they refrained from not being French. We were deprived of French nationality during the war: I don't know how they gave it back to us.
>
> (1997: 204)

Cixous finds the notion of nationalism and nationality problematic. She is not keen to accept her French identity overtly. France was a colonising nation and this leads her to question: 'How could I be from a France that colonised an Algerian country when I knew that we ourselves, German Czechoslovak Hungarian Jews, were other Arabs. I could do nothing in this country. But neither did I know where I had something to do. It was the French language that brought me to Paris' (204). However, as she points out, the similarities between the position of women and colonised peoples was not apparent to her at that time. She was far more aware of the consequences of colonialism and its debasing effects:

> the exploited were not even 'workers' but with racism's assistance, something worse – subhuman; and the universe could pretend to obey 'natural' laws. War was on the horizon, partially concealed from me. I wasn't in France. I didn't see betrayal and collaboration with my own eyes. We were living under Vichy: I perceived its effects without knowing their causes. I had to guess why my father couldn't do his work, why I couldn't go to school, et cetera. And I had to guess why, as a little white girl informed me, 'all Jews are liars'.
>
> (Cixous and Clément 1986: 131)

In France, her Jewish identity was not problematised as much as her being a woman. At that point, she was at war when she 'felt the explosion, the odour of misogyny'. The Algerian war is an important metaphor for Cixous. The war is also a war against her as a woman: 'the enemy is all over the place: not only are there class enemies, colonialists, racists, bourgeois, and anti-Semites against me – "men" are added to them' (Cixous and Clément 1986: 74). From 1955 onwards, she 'adopted an imaginary nationality which is literary nationality' (Cixous and Calle-Gruber 1997: 204).

Feminine writing

Jacques Derrida has been a significant influence on Cixous. This is not surprising given their common Jewish Maghrebin background. In particular, they share a suspicion of binary forms of thinking. In her work, Cixous seeks to break down binaries, arguing that Western philosophy and literary thought are locked into an endless series of hierarchical binary oppositions which can be reduced to the male–female binary. In the binary opposition for her there is always one dominant signifier that is victorious – the male. She also locates death in this kind of thought; she denounces the equation of femininity with passivity and death. As Torril Moi points out, her theoretical project can best be summarised as seeking to undo this type of logocentric ideology, 'where logocentrism colludes with phallocentrism in an effort to oppress and silence women' (1985: 105; see also Shiach 1991).

In order to break down this binary way of thinking, Cixous advocates a form of heterogeneous *difference*. The notion of difference is clearly inspired by Derrida and can be discerned also in her concept of feminine writing. It is through the concept of difference that the dominant phallogocentric logic can be undermined. However, Cixous is not comfortable even with the term feminine writing, because the very terms 'masculine' and 'feminine' remain entrapped within a patriarchal binary logic. It is not the sex of the author that is important for her but the writing itself. Her abhorrence of the binary logic can be seen in her claim that all humans are bisexual. It is clear that what Cixous wants is to claim an interstitial space. This means that feminine writing is not simply the exclusive preserve of women. She notes:

> Most women are like this: they do someone else's – man's – writing, and in their innocence sustain it and give it voice, and end up producing writing that's in effect masculine. Great care must be taken in working on feminine writing not to get trapped by names: to be signed with a woman's name doesn't necessarily make a piece of writing feminine. It could quite well be masculine writing, and conversely, the fact that a piece of writing is signed by a man's name does not in itself exclude femininity. It's rare, but you can sometimes find femininity in writings signed by men: it does happen.
>
> (Cixous 1981: 52)

Cixous argues that it is not possible to define or theorise the feminist practice of writing, because it is not easy to theorise, enclose or even encode such a practice but that does not mean that it does not exist. On the contrary, she points out that 'it does and will take place in areas other than those subordinated to philosophico-theoretical domination' (Cixous 1980: 253). For Cixous, a binary indicates not only patriarchy but also hierarchy and domination. Hence, Cixous continuously seeks a way out of the binary structure, which she finds stifling. She looks for a way out where there would be a mutuality of recognition through knowing, where one takes a risk for the other, where one is not threatened by otherness but rather where one is delighted: 'delighting to increase through the unknown that is there to discover, to respect, to favour, to cherish' (Cixous and Clément 1986: 78).

It is not surprising, then, that her opposition to all binaries is intimately linked to her call for a feminine practice of writing that relates to the body. For Cixous, the patriarchal order itself can be challenged through feminine writing. She utilises the Hegelian Master-Slave dialectic to illustrate how dialectic structures dominate the formation of subjectivity and sexual difference. Susan Sellers has defined Cixous's theory 'as an/other writing' (1996: xi). The recognition of the 'other' is an important means for the individual to differentiate themselves. However, this recognition is experienced as threatening and so it is repressed. For example, in the binary man–woman it is the woman who acts as the 'other', where sexual difference is tolerated only when repressed. To exemplify this point Madan Sarup cites the example of *Sleeping Beauty*: 'the woman is represented as sleeping, as possessed of negative subjectivity until she is kissed by a male. The kiss gives her existence, but only within a process that immediately subordinates her to the desire of "the prince" ' (1993: 110).

For Cixous, the way out of these patriarchal structures is to engage in the subversive act of feminine writing practices. Her engagement with such a form of writing is centred on unearthing myths that perpetuate the logic of patriarchy; she seeks to undo their 'naturalness'. She rejects both the Lacanian and Freudian models of sexual difference on the grounds that these condemn women to negativity, because they privilege the phallus. In contrast, she calls for an interstitial space: bisexuality, which does not deny sexual difference but which recognises plurality where there is a copresence of both masculinity and femininity within a single subject. In this process, Cixous is interested in disturbing the notion of individual subjectivity as unified and stable and is keen to expose the boundaries of the self.

This form of bisexuality can best be explored in writing where alternative economies can be explored without merely reproducing the system. Such a form of writing practice, one that embodies bisexuality and promotes the interest of women, underpins Cixous's project. These concerns lead to her focus on the body, arguing that women's relations to their bodies are culturally determined. As Sarup points out, 'It is clear that she favours texts that are excessive in some way, texts that undermine fixed categories' (1993: 111). It is not surprising then that she is attracted to the texts of Shakespeare, Poe and Genet, who all embody such excess.

For Cixous, gender is central to her notion of the feminine, which she derives from a particular reading based upon laws that govern patriarchy. Her project is to formulate responses that challenge these laws through her notion of the feminine. She finds Freud's Oedipal process a 'useful model for the process by which the amorphic, desire-driven human infant is socialized to assume its adult role' (Sellers 1988: 1). In the text 'Extreme fidelity' (1988a), Cixous equates the classic response to patriarchal law to submission. She points out that women accept the supremacy of such law by internalising and accepting its supremacy. By drawing on Derrida's notion of the 'logos', Cixous points out the manner in which Eve in the garden of Eden reinforces logocentrism. Despite seeing Eve as the cause of the loss of paradise, Cixous views Eve's decision to pursue her desire as an alternative interpretation. Cixous sees this response to patriarchal law as the 'feminine', because it is separate from the 'masculine' response. The story of Eve and the Garden of Eden symbolises the manner in which we are all forced to deal with social schema. It provides us with choices either to conform or, like Eve, 'we can ignore and defy the law, searching for the means to inscribe our defiance in the attempt to subvert its power' (Sellers 1988: 2).

In 'Tancrede continues' (1988b), Cixous turns her attention to famous lovers in order to illustrate how both the 'masculine' and the 'feminine' are found in both sexes. This allows her to argue that gender identities are not fixed but that a range of possibilities exists between the two poles. Although Cixous argues for a feminine position for women and men, she recognises that the pure adoption of either position is untenable. This does not entail the rejection of biological sexual differences but rather recognition that these differences are grounded in culture. As Sellers points out, for Cixous because of the way society has determined sexual difference 'women remain closer to a "feminine economy" than men, and that it is women who must initiate the changes that will revolutionise social and political order' (2).

The biological sexual differences, however, necessarily entail different bodily experiences resulting in different sources of knowledge. These different experiences give rise to different perceptions and different potentialities of understanding. For Cixous, these differences are symptomatic of a valuing of all sorts of differences ranging from language to the manner in which identity is constructed. Sellers points out that the centrality of difference heightens the perception of difference: 'pioneering studies such as … Foucault's … have identified the acknowledgement and articulation of difference as the organising principle underlying the formation of all social groups' (1998b: 2–3). In this way, Cixous argues for a new attitude to difference, an attitude that would involve a 'feminine' acceptance of the 'other'. Through feminine writing, the binary logic of the present system can be overcome.

The way out is through challenging phallocentric and logocentric authority through an exploration of female pleasure. It is through this exploration, and through understanding bisexuality, that a woman may come to writing. For Cixous bisexuality is not some sort of biological essentialism albeit she is often accused of being essentialist (Aneja 1993; Lie 1999: 17). She notes:

> One can no more speak of 'woman' than of 'man' without being trapped within an ideological theater where the proliferation of representations, images, reflections, myths, identifications, transform deform, constantly change everyone's Imaginary and invalidate in advance any conceptualisation.
>
> (Cixous and Clément 1986: 83)

Cixous' message is in essence 'write yourself'. As Conley points out, this call is carried into her fictional texts where 'the endeavor is double: to re-traverse all the loci where women had been excluded (fiction, myth, psychoanalysis and others) and to produce a subversive fiction that is not a representation of the real but a phantasmatic writing undoing censorship and repression, toward and from woman' (1984: 52). In this way, her notion of feminine writing is a political strategy that seeks to redress the wrongs that the system perpetuates; it is in short a way out, a way to be newborn.

After many years of writing, Cixous found that the writer who most espoused what she advocated, somebody who practised feminine writing, was the Jewish Brazilian novelist Clarice Lispector. The attraction of Lispector can be readily discerned by the common heritage that they share. Lispector was born in Podolia in the Ukraine and immigrated with her parents to Brazil when she was a child as the country was engulfed by political turmoil. She also experienced the loss of a parent when her mother died when she was only nine. What is remarkable is that in Lispector Cixous found a Jewish woman who shared many of her theoretical concerns: the exploration of subjectivity, alternative relations to otherness and the focus on ethical issues.

This commonality of experiences with Lispector resonates with Cixous. For both, writing is a utopian space where one can dream and invent new worlds, better worlds. As Cixous points out, when we hear the 'voice of the mother', all sovereignty, sadism, geometric rigidity, standing at attention and states of erection will collapse in revolutionary effervescence and laughter (1981: 51–55). In this way, the practice of writing is tied inextricably for Cixous to the body and through this she expounds the notion of a feminine practice of writing. By drawing a parallel with feminine sexuality expressed through her notion of *jouissance*, Cixous argues that patriarchy can be challenged through feminine writing. As Morag Shiach has noted, her readings of any author are aimed at ensuring that she disrupts the habitual, 'to move beyond the hierarchies of dual opposition, and to challenge the deathly economy of intersubjectivity' (1991: 38).

The Gift

In his seminal study, *The Gift*, Marcel Mauss (1969), examined the notion of gift giving which, he argued, although seen to be a voluntary act entails systems of repayment and obligation. His focus was on prestations which signified gifts given either freely or under obligation and could include not only material goods but also services, entertainment, courtesies, ritual, military assistance, women, children, dances and feasts (1969: 3). This system of exchange between ethnic groups in which individuals and groups exchange everything was characterised by Mauss as total prestations and he called it potlatch. He explained that: 'Total prestation not only carries with it the obligation to repay gifts received, but it implies two others equally important: the obligation to give presents and the obligation to receive them' (10–11).

The gift has clear implications in the 'primitive' societies he examined. It was meant to confer meaning and establish a complex system of exchange defining social, political, economic and cultural relations between different groups. It represented mechanisms through which a sense of stability and coexistence could be fostered. However, for Mauss, when reason is opposed to emotion, 'peoples succeed in substituting alliance, gift, and commerce for war, isolation, and stagnation' (1969: 80). The squandering of fortunes during ritual was an important part of those societies, because those who had excess wealth could not consume their wealth in private. In short, fortunes had to be 'wasted' but the process entailed the possibility of gaining status. In his book, *The Accursed Share*, Georges Bataille (1991), the theorist of expenditure as excess, examines aspects of human culture that cannot be reduced simply to the classical economic balance between production and consumption. Bataille seeks to illustrate the difficulties associated with viewing human existence in a mechanistic manner. He argues thus that the sun is an example of giving without receiving:

> Solar energy is the source of life's exuberant development. The origin and essence of our wealth are given in the radiation of the sun, which dispenses energy – wealth – without any return. The sun gives without ever receiving. Men were conscious of this long before astrophysics measured that ceaseless prodigality; they saw it ripen the harvests and they associated its splendour with the act of someone who gives without receiving.
> (1991: 28–29)

By drawing on the analogy of the sun, Bataille examines the theory of the potlatch, which Marcel Mauss had posited, arguing that the system of exchange did not necessarily entail reciprocity. For Bataille, the purpose of gift giving is not merely to receive gifts in return, but rather power is acquired through the act of giving. Moreover, this action that is brought to bear on others is precisely what constitutes the gift's power, which one acquires from the fact of losing (70). Nevertheless, the one who receives then feels obligated to return a gift, and in the process seeks to outdo the original gift giver in order to obliterate the obligation. Yet, for Bataille, the ideal potlatch would be one that could not be repaid. It is this sense of spending and dissipation that determines and measures wealth. He points out that the purpose of the potlatch is not simply reciprocity but to confer rank upon whomever has the last word. The potlatch thus should be seen as an example of the general economy where excess and luxury are the key defining aspects. The general economy is an economy without equilibrium, one characterised by loss and expenditure without return. In short, gift giving without the expectation of return within the principle of the general economy is a luxury – the excess that is necessary to keep the system in balance.

Hélène Cixous appropriates this notion of the gift from Bataille. Much like the distinction which Bataille makes between the economy proper and the general economy, Cixous distinguishes between the Realm of the Proper and the Realm of the Gift with the former equated to masculinity and the latter to femininity (Derrida 1995; Fisher 1999; Stil 1999; Schrift 2001). For Cixous, then, there are two types of gift giving: one masculine and the other feminine. The former is tied up in mechanisms of exchange with expectations of immediate return whilst the latter is a form of giving without receiving. She points out:

> Can one speak of another spending? Really, there is no 'free' gift. You never give something for nothing. But the difference lies in the way and how of the gift, in the values that the gesture of giving affirms, causes to circulate; in the type of profit the giver draws from the gift and the use to which he or she puts it.
>
> (Cixous and Clément 1986: 87)

Cixous argues that these differing conceptions of giving are characteristic of an alternative feminine writing practice. The notion of the gift, Conley notes, is an important one for Cixous: 'the gift as excess, as spending and abundance, becomes, because of her cultural position in (Western) society, woman's essential attribute; because she has always been repressed culturally, she is more capable of giving than man' (Conley 1984: 18).

While Cixous is interested in determining differing writing practices, she advocates a feminine form of writing. This form of writing breaks down binaries, rejects fixed categories and recognises the possibility of multiple identities and subjectivities that are plural and dynamic. Torril Moi points out that the Realm of the Gift appears to correspond closely to Derrida's definition of writing: 'the feminine/female libidinal economy is open to difference, willing to be "traversed by the other", characterised by spontaneous generosity; the Realm of the Gift isn't really a realm at all, but a deconstructive space of pleasure and orgasmic interchange with the other' (1985: 113). Indeed, Cixous's vision of feminine writing 'is firmly located within the closure of the Lacanian Imaginary: a space in which all difference has been abolished' (117).

Such writing, Cixous argues, is not easily defined albeit it is closely associated with speech because of its link to music. She explores this link on the grounds that speaking is a transgressive act for women and that writing is the space for transformation. Such writing is best understood in relation to the body. Rationality, Cixous argues, is far too often asserted around the separation between the mind and body, which is only possible through erasing and hystericising the body. This relation between mind and body and their artificial separation leads her to the unconscious, with myths and dreams occupying an important place in her texts.

In Lispector's texts, Cixous stresses, 'there is a return of the living, a dazzling revaluation of primary values. One is no longer in the economy of the gift. And of love. Of how to give' (Sellers 1994: xxx). In Lispector,

Cixous finds a writer who is not only able to portray opposition but also one who has the ability to find alternatives without succumbing to forms of domination:

> How can the gift be given without creating the other the prisoner of the gift? This is extremely hard to do in reality, even in the strongest and most generous relationships. It is the subject of Clarice Lispector's writing. She does not make a theory of it, she gives concrete examples. Her narratives contain the possibility of a practice. Perhaps this possibility can only exist in texts. But at least in her writing it is there, it makes itself felt, it appears.
>
> (Sellers 1994: xxxi)

Fiction and theory

Cixous's fictional writings have provided her with a space in which her theoretical writings can be deployed. It is here that her concerns with subjectivity, and representation are explored. A large part of her oeuvre is dedicated to a critical interrogation of the founding works of Western culture (Leonard 2000: 121). In *The Newly Born Woman*, Cixous and Clément (1986) trace the manner in which women have been represented. In the first part, Clément focuses on images of women such as the sorceress and the hysteric. In the second part, Cixous points out ways to liberation. The third part is an exchange between Clément and Cixous, pointing to the similarities and differences between their works. However, above all, there is a common sharing of the need to give voice to silenced, marginalised women.

Cixous points out the manner in which women have been marginalised in both philosophy and literature and questions the solidarity between logocentrism and phallocentrism. She equates the oppression and repression of women to the 'dark continent', arguing that:

> She has not been able to live in her 'own' house, her very body. She can be incarcerated, slowed down appallingly and tricked into apartheid for too long a time – but still only for a time. One can teach her, as soon as she begins to speak, at the same time as she is taught her name that hers is the dark region: because you are Africa, you are black. Your continent is dark. Dark is dangerous. You can't see anything in the dark, you are afraid ... And we have internalised this fear of the dark. Women haven't had eyes for themselves. They haven't gone exploring in their house. Their sex still frightens them. Their bodies, which they haven't dared enjoy have been colonised. Woman is disgusted by woman and fears her.
>
> (Cixous and Clément 1986: 68)

In this way, men have committed the greatest crime against women: they have appropriated the colonial strategy of divide and rule to ensure that women hate women and thereby do men's dirty work. 'The "*Dark Continent*" *is neither dark nor unexplorable*' (1986: 69), writes Cixous; the way out is through challenging the phallocentric and logocentric authority that represses women. Through this challenge, a woman comes to writing.

Theatre and myth

Increasingly, Cixous has begun to write for the theatre, giving her a space in which to explore her analyses of subjectivity and their relationship to the body. It is particularly in the theatre that women have been objectified and served as the other to men, thereby silencing women and negating their bodies, rendering them as objects of display. In this context, she utilises the theatre as a space where it is possible to expose visually the forms of representation, oppression and repression that women experience (Fort 1997). As Madan Sarup notes, Cixous is able to illustrate that the 'theatre functions as specular fantasy, where women characters function as mirrors of male heroism. Women in such theatre are silenced and repressed, their bodies both negated and elevated to the level of display' (1993: 114–15). Cixous has pointed out that she sees her theatrical writing as being different, that she writes her fiction with one hand and her theatre with another (1989: 126).

In her early plays, Cixous was interested in exploring women's relations to patriarchy while her new plays seem to be increasingly concerned with issues of ethnicity and nationalist struggle. Hence, her work on Cambodia and India become metaphors for the 'competition between different conceptions of personal and social relations' (Sarup 1993: 115). It also illustrates her interest in resistance. As Sarup points out, writing for the theatre has opened up new avenues for Cixous's project, allowing her to explore 'different relations to otherness, to develop her theorisation of the bodily dimensions of language, to posit the existence of alternative social and subjective economies, and to tie her theoretical work to the mechanisms of historical change' (115). This transformation has meant that Cixous's work is now directed at understanding women's struggle as part of a larger movement, 'to realise the subjective and collective dimensions of a feminine economy, to preserve cultural diversity in the face of homogenisation, and to resist the different forms of social domination' (116). As Cynthia Running-Johnson has pointed out, the transition to the theatre was a turning point for Cixous where she moved the focus from 'the body to history, from the self to others' (1999: 247). However, it is important to note that Cixous's work on the cultural other has not escaped criticism on the grounds that it borders on a kind of orientalism that homogenises and silences the other woman (Aneja 1993; Davis 1999; Manners 1999; Sellers 1996; Shiach 1991: 65–66; 122–23).

Although Cixous argues that it is not possible to define feminine writing, it is proximate to speech. Speech is important, because it is related to song and the unconscious. Indeed, speech 'is a powerfully transgressive act for women, and writing is a privileged space for transformation' (Sarup 1993: 112). Writing, however, is best understood and produced in relation to the body. The separation between mind and body comes at the expense of hystericising the body. Through the use of myth and dream Cixous explores the repressed and seeks to unsettle the notion of subjective autonomy and conscious control. For Cixous, moving beyond the rational and that which can be known 'towards the site of creation, multiple subjectivity and the bodily roots of human culture derives from a close study of Nietzsche' (Sarup 1993: 112).

Ann Rosalind Jones has characterised Cixous's writing as a 'growing collection of demonstrations of what id-liberated female discourse might be' (1985: 365). Her texts are fictions in which 'tableaux, poems, fables, images intermingle endlessly' (Micha 1977: 115). Cixous's texts are replete with myth. She uses and rewrites myths so that female mythic figures reappear breaking down the dominant patriarchal portrayal of women. Cixous uses myth, because in earlier times it took the place of analysis. She notes:

> I am passionately interested in the myths, because they are always (this is well known) outside the law, like the unconscious. Only afterwards there is the story, which signifies that there has been a clash between the in-law and the out-law ... What happens? Interpretation, of course, because we do have myths and their interpretations. One never questions enough the traditions of interpretation of myth, and all myths have been referred to a masculine interpretation. If we women read them, we read them otherwise. That is why I often nourish my texts, in my own way, at those mythic sources.
>
> (Conley 1984: 155–56)

The law that Cixous is referring to is the law of patriarchy, the conventional social order where women are suppressed. The use of myths is a way to subvert and reinscribe the dominant social order. As Tilde Sankovitch points out, 'the use of myths (transformed, remade, inverted) is therefore the key-stone of a methodology of female self-discovery and self-expression, of rebirth, recovery, rewriting' (1988: 129). Just as the reinterpretation of myths restores woman to herself, the act of writing reinstates woman in the realm of the Book so that 'her truth may be expressed' (130). It is in the Book that *écriture féminine* is born. The very idea of feminine writing, Cixous warns, is 'a dangerous and stylish expression full of traps, which leads to all kind of confusions' (Conley 1984: 129). Sankovitch has observed also that Cixous's writing 'may be seen as the culmination of a long myth-making past, during which women writers have taken up, each in turn, the task of finding access to the promised Book by creating, inventing, or adapting the necessary empowering myths of strength and creative courage' (1988: 148).

Feminine writing is a means to displace writing from the patriarchal domain to the 'libidinal maternal realm of fémininité, a realm of desire, of passion, of love, where the experience of the body is valorized and linked with the experience of language' (131). As Sandra Gilbert has noted, feminine writing may be used as 'a fundamentally political strategy, designed to redress the wrongs of culture through a revalidation of the rights of nature' (Gilbert 1986: xv).

Cixous steadfastly believes that it is not possible to define feminine writing, because defining it would entail theorising and encoding thereby rendering it static as opposed to what it should be: dynamic. It is for this reason that she refuses to produce theory for the sake of theory itself albeit her work has made a considerable theoretical contribution. Cixous has likened her work to poetry that is not encumbered by the rules of theory. The example she cites of such work is the poet Rilke, who, she says,

> did not have to produce theory. Heidegger did that for him. Rilke, with the peculiar instrument infinitely freer than philosophic discourse, produced a series of works that are living objects in which you see, for example, how a rose opens up. In a certain way, poetry is disenfranchised from the obligation that philosophy has: to demonstrate, justify.
>
> (Conley 1984: 152)

Cixous sees the combination of myth and poetry most clearly in the Brazilian writer Clarice Lispector. Carol Armbruster has noted that Cixous sees Lispector's works as a space where she 'receives the other in its living totality and attempts to relate its life and fullness through a language that calls and names it without possessing or dominating it, without transforming it in any way, and without denying its difference' (1983: 150–51).

Death and loss

Cixous has described the death of her father of tuberculosis when she was eleven as having a formative influence on her writing, with loss and the need of reparation becoming motivating forces. Death remains a powerful metaphor that links writing, motherhood and love (Lie 1999: 14). For her, language provides a compensatory role and a way to live and inscribe loss. Writing is a path of discovery linked inextricably to 'the experience of disappearance, to the feeling of having lost the key to the world. Of having been thrown outside. Of having suddenly acquired the precious sense of the rare, of the mortal. Of having urgently to regain the entrance, the breath, to keep the trace' (Sellers 1994: xxvi). For Cixous, writing is living; it is about surviving and existence. It is a product of the world that she grew up in, a violent world. She explains what drives her to write:

> It is out of fear, despair, against reality – because there was the war, there was death, because there were massacres, because there was betrayal, because there was barbarity, because there was no language, and too many languages and not enough languages, because my father died, because the

> Jews were massacred, because the women were exploited, because the Arabs were expropriated … I gathered up twigs, magic words. Gaining on time, competition with time? Gaining earth, fabricating a ground, rather than gaining time. But maybe I'm just telling myself stories.
>
> (Cixous and Calle-Gruber 1997: 95–96)

Cixous's first major work of fiction, *Dedans* (in English, *Inside*) is about loss and death. The notion of 'inside' can be seen as representing her father's death as well as that idyllic stage of childhood before the experience and knowledge of the world. Cixous notes that the text 'wrote itself inside the father, in looking for him even into death and in returning. There is something simple and mysterious in the origin of a writing: "I" am in the father whom I carry, he haunts me, I live him. There is a relationship between father and language, father and "symbolic"' (Sellers 1994: 19).

In the essay, 'Writing Blind' Cixous talks about herself as author and the manner in which her father's death has left an indelible mark on her:

> I have often said that my father, in going off precipitately, took with him the floor of the world and all the temple. It was terrifying to see that ruin. And what happened to the family? Each one made a gesture to saturate the abyss. My mother became a midwife. My brother is almost a midwife, he is a pediatrician. Each one of us got busy around the process of bringing into the world. I set myself to weaving time. A year without a book – this has never happened to me, a year without the fabric of life.
>
> (1998: 149)

In the essay entitled, 'La Venue à l'écriture' ('Coming to Writing') published in 1977, Cixous describes that writing for her is a way of ousting death, of relegating it into a manageable place where one cannot be surprised. Writing provides 'the means to overcome separation and death, to "give yourself what you would want God-if-he-existed to give you"' (Sellers 1994: 64). Martine Motard-Noar points out that Cixous's fictional writing has been aimed at analysing her father's death. Through writing, she is able to deal with the binaries that have plagued her and which she has sought to overcome. Writing makes 'for fictional vertigo' (1995: 197; 1999)

As a Franco Maghrebin Jewish woman who has experienced loss and exclusion Cixous's emphasis on writing as a political strategy is all the more important. Cixous has been identified closely with a movement of women (*Psychoanalyse et Politique*) who sought to develop revolutionary theories of the oppression of women in relation to psychoanalytic theory. This group engendered hostility towards those who described themselves as 'feminist' on the grounds that they were merely working to gain access to, and reproducing, the very structures of masculine power.

The female text that emerges through feminine writing is for Cixous one where 'the act of speaking and, even more of writing as a female represents a fundamental birth drive which will destroy the old order of death, not merely its material, economic, social and political manifestations, but the generative system, which determines the production of meaning' (Stanton 1980: 78). Given that Cixous's writing is deeply embedded within a sense of loss, Anne-Marie Picard has observed that 'it has become a feat of transforming *bereavement into benediction*', the title of one of Cixous's seminars (1999: 24).

The death of her father clearly left a huge void and Cixous explains that she thought that it was '*The* End and *The* First Cause'. However, she realised that it was just the first apocalypse and that other apocalypses could follow: '*The* End is not the end. No more than *the* beginning begins' (2002: 406). Cixous's life story has been at the forefront of her writing and in *Le jour où je n'étais pas la* she writes about the loss of her Down's syndrome child. In this text, she returns to the death of her son, another apocalypse, some forty years later. Here, Cixous writes about the turmoil she experienced when her son dies, particularly because she had placed him in the care of her mother (Hanrahan 2003: 99). Cixous writes how the death of her son was a new beginning:

> Once my first son died, I was begun again … The inexact child was an irruption of the unforseen, the incalculable, into the presumption of calculations. I was twenty-two years old, unknowing and totally calm. I was at anchor. I remained in the silence of its inexactness for exactly thirty-nine years.
>
> (2002: 406)

In an interview on her notebooks, Cixous points out that she had tried to write about this experience but she did not know she could not be explicit. Nevertheless, she points out that 'very often the character of this baby would roam in my texts, but it was always in a disguised form, and not directly, because I simply couldn't bear or couldn't … translate it in a way that would satisfy me, that wouldn't betray the story, (2004a: 119).

Mairéad Hanrahan has noted that for Cixous writing is a three-legged process that allows 'her a way to step out of herself, come at herself from another angle, it enables her to meditate – that is, re-meditate, work through again-for-the-first-time – the relationships that make her who she is' (2003: 99). It is not surprising that Cixous has poignantly observed that 'books are characters in books'. As she points out, 'The story I have to tell is the story of writing's violence. I want to write what I cannot write. The book helps me. The book leads me astray, carries me away' (Cixous 2002: 403).

Cixous and Bakhtin

Lisa Gasbarrone has noted the similarities between Cixous and Mikhail Bakhtin's writings. She likens Cixous's notion of feminine writing to that of Bakhtin's dialogic discourse. The resemblance lies in the manner in which feminine writing describes the relationship between self and other which they seek to establish through literary expression. Gasbarrone suggests through a Bakhtinian reading of Cixous that the promise of the relationship between self and other is not realised.

Gasbarrone argues that 'Laugh of the Medusa' needs to be seen as the text in which Cixous seeks to uncover the *féminin futur* and which serves 'as both a model and an invocation' (1994: 3). In this text, Cixous's call to a project of feminine writing is, she argues, framed figuratively as a call to arms. It is important to recall Gasbarrone's argument at length:

> There can be no mistaking her assertion that the break with the past must be immediate, violent and complete. Women's writing must not reinforce the mistakes of history ... Her look to the future to a time when feminine *écriture* in all its promise may be fully realised, is all the more significant in that she believes no dialogue with the past is possible ... The relationship between women's writing and the masculine order of both history and literature is more than confrontational; it is openly combative. The language Cixous uses to describe the 'struggle' of women's writing is suffused with violence: 'we must kill the false woman who is preventing the live one from breathing. Inscribe the breath of the whole woman'. The whole woman emerges only with the violent death of her false counterpart, and women's writing with the toppling of the male literary order. Woman must make 'her shattering entry into history, which has always been based on her suppression. To write and thus forge for herself the antilogos weapon'.
>
> (1994: 3)

This idea of a rupture, of a break with the past, has led to a reading that suggests an affinity between Cixous's feminine writing and Bakhtin's literary theory. As Gasbarrone argues, 'the observation is not farfetched. Bakhtin locates the beginnings of the novel, the privileged form of dialogic exchange, in a definitive break with the patriarchal world of myth and epic' (1994: 4). The phallogocentric order that Cixous seeks to overturn has much in common with Bakhtin's world of the epic. 'Both are types of what Bakhtin would call monologic discourse, grounded in patriarchal myth, deaf to other voices and discourses, and subvertible only through transgression of the linguistic and literary laws that govern them' (4). Despite these similarities, Gasbarrone argues that it is not at all clear that Cixous's text is what 'Bakhtin might have called dialogic, or even transgressive' (5). The basis of her argument is that Cixous's text is utopian whereas Bakhtin's dialogic discourse is about the radically present. Gasbarrone argues that Cixous's 'location of otherness totally within the parameters of the self results in its negation. In short, she cancels otherness out' (8).

Gasbarrone concludes that she has a preference for Bakhtin's dialogic discourse over Cixous's feminine *écriture*. Gasbarrone's conclusion is hardly surprising. Cixous is clearly inspired by a number of theoreticians including Derrida, but she has marked out a certain distance from them. Hence, while it is easy to point to affinities it is far more difficult to map her intellectual pedigree. It is precisely for this reason that Cixous finds the very idea of theory an anathema. Nevertheless, it is possible to see in Cixous far greater affinity with Frantz Fanon. This is not because Cixous is informed by his Marxism but rather his analysis of the colonial world in which she was born and where she grew up conditions the very practice of her writing. She has herself noted that she learned everything from the Algerian spectacle. Her apparent call to arms, the notion that the break with the past must be immediate, violent and complete, her looking into the future which characterises her utopianism, the idea of being born again as suggested by the title of her book (*The Newly Born Woman*) all resonate with Fanon's characterisation of the colonial condition.

Cixous and Derrida

Hélène Cixous and Jacques Derrida have a great deal in common. They share a common background, with Jewish Algerian roots, a deep interest in cultural and philosophical matters, a radical questioning of European thought as well as a certain ethical and political project (Still 1999: 124). If Cixous is deeply influenced by anybody it is Derrida, with whom she has had an ongoing exchange from her particularly 'feminine' perspective. Conley argues that Cixous is engaged in extending Derrida's project of undoing paternal authority 'from a "masculine border", yet [he] does not broach the possibility of a maternal, a matrical. This is where *her* work "begins"' (1991a: 8). In her classes, Cixous sets out the task of her texts: the role that they perform is both a philosophical and analytical reading 'that combines both dimensions but without attempting to enclose the world in its discourse, as a kind of total analysis. To this must be added a reading on the semantic level, a graphico-phonic reading, which listens to silences, looks at graphic tracings' (9).

Although Cixous is deeply influenced by Derrida, there are important points of departure as in the case *Of Grammatology*, where Derrida articulates his position on writing and the text. Cixous points out that she has a different conception of writing; her purpose is not to analyse it as Derrida's methodology demands. Rather, she says, 'I speak in a more idealistic fashion. I allow this to myself; I disenfranchise myself from the philosophical obligations and corrections, which does not mean that I disregard them' (Conley 1991a: 150–51).

Cixous explains how Derrida was the first person with whom she shared her writings and the profound influence that he has had on her.

> In an inaugural way, when I began to write, the first person I showed my texts to was Derrida. I was in such a desert, an absolute desert that no

> one in the world, not even I, could imagine now. A desert leading to an effect of a temporality. There was no time. The presence of J.D., whom I read was inscribed in the timeless space where I was, as the contemporary presence of Montaigne is inscribed in me – or even better of Archimedes, as he appears to me, evoked by my son, quite alive on his sand, writing today as 2,500 years ago, and still discovering the experiences of thought, the secrets, the cosmic levers.
>
> (Cixous and Calle-Gruber 1997: 83)

This special relationship, given their common Jewish Franco-Maghrebin background, is discernable in the way they engage with the French language. This relationship is based on their foreignness, and can be likened to Joseph Conrad's relationship with English.

> He [Derrida] has a way of listening to the French language that is meticulous, vibratile, virgin: new, young. He hears as quickly as it speaks. Like a second language: as one reads languages by the roots. Talking is a marvellous act that escapes us: it is to hear Language speaking its languages in language. To hear onself, to overhear oneself, to catch one's own hints. To accept this surprising phenomenon: when we swim it, when we gallop it, language always tells us volumes more than we think we are saying. I recognise his foreign relationship to the French language. I also have a foreign relationship to the French language. Not for the same reasons but from the start it was there. He has himself made the portrait of his own foreignness. My foreignness is all-powerful in me. When 'I speak', it is always at least 'we', the language and I in it, with it, and it in me who speak.
>
> (Cixous and Calle-Gruber 1997: 84)

It is not surprising that Derrida claimed that for him Cixous was the greatest writer in the French language. The bond that they share is easily discernable in *Veils*, a book that they co-authored where the play of the visible and the invisible as a result of Cixous's myopia leads to an extended meditation on friendship (Cixous and Derrida 2001; Derrida 2006; Cixous 2006a). In the text, *Portrait of Jacques Derrida as a Young Jewish Saint* Cixous writes of their shared experiences of Algeria:

> … we do mirror a number of precise stigmata, dated Algiers (1867, 1870), Oran (1940, 1942, 1954, 1956), all those dates of Passovers, transfers, expulsions, naturalizations, de-citizenships, exinclusions, blacklistings, doors slammed in your face, dates of war, of colonization, incorporation, assimilation, assimulation, indigene/ni/zations that constitute the archives of what he calls 'my nostalgeris' and that I call my 'algeriance', dates and plaques, my doctor father's nameplate yanked off the wall by Vichy, the psychic rash of plaques at the evocation of

> the nationalist-racist outbreaks, tremors and symptoms at the portals of Schools.
>
> (2004b: 5)

Conclusion

Hélène Cixous has recently written that she never wanted to write about Algeria, 'this native land whose high closed blankness I skirted for so many years'. Yet, Algeria keeps announcing itself to her, forcing itself to the forefront: 'I could no longer put off the book which didn't stop calling me whenever I opened the window of darkness ... *The whole time I was living in Algeria I would dream of one day arriving in Algeria'* (2006: 96). It is not surprising then that Cixous has described herself as 'pregnant with beginnings' (Lie 1999: 11). Her Jewish French Algerian Maghrebin beginnings have fuelled her imagination. It was there that she realised how powerful writing could be as a means to escape the vagaries of life: the brutality of colonialism, the death of her father, the taking away of her citizenship, exile, a world war and decolonisation. It was in the reality of experiencing otherness that she discovered the pleasures of writing and through which she could envision alternative worlds, better worlds. It is only in writing, Cixous notes, that 'there is a somewhere else that can escape the infernal repetition, it lies in that direction, where *it* writes itself, where *it* dreams, where *it* invents new worlds' (Cixous and Clément 1986: 72). Through writing, and writing the body that has been so vividly marked by the spectre of Algeria, she is able to seek another world (Cixous 2006). It is only in writing that Cixous is able to unleash 'uncontrollable resources' (Cixous and Clément 1986: 97).

Chapter 6

Althusser, Bourdieu, Foucault and Lyotard

> A Philosophy does not make its appearance in the world as Minerva appeared to the society of Gods and men.
>
> (Louis Althusser)

> … the Algerian war, by its mere existence as well as by its special form and its duration, transformed the situation in which and by which it was brought into being.
>
> (Pierre Bourdieu)

> A progressive politics is a politics which recognises the historical and the specified conditions of a practice, whereas other politics recognise only ideal necessities, univocal determinations and the free interplay of individual initiatives.
>
> (Michel Foucault)

> The postmodern would be that which in the modern invokes the unpresentable in presentation itself, that which refuses the consolation of correct forms, refuses the consensus of taste permitting a common experience of nostalgia for the impossible, and inquires into new presentations – not to take pleasure in them, but to better produce the feeling that there is something unpresentable.
>
> (Jean-François Lyotard)

Louis Althusser, Pierre Bourdieu, Michel Foucault and Jean-François Lyotard are all border intellectuals whose names are inextricably linked with the revolution within social theory in the twentieth century. Respectively, they have left an indelible mark on theory and challenged prevailing orthodoxy. Significantly, each in their own way was an insider and outsider within their own society. Although only Althusser was born in Algeria, all four were shaped by events there. Bourdieu and Lyotard spent a considerable time in the colony and this without doubt marked their subsequent writings. Foucault was not directly associated with Algeria but no scholar of his generation could escape the ravages of the French colonial project and its effects on the metropole. Indeed, in Foucault's case, his transformation and politicisation came about during a self-imposed exile in the neighbouring colony of Tunisia.

It is remarkable that the postcolony defined the work of these most significant French post-structuralist and post-modern thinkers.[1] Each was reacting also to the influence and impact that Jean Paul Sartre exercised over French intellectual life. Sartre's existential humanism despite his vehement opposition to the French presence and the war in Algeria was being questioned as these thinkers, each in their unique way, brought the universalism and certainty of modernity into crisis.

Althusser

Louis Pierre Althusser was born in October 1918 in Birmandrëis, Algeria to a father of Alsatian background, Charles Althusser and a French mother, Lucienne Berger. His mother was in love and engaged to Charles' brother Louis who died during the First World War. As was the Levirate custom at the time, his father proposed to Lucienne. He was named after his dead uncle who was a brilliant *lycée* student in Algiers preparing to study at a prestigious national academy. As he recounts in his autobiography, 'from the earliest childhood I bore the name of a man who still lived and was loved in my mother's thoughts: it was *a dead man's name*' (Althusser 1993: 54). He also had a younger sister Georgette. His father eventually established himself in the banking industry and worked his way into management. His mother worked briefly during the War in what Althusser describes as one of the best periods of her life. However, after his father returned from the War, his mother ceased to work.

From an early age, Althusser was strongly influenced by his mother. His recollection of his time in Algeria as a child is that he was rather lonely, because his mother was 'intent on preventing us (herself) from having any contact with dubious acquaintances, keeping us away from germs and impulses which might have led to goodness knows what!' (1993: 57). Catholicism and the Church became an important part of his life, as his mother was deeply involved and devoted to the faith. His involvement in the church remained for a long time as he became involved in the Catholic workers' movement. He was certainly a practising Catholic until well after the Second World War. During the War, he served briefly with an artillery unit in Bretagne. He was eventually placed in a POW (prisoner of war) work camp in Schleswig, Stalag XA in Germany where he remained for nearly five years. His recollection of that period was that it was a time when he found life relatively easy, because he was able to enjoy the comradeship of men behind barbed wires where he felt protected.

After the War, Althusser enrolled at *Ecole Normale Supérieure* (ENS) where he came first in the *aggregation* examination in philosophy in 1948. In the same year, he was appointed to be *caîman* with the responsibility of preparing students for the *aggregation*. Althusser remained at the ENS until 1980 when he strangled his partner Hélène Rytmann, whom he had met in 1946. At the ENS, Althusser noted that he always felt like an outsider and a complete stranger. Rytmann had been deeply involved with the French resistance and with the Communist Party with which she was engaged in a struggle to be readmitted as a member. She was highly influential in Althusser's move to the left and he finally joined the Communist Party in Paris in 1948. Together, they shared an interest in the working class and argued for revolutionary change. Since his childhood, he was prone to anxiety and depression, and these episodes became more acute from 1947 onwards, no doubt fuelled by his internment.

Althusser's internment during the War as well as his commitment to the Church and his position at the ENS (where he lived for most of his life), as well as his membership in the French Communist Party, all signify the passion, commitment and loyalty that underpinned his life. Yet, there remained an ambivalence that 'required the security of an ideological structure (the fantasy of being contained) and the freedom to be critical of that structure' (Kirshner 2003: 215). These institutions provided Althusser with a degree of anonymity but ultimately they 'were surrogate homes for one of nature's asylum-seekers. To be in, but not fully of, an institution was always Althusser's need' (Sturrock 1998: 50). Althusser was, as Lewis Kishner argues an ' "outsider on the insider" of the Church, the Stalag, the Party, and psychoanalysis, accepting no master in the flesh and having immense difficulty with symbolic ones' (2003: 225). Althusser, as an Algerian born *pied noir*, was of course always used to being an outsider on the insider, this was the condition that was part of his formative years.

Louis Althusser is perhaps best known for a series of essays that deeply influenced Marxist thought in the West. The works *Pour Marx* (1965) and *Lire de Capital* (1965) were profoundly influential in a rethinking of the Marxist project. Althusser's project was aimed at rescuing Marx from Soviet dogmatism and humanistic interpretations. He was known particularly for arguing that the 'later' Marx made an epistemological break with the romantic 'humanism' of the young Marx – when he made a commitment to explore the scientific basis of the structure of bourgeois society. As Althusser pointed out:

> Marx broke radically with every theory that based history and politics on an essence of man ... This rupture with every *philosophical* anthropology or humanism is no secondary detail; it is Marx's scientific discovery ... The earlier idealist ('bourgeois') philosophy depended in all its domains and arguments (its 'theory of knowledge', its conception of history, its political economy, its ethics, its aesthetics, etc.) on a problematic of *human nature* (or the essence of man) ... By rejecting the essence of man as his theoretical basis, Marx rejected the whole of this organic system of postulates.
>
> (cited in Davies 1997: 58)

For him, Marxism was not an ideology, it was a revolutionary science, the science of society. Indeed, the Structualists, of whom Althusser was a leading proponent, stressed the importance of structures that underpinned all human cultures with little capacity for historical change or human inventiveness. In such a formulation, 'there was no place for agency, cohesive selfhood, or intentionality' (Kirshner 2003: 212). As Robert Resch points out, 'it is no exaggeration to say that Structural Marxism constitutes a comprehensive and largely successful response to a century of accumulated problems within the Marxist tradition' (1992: 3).

Althusser was reacting against the existential humanism of Jean Paul Sartre whose work he saw as being bounded in the philosophy of the subject and consciousness thereby rendering 'expendable the notion of a conscious subject as the agent of history' (Kirshner 2003: 223; Ferretter 2006). Nevertheless, he doggedly held on to a political position that was often rejected by the post-structuralists. He points out the ideological basis of humanism:

> In ideology men do indeed express, not the relation between them and their conditions of existence, but *the way* they live the relation between them and their conditions of existence: this presupposes both a real and an '*imaginary*' '*lived*' relation … In ideology the real relation is inevitably invested in the imaginary relation, a relation that *expresses a will* (conservative, conformist, reformist or revolutionary), a hope or a nostalgia, rather than describing a reality.
>
> (Althusser 1969: 223–34)

Althusser's break with Marxism came in his characterisation of humanism. He did not see humanism as a progressive or emancipatory force that resulted from the inhumane conditions of capitalism (Feretter 2006: 23; Johnson 1993). Althusser's antihumanism had much in common with the new humanism that Fanon and other postcolonial revolutionaries such as Che Guevara articulated (Ahluwalia 2009; Ahluwalia and Nursey-Bray 1997; Said 2004). This was necessarily so, given Althusser's own Algerian experience of colonialism. Hence, what was essential 'was either to do away with the concept of humanism altogether, or, more positively, to articulate a new antiracist humanism, which would be inclusive rather than exclusive, and which would be the product of those who formed the majority of this totality' (Young 2001a: xiv).

One of Althusser's concepts that continues to have a great deal of resonance in cultural theory is the idea of interpellation.[2] In his discussion about ideology he says there are certain moments of recognition when we recognise ourselves by the mere way in which we are addressed or called as in 'Hey! You!' Our response to that call albeit from a policeman, teacher, or priest renders us as:

> subjects because we are subjected to an authority, a Subject with a capital S. We are located, in relation to that Subject, as biddable small *s*

> subjects precisely because we recognize ourselves, and (this is crucial) *because we have no choice*. We are turned into biddable subjects because it becomes instantly obvious to us that we *are* that way and that we *know* that way.
>
> (Law 2000: 14)

This scene of interpellation is often theorised as the inadvertent way in which the values of a system were appropriated by a subject. However, in Althusser's case, as Robert Young has so astutely noted, his 'ideology starts with a brutal colonial address to a subject regarded as already degraded, a member of the debased cultural system who must be apprehended within an apparatus of power' (Young 2001: 416).

A particular aspect of the radicalisation of the 1960s was the emergence of a form of French Maoism that Belden Fields labels as 'antihierarchical Maoism' with which Sartre, Lefebvre, Althusser and Foucault were all associated. Antihierarchical Maoism, he points out, 'raised basic questions about the nature of oppressive power, about the problematic of the personal/cultural/political, and about the criteria of emancipatory struggle' (Fields 1984: 148). In Althusser's unpublished papers, Gregory Elliot (1987) found considerable criticism of the Communist Party and its failure to deal with the Algerian question (also see Badiou 2005; Majumdar 1995: 19). As Benita Parry has suggested, in the 'revolt against the economism of orthodox historical materialism, and the turn to the historical-materialist concept of social *practice*, Althusser had endorsed the revolutions in Cuba and China, regarding the latter as a "concrete critique" of Stalinism and undertaking to theorize it as such' (Parry 2004: 77).

It is clear that Althusser's anticolonial concerns can be ascribed to his Maoism as Parry has also suggested. Nevertheless, there is clearly a deeper source which are his Algerian roots and the colonial experience itself. It was through his particular Marxism that he could be seen to 'be counteracting in some measure one of the weakest features of the tradition, its Eurocentricity and preoccupation with things "western" in a provincial sense' (Parry 2004: 77).

Central to this is the position of Algeria and the Algerian War which was significantly different from the war in Indochina, especially in terms of its impact on the political system within France itself. In the Algerian War, conscription was a central element that was not used in Indochina and this immediately embroiled the metropole and led to the radicalisation of a whole generation. For Althusser, given his personal itinerary, this was all the more important (Majumdar 1995: 8). As Fields argues, 'The war in Algeria resulted in the fall of the Fourth Republic and the institution of the more authoritarian Fifth Republic under de Gaulle. It also stimulated a considerable antiwar movement in which students played a major role' (1984: 149).

The work of Althusser, particularly his views on ideology, were a vital part of that radicalisation process. His views, however, pitted him against the French Communist Party which saw him using his position at the ENS to subvert the official party line largely in the way he read Marx's work. However, it was not until the late 1970s when relations between the Socialists and Communists ruptured that he launched a severe attack on the party for not being able to engage in any self-criticism. Despite such a virulent attack, Althusser was never purged from the party, primarily because 'purging would have had negative national and international repercussions for the party' (Fields 1984: 175).

The significance of the uprising of 1968 was that it challenged the neo-Marxist rhetoric that originated 'out of the corridors of the privileged and before which the professional voices of criticism, such as Louis Althusser, were helpless' (Olson 1984: 174). Nevertheless, during the 1970s when there was a great deal of upheaval in France, Althusser questioned whether 'even forms of working-class *resistance*, far from embodying the promise of any alternative, were *in effect* the ideological props and struts of the status quo' (Lloyd and Thomas 1998: 184). What was central to such an assertion was the question about how we could be certain that such resistance was not part of an ideological apparatus. As David Lloyd and Paul Thomas point out, 'what does it matter if school children crucify their teachers if they go on to work in factories? The educational system will have done its work well enough' (Lloyd and Thomas 1998: 185).

In the aftermath of Althusser strangling his wife, there was much talk about the leniency towards him given that he was placed in psychiatric care rather than a prison. His position in French intellectual life, it was often claimed, allowed him to escape from the punishment. However, what remained less clear in the media frenzy that ensued was the persistent bouts of depression and mental illness that he had endured. We glean some insight into the violence with which Althusser grew up first in Algeria and then during the Second World War. He was after all a child of violence 'produced by the violent praxis of their fathers – which takes them back to the History from which they wished to escape' (Sartre as cited in Young 2001: 295).

The institutions that defined Althusser, his family, the Church and schools, what he described as the 'ideological state apparatus' were for him not only exploitative but also inherently violent social formations that embodied the ideology of the state. As John Sturrock puts it, 'the "unmasking" of his own mother and father as the two people bearing ultimate responsibility for his problems of affect is simply a domestic version of the larger theory, with Althusser now cast as "the concrete individual" and his own circumstances representing what, in writing about the young Marx, he describes as "the irruption of real history into ideology" ' (Sturrock 1998: 45).

There are few critics today who would consider themselves to be strong Althusserians.[3] Neverthless, Althusser's work has been highly influential since the 1960s. In virtually every field of critical theory including, 'New Historicism, cultural materialism, postcolonial and race oriented criticism, gay, and queer theory, feminism, post-structuralism and cultural studies' his work and especially his conceptualisation of ideology is foundational (Ferretter 2006: 143). There is little doubt that Althusser's work was born out of the experiences of the postcolony and his locatedness as a border intellectual who remained out of place.

Bourdieu

Pierre Bourdieu was born in 1930 and grew up in Lasseube, a small village in the south of France. He was the first in his family to complete high school. His early years were spent in the rural area of Béarn. He eventually moved to Paris where he was able to gain entrance to the highly influential École Normale Supérieure (ENS) and studied philosophy with Louis Althusser. At the ENS, Bourdieu not only experienced the rigours of the academic selection process but also the problems associated with being an outsider from the countryside and not part of the élite. His origins made him particularly sensitive to the question of power and prestige and this no doubt had a great deal of resonance with his later experiences in Algeria.

This personal experience of being the outsider to French academe's premier institution eventually 'motivated him to submit French schooling – indeed all institutions – to critical examination' (Swartz 2002: 548). These personal experiences were important in defining the research that he was to undertake as well as his role as a defender of the underprivileged (Reed-Danhay 2005). From the very beginning, Bourdieu's main interest was in capturing 'human relations in action' (Robbins 1991: 1). It is in this context that Derek Robbins observed that 'Bourdieu is a humanist existentialist who tries to be authentic – not to a "self" but to the social conditions which have generated his functioning persona' (Robbins 1991: 172).

After the ENS, he went on to teach at the Lycée Banville in Moulins from 1954 to 1955, just outside of Paris. However, the war in Algeria meant that he was called to military service. The Algerian War, and in particular, the battle of Algiers had a profound impact not only on Bourdieu but also on a whole generation of French intellectuals. These intellectuals witnessed the excesses of colonial power administered by the state through betraying what was fundamental to the French colonial project – the mission of liberation and civilisation. Bourdieu sought to redress this injustice in his work with 'direct opposition and with research into the nature of domination itself' (Calhoun 2006: 1403–4).

During his military service, Bourdieu was assigned first to an air unit in the Chellif Valley that was about 150 kilometres west of Algiers. He was subsequently transferred to Algiers where he worked in the documentation and information service of the General Government.[4] In Algiers, there was an excellent library of which he took full advantage and read virtually everything that had been written on the colony. When he finished his military service, Bourdieu joined the University of Algiers where he taught philosophy and sociology and began his ethnographic research. His research and views brought him to the attention of the far-right Algerian settler population and on the advice of friends in May 1961, he fled Algeria at night fearing that he would be assassinated. Bourdieu eventually moved back to Paris due to the threats on his life and worked with Raymond Aron who helped him gain a position as his assistant at the Sorbonne. In the following year, he began teaching at the University of Lille. He subsequently founded and established the Centre for the Sociology of Education and Culture and was eventually honoured with a chair at the College de France in 1982 upon the recommendation of Michel Foucault.

His reputation as a scholar began with the publication of his book *The Algerians* (1962). Bourdieu describes the genesis of this book:

> I left for Algeria while I was in the army. After two hard years during which it was not possible to do anything, I devoted myself to fieldwork. I began by writing a book with a purpose of casting light on the drama of the Algerian people and also on the colonialists, whose situation was no less dramatic, beyond their racism.
>
> (Bourdieu 1986: 38)

The Algerians, based on fieldwork amongst the Kabyle, marked the turning point of his move from philosophy to sociology because of his belief that empirical work was essential. As Yacine points out, it was in Algeria where Bourdieu witnessed the daily impact of the war that 'an original thought was forged, nourished by the most quotidian, alive to the complexity of the real, and fiercely resistant to theoretical simplification' (Yacine 2004: 495). For Bourdieu, Algeria became the object of study because of the 'clash of civilisations'. As he put it:

> This study, which is a conceptual outline of a more extensive analyses, includes a description of the original social and economic structures … which, although not the main purpose of this book, is indispensable for an understanding of the breakdown of the social structures caused by the colonial situation and the influx of European civilization.
>
> (cited in Robbins 1991: 14)

In his early work on Algeria, Bourdieu was concerned with three main areas. First, he sought to understand a society in transition from a precapitalist to a capitalist economy. Second, he tried to capture how the transition affected the attitudes of those who were caught up in it, in particular, their conception of time. Finally, he examined the revolutionary potential of both the peasantry and industrial workers (Wacquant 2004: 390). In Algeria, Bourdieu was to witness firsthand the colonial excesses and it was there that he began his social scientific work among the Kabyle peasants as an amateur ethnologist. His empirical studies were not driven by the motivation to analyse these societies on the basis that they were previously autonomous. Rather, 'his scientific activity was a way of operationalizing an appropriate response to the colonialist oppression which he had witnessed with revulsion' (Robbins 2002: 115).

As a result of this research, he coined the terms 'acculturation' and 'deculturation' dividing Algerians into four major categories of people – the Kabyles, the Schwia, the Mozabites and the Arab speaking. Bourdieu argued that these various groups had distinct cultures albeit with considerable overlap and interpenetration. The war for liberation, however, had assisted in breaking down differences and had fostered the development of a national consciousness. Bourdieu argued that the Algerians had a 'stage personage' which meant that they never revealed to others their inner self and consequently they were perceived as existing for others. He argued that although Islam was partly responsible for the irruption of war, the real reason could be discerned in Algeria's complex social structures (Le Sueur 2001: 225).

It was because of this familiarity that Bourdieu was one of the critics who strongly rejected Fanon and Sartre's characterisation of colonial identity and the role of violence. In the preface to Bourdieu's book, *The Algerians*, Raymond Aron wrote, 'For almost eight years the drama of Algeria weighed on the French like an obsession, a guilt, and also like a duty. It precipitated the fall of a regime, split a nation asunder. It imperilled domestic peace and spread throughout the mother country a climate of passion and crime. It could no longer be considered a simple episode in a historically irresistible movement called decolonisation' (cited in Le Sueur 2001: 250). Aron argued that Bourdieu's work showed that reconciliation was not possible because of the cultural differences that existed between the colons and the Algerians.

Nevertheless, Bourdieu recognised that violence was a product of the colonial system. However, in contrast to what he considered to be Fanon's utopian position, he argued that Algerian society would be altered fundamentally after the war. The effect of the war was that Algeria had become highly revolutionary. In an interview in 1994 with Le Sueur, Bourdieu was highly critical of Fanon and Sartre arguing that what

> Fanon says corresponds to nothing. It is even dangerous to make the Algerians believe the things he says. This would bring them to a utopia. And I think these men contributed to what Algeria became because they told stories to Algerians who often did not know their own country any more than the French who spoke about it, and therefore, the Algerians retained a completely unrealistic utopian illusion of Algeria …
>
> … the texts of Fanon and Sartre are frightening for their irresponsibility. You would have to be a megalomaniac to think you could say just any nonsense. It is true, of course, that I do not have a lot of admiration for these two here … even when they are right, it is for bad reasons.
>
> (Le Sueur 2001: 252)

For Bourdieu, what is particularly disturbing about Sartre and Fanon is that they failed to see the specificity of the Algerian situation, and that instead they used the situation to universalise and depersonalise the Algerian revolution.

In particular, Bourdieu finds their misreading of the peasantry especially disturbing. The peasantry, he notes, was completely overwhelmed by the war, 'by the concentration camps, and by mass deportations' so to claim that it was a revolutionary force was 'completely idiotic' (254).

Bourdieu believed that Fanon's analysis was fundamentally incorrect because he was deploying categories of blackness which held little relevance in the Algerian context:

> I think this is very important. ... The black's problems are not the same as the Algerian's problems. For the Algerians, there are poverty, humiliation, the Frenchification, and linguistic issues, but they are not concentrated to the degree to which Fanon claims on corporeality. There is a huge difference. ... The Algerian women have a relationship with their body that is not the same. I think that logic that Fanon develops does not have the same importance for the North Africans [Maghrébins] as it does for Fanon.
>
> (Le Sueur 2001: 253)

For Bourdieu, it was the European who 'gradually created an environment that reflected his own image ... a world in which he no longer felt himself to be a stranger and in which, by a natural reversal, the Algerian was finally considered to be a stranger' (cited in Naylor 2000: 131). Although he was stridently opposed to the Algerian war, Bourdieu did not proclaim himself as a nationalist champion. Rather, from his very first writings he 'pointed to the *causative role of colonization*, the source of the main economic and social evils visited upon Algeria' (Yacine 2004: 498). The conclusion that Bourdieu was able to derive as a result of his fieldwork was that colonialism 'provided a "pathological acceleration" to trends which were already latent – arising, amongst other factors, from the contact of the rural poor with urban employment in periods of economically enforced emigration to mainland France' (Robbins 1991: 26). As he later put it, Algeria in the 1960s with the benefit of hindsight, was a veritable social experiment:

> Owing to the war of national liberation and to certain measures of the military policy of repression, such as the forced relocation of population carried out by the French army, this country – in which some remote and isolated mountain peoples, such as those I was able to study in Kabylia, had preserved almost intact the traditions of a precapitalist economy quite alien to the logic of the market.
>
> (Bourdieu 2000: 18)

The Algerian experience and the fieldwork that he carried out amongst the Kabyle was 'at the basis of his epistemological position and of the original political perception that animates his works and led him, like Durkheim before him, to fuse ethnology and sociology, and thereby set off the ongoing scientific revolution henceforth associated with his name' (Yacine 2004: 488). In Bourdieu's work Kabylia played precisely 'the role that prehistory played in George Bataille's works … ' (Fourny 2000: 110).

In reading Bourdieu's earliest writings, one discovers the antecedents of his subsequent project. By concurrently carrying out fieldwork in Algeria and in his own childhood village in southwestern France, Bourdieu was able to reflect on two crucial moves which came to define his entire oeuvre. First, he used the fieldwork in the two disparate areas as a 'living laboratory to cross-analyze the other' enabling him 'to discover the specificity of the "universally prelogical logic of practice" and to initiate the decisive break out of the structuralist paradigm by shifting his analytical focus "from structure to strategy" from the mechanical mental algebra of cultural rules to the fluid gymnastics of socialized bodies' (Wacquant 2004: 389). Second, Bourdieu turned the anthropological gaze of the 'other' on his own society and people paving the way 'for elaborating and deploying the stance of epistemic reflexivity that is the trademark of his work and teaching' (389).

In subjecting the two very different sites of research, Algeria and France, to the same forms of inquiry meant that Bourdieu 'may be seen as an odd precursor of "multi-sited" ethnography decades before it became identified as a distinctive methodological genre' (396). Algeria and Béarn provided the context that allowed Bourdieu to 'perceive the social phenomena in both cases in terms of a process of transition from traditional to modern culture' (Robbins 1991: 50). In Bourdieu's case, the personal simply cannot be excluded from the social and it is important to note that he argued that, 'progress in the knowledge of human matters cannot be separated from progress in understanding the subject who knows' (Bourdieu cited in Jenkins 2006: 47). Bourdieu's own position as an outsider meant that he was acutely aware of alienation and the effects that it produced. As he so poignantly points out:

> My main problem is to try to understand what happened to me. My trajectory may be described as miraculous, I suppose – an ascension to a place where I don't belong. And so to be able to live in a world that is not mine I must try to understand both things: what it means to have an academic mind – how such is created – and at the same time what was lost in acquiring it. For that reason, even if my work – my full work – is a sort of autobiography, it is a work for people who have the same sort of trajectory, and the same need to understand.
>
> (Bourdieu and Eagleton 1994: 272)

Indeed, as Fourny points out, despite avoiding the word alienation, 'Bourdieu's complete work could somehow be read in light of the Marxist concept of alienation … ' (Fourny 2000: 4). Bourdieu's Algerian and subsequent work in Béarn were undoubtedly 'motivated by a certain pathos to discover, articulate, formalize and develop a series of theory-laden concepts contained synoptically in his own autobiographical experience' (Jenkins 2006: 67).

For Bourdieu, ethnology and sociology were restorative disciplines in both the colonial context as well as in terms of his childhood village. These disciplines had the opportunity to redress the degradation that they had endured. As Angela McRobbie has so astutely pointed out, Bourdieu 'reinvented sociology as a more critical instrument for the extension of democracy and the politics of social transformation in the post-industrial era' (McRobbie 2002: 130). His conceptualisation of these disciplines was also based upon his reactions to Sartre's existentialism and the structuralism championed by Lévi Strauss as he sought to overcome the dichotomy between the individual and society. In short, he challenged the 'opposition between subjectivism and objectivism' (Jenkins 2002: 18).

Central to this process was Bourdieu's reflexivity as he sought to define the distance between himself and the subjects of his research in order to understand how he was 'inserted within them' (Robbins 1991: 25). His obsession with reflexivity gave rise to his conception of a society comprised of a series of overlapping social fields of activity. Such a conception allowed him to undertake a nuanced analysis of social positionality. It is also a key way to understand his views of the game and the manner in which different social actors are 'relationally positioned within a field, this position determining his or her situated viewpoint of the activities of this and other fields. Thus, each actor has only a partial view of the game, acting accordingly' (Maton 2003: 56).

Habitus

One of Bourdieu's best known and most useful concepts, habitus, was conceived in Algeria in opposition to the modernist policies that were being pursued by the Governor-General Jacques Soustelle who tried to 'contain the opposition by modernizing the economy, but also to Marxist or Sartrean hopes that Algerians could be turned into rational revolutionaries' (Vincent 2004: 140). Habitus as a concept emerged from the depths of the disintegrating colonial world as a 'mediating category, straddling the divide between the objective and the subjective' (Wacquant 2004: 91). It is not surprising then, that for Bourdieu, habitus represented 'a set of embodied durable dispositions that tends to reproduce the society that produced it' (Cresswell 2002: 380).

The conceptualisation of habitus was crucial for Bourdieu to avoid Marxist determinism and to recognise the conditions within which subjects find themselves. For example, through the analysis of Kabyle social organisation, 'Bourdieu deliberately made available a vision of how societies might still organize themselves if human agents were to choose to be habituated by that vision' (Robbins 1991: 170). In such a context, the concept of habitus represents the cultural unconscious thereby widening 'the sphere of sociological intervention to include culture in all its manifestations' (Kauppi 2000: 11).

Habitus is a generating principle that can be best described as 'social practice' where an individual's history or past experiences are inscribed, where the past continues to effect the present. The manner in which one thinks, the perspectives adopted, the patterns of perception, the values and mores that define a particular society, are all part of the habitus. It is these cultural orders that 'structure all the expressive, verbal, and practical manifestations and utterances of a person' (Krais 2000: 56). Bourdieu's explicit definition of habitus:

> A system of schema [that] constantly orient choices, which, though not deliberate, are nonetheless systematic; which, without being arranged and organized expressly according to an ultimate end, are nonetheless imbued with a sort of finality that reveals itself only *post festum*.
>
> (cited in Dianteill 2003: 530)

The metaphor of a game is one that Bourdieu often used to capture the manner in which the habitus operates. For example, in a soccer game, it is the player with experience who dominates play and when a ball comes to him or her, the player intuitively knows what to do with it. There is an unreflexive ability to deal with what is thrown at the player. As Lenoir points out, the concepts of habitus, field and capital are 'only defined within the theoretical system which gave them meaning' (Lenoir 2006: 36). These concepts are most clearly manifested in the body where the social framework – our class, gender, ethnicity and sexuality – becomes activated through practice which tends towards the reproduction of the social framework (Cresswell 2002: 380). It is in the body that the social world is inscribed with power integral to that process. The habitus represents the 'internalisation of the social order, which in turn reproduces the social order. Power, then, is reproduced through the practices of people who act in accordance with internalised (embodied) schemes of perception' (Cresswell 2002: 380).

Structuralism

Bourdieu's intellectual project needs to be seen as a reaction to two major intellectual trends that were dominant in the 1960s and 1970s – existentialism and structuralism. Structuralism for Bourdieu was essentially a reaction to existentialism and in that respect the very notion of habitus which was also a reaction to existentialism, sought to ensure that social agents were not simply viewed as automated machines. His antipathy towards Sartre meant that he was concerned to 'overcome the opposition between the subjectivist emphasis on individual consciousness and the objectivist preoccupation with social structures' (Garrett 2007: 226). Habitus was a means to explain the manner in which subjects adapted to the structures that were inherent in their particular social framework. Bourdieu's work engaged with structuralism in order to provide a nuanced version that had the capacity to recognise the role of individual social actors (Reed-Danhay 2002: 377). Bourdieu's major problem with the structuralists was that in their theoretical formulation there was no capacity for human agency. Bourdieu spoke of his work as '*constructivist structuralism* or of *structuralist constructivism*' (cited in Garrett 2007: 230).

Bourdieu was unquestionably a modern thinker who deployed rational scientific tools to analyse specific historical fields and his work was deeply grounded in rationalist epistemology (Robbins 2002: 113). Bourdieu himself noted:

> My entire scientific enterprise is indeed based on the belief that the deepest logic of the social world can be grasped only if one plunges into the particularity of an empirical reality, historically located and dated …
>
> (Bourdieu 1998: 1–2)

Moralism

From the 1990s onwards, Bourdieu increasingly came to occupy the mantle of the public intellectual. Bourdieu became a vociferous advocate of the unemployed and regularly denounced neoliberal economic policies. This appeared to be a curious shift, primarily because he did not have a strong record of public activism. Nevertheless, he was part of a continuing tradition that had been championed by Jean Paul Sartre. It was a tradition that embraced the defence of Republican values. Nillo Kauppi has argued that moral values are embedded deeply within Bourdieu's theory and this provided the impetus for him to adopt the stance of the public intellectual. These values are inseparable from his mission that sought the 'construction of a just and equal society, a background against which reality, as Bourdieu sees it, is staged' (Kauppi 2000: 14). Furthermore, his moral values and ethics were determined by his recognition of the centrality of class within the French context. His work on French society clearly showed that despite the rhetoric of equality, France continued to function as 'a class society where the dominant fractions define intellectual excellence and taste' (Kauppi 2000: 13).

The struggle with ethics was no doubt precipitated by his strong reaction to Sartre as well as the idea that you could somehow theorise without conducting fieldwork. This tension between philosophy and empirical work led him to declare that:

> When I finished my formal education, and in order to be finished with it, I deliberately tried not to follow everything Sartre's undertaking represented for me. To go to Algeria, to study the workers there closely, as well as those who weren't working, the unemployed, the sub-proletariat, the landless peasants, was a way of breaking with public discourse … and also with the intellectual ritual of the petition which was politically necessary and sometimes admirable in human terms …
>
> (cited in Forbes 2000: 39)

From the very beginning, Bourdieu's intellectual project has been aimed at demonstrating the affinity of philosophy and lived experience through research where both empirical and fieldwork methods are central to understanding social and cultural phenomena. Jacques Derrida, a classmate of Bourdieu's at the École Normale Supérieure, noted that Bourdieu appeared to be caught in a 'love–hate relationship with philosophy' (cited in Kauppi 2000: 14). It is not surprising that Bourdieu's theory 'joins the two worlds: the world of theory and the world of fact' (14). Consequently, in his later life, Bourdieu's theory and activism came together in that spirit of Republicanism that sought the establishment of a just society. It is in this context that Bourdieu's work needs to be contextualised 'in two interrelated contexts of the French intellectual field out of which it emerged and the shift to late capitalism which it has analysed' (Lane 2004: 7). Algeria, however, remained critical to his work and he often retuned to the fieldwork that he had conducted amongst the Kablye.[5]

Foucault

Michel Foucault was born on 15 October 1926 in Poitiers and was christened Paul Michel Foucault after his father who was a well-known local surgeon. It was expected that he would follow in his footsteps. Initially, he had a rather mixed academic career but eventually excelled and was accepted to study at the École Normale Supérieure (ENS). At the ENS, Foucault studied philosophy, and it was here, that it was later revealed, that he suffered from bouts of severe depression. This probably contributed to his fascination with psychology and he trained for a higher degree in psychology and a diploma in pathological psychology. Like other members of his generation who were students at the ENS, he joined the Communist Party under the influence of Louis Althusser. Although he was a party member from 1950 to 1953, he never really participated in any significant manner. After ENS, he took a position at Université Lille Nord de France where he taught philosophy and psychology.

Although Foucault's career is inextricably linked to that of France's most prestigious academic institutions, it is not often recognised that he had several experiences outside of France including living in Sweden, contemplating a move to Zaire and his two-year residency in Tunisia from 1966 to 1968. In 1954, Foucault decided to have a lengthy self-imposed exile from France by first taking up positions in various universities and cultural centres in Uppsala, Sweden (1954), in Warsaw, Poland (1958) and in Hamburg, Germany (1959). In Sweden, he was appointed to the post of French assistant in the Department of Romance Studies. In an interview, years later, Foucault noted that he left France, because it was where he suffered in French and cultural life whereas, 'at this time Sweden was supposed to be a much freer country' (cited in Macey 1994: 73). During his stay in Sweden, France was rapidly changing with events in Algeria gaining prominence. Foucault had some contact and sympathy with Algerian students at the University of Uppsala but was not known as an ardent supporter. As the Director of the Maison de France, he was present for Albert Camus' Nobel Prize ceremony and subsequent debate at the University of Stockholm. What is remarkable is that Foucault never commented on the momentous exchange between Camus and the Algerian student. As Macey notes, Foucault, years later, did make it clear that he was opposed to the war but regretted that, 'being abroad at the time, he had not himself participated in one of modern France's decisive experiences' (Macey 1994: 83).

He eventually returned to France to head philosophy at Clermont-Ferrand University and met Daniel Defret who became his life-long partner. In 1960, he completed his doctorate and rapidly published several works including *Madness and Civilisation* (1961), a book on the work of the poet, Raymond Roussel (1962) and *The Birth of the Clinic* (1963). After Defret was conscripted in Tunisia (where Foucault often visited him), he decided to take a position at the University of Tunis. It was during this time that he wrote the *Archaeology of Knowledge* (1969). He gained firsthand knowledge of the rebarbative effects of colonialism and its impact on the postcolonial state. The highly volatile student demonstrations that began with the pro-Palestinian demonstrations during the Arab-Israeli War of 1967 developed into a movement against the government of Habib Bourguiba anticipating the events of May 1968 in Paris (Young 2001: 396). In later years, Foucault made the observation that Tunisia 'represented an opportunity to reinsert myself into the political debate' (Macey 1994: 204).

Whilst in Tunisia, Foucault worked on a study of Manet and was active lecturing and meeting key intellectuals. David Macey has pointed out that 'virtually all the lecture tours left time for discussions with political activists, academic, mental-health professionals and even Zen Buddhist monks, but the content of those discussions rarely entered Foucault's actual discourse' (1994: xvii). In an interview with the daily *Presse de Tunis*, Foucault outlined why, as someone whose academic career was taking off, he moved to Tunisia. 'After having stayed in the French University long enough to do what had to be done and to be what one has to be, I wandered about abroad, and that gave my myopic gaze a sense of distance, and may have allowed me to re-establish a better perspective on things'. He was attracted to Tunisia because of its French colonial past and 'the sun, the sea, the great warmth of Africa. In short, I came to look for a Thebaid without the asceticism' (cited in Macey 1994: 185).

As I have noted earlier, a considerable part of Foucault's time in Tunisia was spent on the writing of *L' Archéologie du savoir*, which was written in Sidi Bou Saïd and published in Paris in 1969. However, Tunis and the student demonstrations of 1967 and 1968 were particularly confronting for Foucault especially given the manner in which they rapidly became anti-Semitic with the students expressing solidarity with the Palestinians. In a letter to Canguilhem, Foucault wrote:

> Nationalism plus racism adds up to something very nasty. And if you add that, because of their *gauchisme*, the students lent a hand (and a bit more

> than a hand) to it all, you feel quite profoundly sad. And one wonders by what strange ruse or (stupidity) of history, Marxism could give rise to that (and supply a vocabulary for it).
>
> (cited in Macey 1994: 204)

He returned to Paris in the autumn of 1968 to become head of Philosophy at Vincennes University. In 1970, he accepted the chair of the History of Systems Thought at the Collège de France. This began a period of high productivity and a great deal of prominence for Foucault, especially in the United States where his work was being celebrated. He published major works at this time including *Discipline and Punish* (1975) and from 1976, he began publishing his three-volume *History of Sexuality*.

Foucault died in June 1984, aged fifty-seven, at a time when he was seen to be one of the most significant intellectuals of the twentieth century. In France, he was a living national treasure and upon his death the Prime Minister, as well as the daily newspapers, paid tribute to his remarkable career and the impact of his ideas.

Michel Foucault's work evolved over time and needs to be seen within the context of the social and political changes that characterised the 1960s and 1970s. As Sara Mills has observed, prior to the 1960s, 'his work was mainly focussed on the analysis of anonymous production of knowledges and discourses' (Mills 2003: 23). The moves within his writing can be seen as a concern from archaeology to genealogy. As Foucault noted, 'if we were to characterise it in two terms, then "archaeology" would be the appropriate methodology of [the] analysis of local discursivities, and "genealogy" would be the tactics whereby, on the basis of the descriptions of these local discursivities, the subjected knowledges which were thus released would be brought into play' (Foucault 1980: 85). This transition in his work was undoubtedly triggered by his residence in the postcolony of Tunisia.

Michel Foucault's work has been highly influential within postcolonial studies, from informing Edward Said's *Orientalism* (1978) to the work of subaltern studies and beyond, his analysis of power, authority, modes of surveillance and governmentality have been vital to understanding the dynamics of the colonial world. Nevertheless, as Robert Young has pointed out there is almost a calculated absence of the colonial world in his work. It is curious that 'for the most part he preserved a scrupulous silence on such issues and has, as a result, been widely criticized for alleged eurocentrism' (Young 2001: 397). This seems all the more surprising given Foucault's deep awareness of France's policies towards its colonies and the violence in Vietnam and the Algerian War of Independence as well as his extended period in Tunisia.

Foucault neither wrote nor commented on his experiences in Tunisia. Although he was supportive of the student movement, he never expressed his solidarity in writing and it was only much later that he began to speak about the impact of this experience. In the 1970s, Foucault increasingly became vocal and 'was always prompt to denounce what he saw as the "intolerable", would not have remained silent in this way. One can only speculate that it was precisely his Tunisian experience that allowed a much more vocally militant Foucault to emerge' (Macey 1994: 206). The impact that Tunisia had on Foucault cannot be underestimated. His overtly political stances later in life made it evident that it was vital to engage in work that had political meaning.

The writing of the *Archaeology of Knowledge* in Tunis is particularly significant because 'he used his distance from France while working in a postcolonial state the better to develop an ethnological perspective on French culture' (Young 2001: 396). Foucault's use of ethnography entailed examining one's own culture as opposed to colonial anthropology that was focussed upon studying other cultures. He argued that ethnology had its roots embedded within the history of one's own culture. Ethnology, Foucault pointed out, 'is possible only on the basis of a certain situation, of an absolutely singular event which involves not only our historicity but also that of all men who can constitute the object of an ethnology (it being understood that we can perfectly well apprehend our own society's ethnology)' (cited in Young 2001: 377).

The time that he spent in Tunisia was critical, as it allowed Foucault to gain a different insight on French culture. The distance allowed for a kind of reflection that comes from being an outsider, one was able to see the excesses and pitfalls of their own society. It exposed Foucault explicitly to questions of alterity even though he was aware of some of these issues given his own sexuality. The result was unquestionably a Foucault more attuned to the political vicissitudes of his time. In his academic work, there is a significant shift 'against the earlier current developed in *Madness and Civilization* (1961), [in which he] came rather to deny the possibility of the other's separated existence and reduction to silence. In its critique of the central thesis of *Madness and Civilization*, the *Archaeology* signals a major revision in his thinking' (397). *The Archaeology of Knowledge*, Foucault's major work produced during his residence in Tunisia, marks a significant break where the role of discourse becomes central to the 'creation of categories, such as deviance, mental illness or sexuality, through which society is organized' (398). It was a book that Foucault argued was 'written simply to overcome certain preliminary difficulties' (cited in Wandel 2001: 373). This book has been described as perhaps the most important text of his oeuvre. As Torbjorn Wandel points out, it is 'a revolutionary work which in its formulation of the concept of discourse/practice created the necessary condition of possibility for the positive conception of power to come' (Wandel 2001: 371). The term 'épistèmé' is one that Foucault developed in *The Archaeology of Knowledge*. This allowed him to conceptualise 'the body of knowledge and ways of knowing which are in circulation at a particular moment' (Mills 2003: 28).

Foucault's Tunisian experience provided the impetus for him to develop frameworks which could comprehend the complexity of the political scene post-1968 forcing a rethinking of key social and political institutions.

This new form of analysis is one that eventually paved the way for his conceptualisation of govenmentality, the analysis of who can govern and who is governed but also the means by which that shaping of someone else's activities is achieved (Foucault 1991). Foucault's essay on 'Governmentality' was originally given as a lecture at the Collège de France in February 1978. Here he developed his views on the nature and origins of the modern state, views already canvassed in earlier works, for example *Discipline and Punish*. He is concerned with the workings of what he terms 'the problematic of government', and how there are marked changes between a medieval conception of the subject/sovereign relationship where the management of the subject is crucial, to a position where, taking the family as a model, there arises a modern conception of state and society based on the science of political economy. Governmentality then is equivalent to:

> The ensemble formed by the institutions, procedures, analyses and reflections, the calculations and tactics that allow the exercise of this very specific albeit complex form of power, which has as its target, population, as its principal form of knowledge political economy, and as its essential technical means apparatuses of security.
>
> (Scott 1995: 102)

What Foucault tries to do in *Discipline and Punish*, 'is move thinking about power beyond the view of power as repression of the powerless to an examination of the way that power operates within everyday relations between people and institutions (Mills 2003: 33).

Although Foucault was not in France as the events of May 1968 unfolded, his Tunisian experience meant that he had 'developed an abiding passion for politics' (Miller 1993: 15). His work increasingly reflected a form of political urgency as he sought to comprehend the central institutions of Western societies – schools, prisons, hospitals, armies, and the professions that 'strove with sinister efficiency to supervise the individual, "to neutralise his dangerous states", and to alter his conduct by inculcating numbing codes of discipline. The inevitable result was "docile bodies" and obedient souls, drained of creative energy' (Miller 1993: 15). Foucault was often criticised for being Eurocentric and not politically engaged. However, as we have seen, his Tunisian experience had a profound impact on his thinking, and it was in the subsequent events in Iran that he openly engaged with one of the most critical issues of his time.

The Iranian revolution

During 1978 and 1979, as the Iranian revolution unfolded, there was a great deal of support for the overthrow of the Shah. However, as the anti-Shah momentum gathered support and the possibility of an Islamic Republic looked likely, there were many critics on the left who took a cautious approach.

Michel Foucault, however, enthusiastically endorsed the protests in Iran. At this time, Foucault met the Ayatollah Khomeini who was in exile in Paris. In September and November 1978, he visited Iran twice and these trips informed his writings as a special correspondent for the Italian newspaper *Corriere della Sera*. Foucault's journalistic articles on the Iranian revolution are often seen as his misreading of what was taking place in Iran and have been subjected to considerable criticism on the basis of his gender-blindness. His early optimism quickly gave way to dismay and resulted in his open letter of complaint (Afray and Anderson 2005: 260).[6]

Just as he had witnessed in Tunisia, Foucault was acutely aware that something new, different, and unparalleled was taking place in Iran. It was the passion of the struggle against the Shah, often expressed through an Islamic revival, that led him to argue that 'intellectuals will work together with journalists at the point where ideas and events intersect' (cited in Eribon 1991: 282). He believed that the end of colonial rule during the 1960s placed Western thought on a precipice and a crisis that could only be resolved from the outside. As he remarked during a trip to Japan in 1978, 'if philosophy of the future exists, it must be born outside of Europe or equally born in consequence of meetings and impacts between Europe and non-Europe' (1999: 113).

Much has been written about Foucault's folly and his misreading of 'the probable future developments he was witnessing' in Iran (Macey 1994: 410). James Miller, for example, pointed out that it was Foucault's obsession with death that played a crucial role in his writings about the Iranian Islamists. This was particularly resonant with his theme of the 'limit experience' in politics. Janet Afary and Kevin Anderson argue that Foucault's writings on Iran 'represent the most significant and passionate political commitment of his life'. It was an episode, they argue, that ended in failure largely attributable to Foucault's 'silence on Iran after May 1979' (2005: 8). Yet, they claim that his experience in Iran was to have lasting impact on his subsequent work and that 'one cannot understand the sudden turn in Foucault's writings in the 1980s without recognizing the significance of the Iranian episode and his more general preoccupation with the Orient' (4).

Foucault's stint as a visiting professor of philosophy in Tunisia, Afary and Anderson argue, reinforced certain orientalist attitudes such as homosexuality amongst the Arabs (140). In the original preface to the *Histoire de la folie*, Foucault wrote:

> The Orient thought of as the origin, dreamed of as the vertiginous point that gives birth to nostalgias and promises of return … the night of beginnings, in which the West was formed, but in which it traced a dividing line, the Orient is for the West all that the West is not, even though it is there it must seek its primitive truth. A history of this division throughout its western evolution should be written, followed in its continuity and its exchanges but it must also be allowed to appear in its tragic hieratism.
>
> (cited in Macey 1994: 146)

Foucault's time in Tunisia clearly influenced his later attitudes towards the Iranian revolution. Undoubtedly, the encounter with students in Tunisia and the impact of Islam on them made him particularly attuned to the revolutionary potential of the protestors in Iran. Foucault later pointed out that in Tunis he was 'profoundly struck and amazed by these young men and women who exposed themselves to serious risks for the simple fact of having written or distributed a leaflet, or for having incited others to go on strike' (Afary and Anderson 2005: 140). Significantly, his Iranian writings did not change the perception that his work was deeply eurocentric (Said 1983).

It is interesting that what Foucault witnessed in Iran was something very different to the events of 1968 in France. For Foucault, this was necessarily so, 'because the men and women who protest with banners and flowers in Iran have an immediate political goal: they blame the Shah and his regime, and in recent days they are indeed in the process of overthrowing them' (Afary and Anderson 2005: 211). What was puzzling for Foucault was the commitment of the individuals involved in the struggle. He later reflected on this:

> What on earth is it that can set off in an individual the desire, the capacity and the possibility of an absolute sacrifice without our being able to recognize or suspect the slightest ambition or desire for power or profit? That is what I saw in Tunisia. The necessity for a struggle was clearly evident there on account of the intolerable nature of certain conditions produced by capitalism, colonialism, and neo-colonialism.
>
> (Afary and Anderson 2005: 141)

It is Carl Schmitt (1985) who reminds us that all political actions and intentions could be summed up in the distinction between friend and enemy. Politics itself was underpinned by the notion that it was possible to kill without hate. The politics of commitment whether motivated by religion or indeed by a secular cause meant that one could, and did, transcend oneself to kill the *public enemy*. This rendition of politics that Foucault witnessed in Tunisia is, I want to suggest, germane to his later lectures that were released as *Society Must be Defended* (2003). For Foucault, the events in Iran were not a revolution, as it is commonly understood or in a literal sense of the term. Rather, as he pointed out, it was the 'first great insurrection against global systems, the form of revolt that is the most modern and the most insane' (Afary and Anderson 2005: 222).

Foucault's critique of modernity found a certain resonance with the antimodernist stance that was at the core of the demonstrations on the streets of Iran. Foucault's critique of modernity articulated in the ways in which categories such as sexuality, incarceration and mental illness were policed by modern liberal societies had a certain affinity to the counter discourse of the Iranian revolutionaries. The Islamist movement in Iran and Foucault shared several passions. First, they were both opposed to the West's colonialism and imperialism. Second, they rejected the cultural and social aspects of modernity that had changed gender roles and social hierarchies in their respective societies albeit that Foucault had romanticised what this entailed especially in terms of the politics of sexuality. Third, they both had a preoccupation with the discourse of death as a path towards authenticity and salvation (Afary and Anderson 2005: 39).[7] Death, for Foucault, is the ultimate form of resistance against forms of injustice, a kind of political spirituality. It is a conception that becomes pronounced in his later analysis of bio-power where 'death is power's limit, the moment that escapes it' (Foucault 1978: 138). The Iranian situation impressed Foucault who witnessed the global reach of Islam and the manner in which technology was used to mobilise the population against the Shah's regime. In Shiite Islam, he saw a form of Islam that could radically 'change their subjectivity' (Afary and Anderson 2005: 255). James Miller argues that what he sees as being both original and challenging about Foucault's work is his preoccupation with death, 'which he explored not only in the exoteric form of his writing, but also, and I believe critically, in the esoteric form of sado-masochistic eroticism' (Miller 1993: 7).

Critically, he recognised that Islam was being juxtaposed to older forms of left-wing models that appeared to have no salience in Iran. Islam, for Foucault, represented an entirely new form of resistance. It was, he suggested, a 'different way of thinking about social and political organisation, one that takes nothing from Western philosophy' (cited in Duschinsky 2006: 548). The form of technology that was used was the development of a cassette culture that operated as an alternative to the official media. Paradoxically, the very rejection of modernity that Foucault found so attractive used those very means to communicate such propaganda. Afary and Anderson point out that Foucault's stance in his Iranian writings reveal more fundamental problems in his overall theoretical project. They question whether:

> … a poststructuralist, leftist discourse, which spent all of its energy opposing the secular liberal or authoritarian modern state and its institutions, leave the door wide open to an uncritical stance toward Islamism and other socially retrogressive movements, especially when, as in Iran, they formed a pole of opposition to an authoritarian state and the global political and economic order?
>
> (2005: 136)

It is often argued that the events of May 1968 revolutionised a whole generation of French scholars much as the colonial situation and the Algerian War for independence had done for Sartre's generation. However, in Foucault's case it was the student revolts of Tunisia that had the effect of politicising his work. The fragments of Foucault's life, his self-imposed exile, his sexuality and his politics all made their way into his theoretical work. The distinction between the political and the personal was far more blurred than has been previously thought. Each of his works needs to be seen as 'a kind of fragment of an autobiography' (cited in Miller 1993: 31). In an interview in 1983, he made this clear arguing that, 'the private life of an individual, his sexual preference, and his work are interrelated, not because his work translates his sexual life, but *because the work includes the whole life as well as the text*' (cited in Miller 1993: 19).

Lyotard

Jean-François Lyotard was born in Vincennes, France, on 10 August 1924 to Jean-Pierre Lyotard and Madeleine Cavalli. He was educated at the Paris Lycées Buffon and Louis-le-Grand. Initially, he was keen to become a Dominican monk, an artist, or perhaps even an historian but ended up studying philosophy and literature at the Sorbonne where he established a deep friendship with Gilles Deluze. He married Andrée May in 1948 and together they had two daughters. In 1950, after passing the *agrégation* he ended up at a lycée in Constantine, Algeria where he taught philosophy. Lyotard recalled that after his marriage and the birth of his children he was compelled to earn a living:

> As you can see, it was already too late to pronounce monastic vows. As for my artistic career, it was a hopeless wish because of an unfortunate lack of talent, while the obvious weakness of my memory was definitely discouraging my turn towards history. Thus I became a professor of philosophy at a lycee in Constantine, the capital of the French department of East Algeria.
>
> (1988b: 1–2)

In Constantine, Lyotard immersed himself in reading Marx as the Algerian political situation unfolded. Subsequently, during 1952–59 he taught at a school at La Flèche. Lyotard wrote that:

> I owe Constantine a picture of what it was for me then, when I arrived from the Sorbonne to teach in its high school. But with what colors should I paint what astonished me, that is, the immensity of the injustice? An entire people, from a great civilization, wronged, humiliated, denied their identity.
>
> (1993: 170)

In 1954, he joined the socialist organisation *Socialisme ou Barbarie* (Socialism or Barbarism), as he became involved in the struggle of Algerian workers against the French settlers. He eventually parted with *Socialisme ou Barbarie* in 1964 over political and theoretical differences. For a short period, he joined the *Pouvoir Ouvrier* (Workers Power), but eventually resigned, as he became disillusioned with Marxism. From 1959 to 1966, Lyotard returned to the Sorbonne as *maître-assistant* from where he finally moved to a position in the philosophy department at the University of Paris X, Nanterre. At Nanterre, he was at the centre of the events of May 1968. The encounter with the Algerian struggle no doubt prepared him for what he witnessed in May 1968, and it was not surprising that he would become actively engaged politically. Lyotard was eventually appointed to the *chargé de recherches* at the Centre National de la Recherche Scientifique where he worked from 1968 to 1970. He then moved to the University of Paris VIII, Vincennes. In 1979, the publication of *The Postmodern Condition* resulted in wide acclaim for Lyotard and he became a regular visitor to several American universities. Lyotard married his second wife Dolorès Djidzek in 1993 and they had a son. He died of leukaemia in Paris on 21 April 1998.

Algeria

Soon after arriving in Algeria, Lyotard rapidly became intimately involved in the struggles of the Algerian workers. His major political commitment of that period came about when he joined the socialist organisation *Socialisme ou Barbarie* (Socialism or Barbarism). As a member of *Socialisme ou Barbarie*, he wrote several essays which were subsequently collected in his *Political Writings* (1993). As Bill Readings points out, these writings 'provide a useful empirical corrective to charges that poststructuralism is an evasion of politics, or that Lyotard's account of the postmodern condition is the product of blissful ignorance of the postcolonial question' (Readings 1993: xiii). Lyotard writes that when he was given responsibility for the Algerian section of the journal, he saw it as an opportunity to repay a debt:

> I owed and I owe my awakening, *tout court*, to Constantine. The differend showed itself with such a sharpness that the consolations then common among my peers (vague reformism, pious Stalinism, futile leftism) were denied to me. This humiliated people, once risen up, would not compromise. But at the same time they did not have the means of achieving what is called liberty.
>
> (Lyotard 1993: 170)

Lyotard was an integral part of the *Socialisme ou Barbarie* journal, and from 1954, when the War for Algerian independence broke, he wrote extensively about the political situation in Algeria and its implications for France. The journal was the theoretical voice of 'a few militants, workers, employees and intellectuals who had banded together with the aim of carrying on the Marxist critique of reality, both theoretical and practical, even to its extreme consequences' (Lyotard 1993: 165).

In these political essays, Lyotard wrote about the possibility of a socialist revolution in Algeria. The colonial occupation meant that Algerians necessarily had to be kept in a state of underdevelopment and poverty. Lyotard outlined the notion of 'terror' and argued that if Algeria was to prosper it was necessary for the occupation to end. However, he was not overtly optimistic about the possibility of a revolution. Nevertheless, he argued for a socialist revolution but, like Frantz Fanon, was concerned about the national bourgeoisie and nationalism which would lead to new forms of inequality and domination.

Bill Readings has pointed out that Algeria was not for Lyotard his Spanish Civil War or Sartre's Algeria. It did not allow him to occupy the position of the other and appear victorious in his vehement opposition to French colonial rule. Rather, his was an account of the anti-imperial struggle. He wrote, 'not of "the Algerian War" but of "the Algerians' war" – a war that is not his, cannot be his, but that nonetheless calls out to him, demands a testimony that can never be adequate, a response that can never redeem his debt or obligation' (Readings 1993: xiv). His political writings then are a record of the impossible and represent a politics that 'cannot speak the language of the political' (xv).

It is not simply the struggle for self-determination that captured Lyotard. The Algerian struggle had a far-reaching impact, because it marked the crisis of the colonial state and exposed the limitations of the modernist imperialist ideology that was formulated upon the principles of historical progress. For Lyotard, 'what counts in these writings is the presentation of a war against the presumed neutrality of "progress" and "development" (capitalist *or* communist) that has been defined in Europe' (xviii). It is the project of 'depoliticization', where there is a recognition that there is no alternative political truth that becomes the most significant moment for Lyotard. He explains that:

> I hope also to make today's reader understand why my picture of the Algerians' war is so unlike the one that appears in memoirs, log books, and chronicles (good or bad) in which people bear witness to their experience of the 'Algerian War'. My picture is only sketched with difficult, only corrects itself from moment to moment over seven years, on the basis of the thought and practice of the group. And these texts are certainly those of a combatant, but one who is neither French nor Algerian, but internationalist.
>
> (Lyotard 1993: 168)

In his essay, 'Algeria Evacuated', which was written after the end of the colonial occupation, Lyotard questions why a socialist revolution did not eventuate. As he had pointed out in earlier writings, this was not possible, because the forms of political struggle were not class based. Algeria, Lyotard pointed out, contrary to the belief of the Communist Party hierarchy was not a classic situation where there was a proletariat that would lead the revolution. The failure of a socialist revolution no doubt contributed to his disillusionment with Marxism and his realisation that such political struggles and the movement for liberation could not easily be captured in a grand narrative.

Lyotard's resistance to and lamenting of modernity and its universalism as espoused by the Enlightenment tradition needs to be contextualised as part of his 'wider argument against what may be called the politics of redemption' (Readings 1993: xxiii). It is his Algerian experience which allows him to attack the politics of representation. He argues that to speak for others merely objectifies them and encodes them within one's own discourse. Lyotard explains this in his essay, 'The Name of Algeria':

> The presumption of the moderns, of Christianity, Enlightenment, Marxism, has always been that another voice is stifled in the discourse of 'reality' and that it is a question of putting a true hero (the creature of God, the reasonable citizen, or the enfranchised proletarian) back in his position as subject, wrongfully usurped by the imposter. What we called 'depoliticization' twenty-five years ago was in fact the announcement of the erasure of this great figure of the alternative, and at the same time, that of the great founding legitimacies. This is more or less what I have tried to designate, clumsily, by the term 'postmodern'.
>
> (Lyotard 1993: 169)

The post-modern condition

From Lyotard's Algerian experience onwards, he was always concerned with questions that centred on politics, justice and freedom. These remain at the core of his writing, 'whether he is discussing a piece of art, a literary text, theological arguments or even the end of the universe, his focus always falls upon the social and ethical issues that they evoke' (Malpas 2003: 2). Although his work is associated with the postmodern questioning of the certainty and rationality of modernity and its universalising tendencies, in his work he 'constantly pursues the question of what it means to think and act responsibly in the absence of such absolute rules or universal rules' (Malpas 2003: 2).

In the late 1970s, Lyotard was approached by the Council of Universities of the Provincial Government of Quebec to write a report that would inform them of the state of knowledge in highly developed societies at the end of the century. He was asked to report on how different ways of knowing and dealing with the world from a variety of disciplines and knowledge systems were understood and valued within contemporary society. The result is *The Postmodern Condition*, a report about the 'condition of knowledge in the most highly developed societies' (1984: xxiii) and the way they treat education, science, technology, research and development. Lyotard's approach and methodology were reminiscent of the type of approach that Theodore Adorno adopted as a member of Paul Lazarsfeld's Princeton Radio Research Project during his exile in the United States. As David Jenemann (2007) points out, Adorno refused to engage in the type of research that his American colleagues were engaged in, rejecting merely quantitative methodologies in order to arrive at 'alternative radio practices' that were more in line with his commitment to social and political change.

Lyotard's work has since become synonymous with postmodernism and it is his often-quoted definition of the post-modern as an 'incredulity toward metanarratives' (Lyotard 1984: xxii) which has led to a post-modern distrust of totalising gestures. It is Lyotard's contention that these meta narratives or 'grand' narratives are the underpinnings of Western civilisation and culture, and serve as a legitimating force. Hans Bertens notes that:

> In Lyotard's analysis, the modern pursuit of knowledge is characterized by the way it legitimates itself through a metadiscourse that makes 'an explicit appeal to some grand narrative, such as the dialectics of the spirit, the hermeneutics of meaning, the emancipation of the rational or working subject or the creation of wealth'.
>
> (Bertens 1995: 125)

The central question posed by *The Postmodern Condition* is how the lives and identities of people are impacted by forms of knowledge production. This is a key question because 'the status of knowledge is altered as our societies enter what is known as the post-industrial age and cultures enter what is known as the post modern age' (Lyotard 1984: 3). What is remarkable is that he had realised how commodified knowledge had become and that it was a major source of power and would remain so for a long term. He argued, 'knowledge in the form of an informational commodity indispensable to productive power is already, and will continue to be, a major – perhaps *the* major – stake in the worldwide competition for power' (1984: 5). The predominance of a scientific methodology that permeated Western society was a concern for Lyotard who recognised that there were narrative forms of knowledge that were also vital. He pointed out that, 'scientific knowledge does not represent the totality of knowledge; it has always existed in addition to, and in competition and conflict with another kind of knowledge; which I will call narrative …' (1984: 7).

In a post-modern world, Lyotard argues, the kind of salience that grand narratives held in organising knowledge had diminished. This is compounded by the fact that efficiency and profit are the organising principles of an increasingly globalised world. To illustrate his argument, he points out that knowledge must be analysed through language games and meta narratives which determine the specific rules that make forms of knowledge production legitimate within specific fields. As opposed to efficiency and profit, he argues, 'for the importance of respecting the differences between language games, and thus for the vital role that resistance to the universal systems of organisation plays today'. The potential for resistance, makes it 'necessary to strive for parology within the system rather than attempting to create a new grand narrative that will bring all language games into line in a different way'

(Malpas 2003: 32). Lyotard is deeply aware of the political imperative and this informs all of his readings of art, culture, or literature. He is cognisant of the importance of recognising others' rights to deploy their own language games so that their point of view is articulated. The inextricable linkage between ethics and politics is teased out:

> There is no politics if there is not at the very centre of society, at least at a centre that is not a centre but everywhere in society, a questioning of existing institutions, a project to improve them, to make them more just. This means that all politics implies the prescription of doing something else than what is.
>
> (1985: 23)

Injustice, Lyotard argues, 'occurs when other ways of thinking, speaking and acting are silenced by the language games of a dominant group or culture' (Malpas 2003: 68).

It is in *The Differend* that he begins to formulate a more complex understanding of the language games through the idea of the 'phrase'. He questions both how different phrases can be brought together as well as the impact of different linkages. For Lyotard, phrases are 'categorised into regimens (such as denotation, questioning or ordering, for example), and genres of discourse (such as science, literature, Marxism etc.) generate sets of principle by which types of linkage between phrases are judged as good or bad' (Malpas 2003: 68). Every time a phrase is linked to another, a differend can occur. The differend, Lyotard argues is that instance when either side in a conflict finds it impossible to phrase. It is these differends that are the most important points from where criticism should begin.

It is in these moments when the universalising accounts of history are no longer adequate and this is the point that marks post-modernity. Certain events which challenge the idea of universal progress become the markers of the very disruption of the grand narratives of modernity. For example, the case of Auschwitz, Lyotard argues, 'the speculative grand narrative founders in the face of absolute barbarity. This and other signs are open to more than just statistical or empirical description, however. Instead, they call for responses from across the range of possible genres of discourse' (Malpas 2003: 85).

Across a range of disciplines and areas, including art, literature, history and politics that Lyotard has written, he is always seeking to disrupt the very discourses and orthodoxy which inform them. His focus on the differend, the sign, the event and the sublime means that he is careful not to suggest a systematic methodology for reading texts and analysing forms of knowledge. On the contrary, 'he urges the critic actively to question such programmes and investigate what they exclude or silence' (Malpas 2003: 121). Lyotard's Algerian experience highlighted the problems with the universalising promises and the civilising mission of colonialism with its notions of progress. For Lyotard it is up to the critic 'interminably to rewrite modernity in order to expose the moments where the genres of discourse that make up grand narratives are opened to question and the possibility of change emerges' (Malpas 2003: 121). In his *Political Writings*, Lyotard wrote that *The War of the Algerians* was written for Constantine almost as a correspondence of a lover. As he points out:

> From a distance, the lover confesses his jealousy of everything that deceives or will deceive the loved one. He admires the loved one, he encourages the loved one. He complains, knowing the loved one will not meet the fate that courage and beauty deserve.
>
> (Lyotard 1993: 170)

Conclusion

It is often argued that the works of Louis Althusser, Pierre Bourdieu, Michel Foucault and Jean-François Lyotard, some of the most prominent theorists of the twentieth century, are not grounded in the world. The avoidance of the worldliness within these post-structuralist and postmodernist theorists is often seen as a problem. Edward Said, for instance, became unhappy with Foucault for what he saw as a lack of political commitment within his work and within post-structuralist discourse in general. Foucault, in particular, suggested Said, 'takes a curiously passive and sterile view not so much of the uses of power, but of how and why power is gained, used, and held onto' (1983: 221). However, little attention is paid to the colonial roots of these thinkers. In the case of each of them, the postcolony and the spectre of Algeria looms large. Their experiences in the postcolony are vital to our understanding of how they challenge modernity and the orthodoxy that they sought to refute. The postcolony sharpened their sense of methodology. In the case of ethnography, for example, this was no longer just a methodological tool that examined exotic societies but rather was an important tool to reflect on one's society. The postcolonial experiences of these thinkers made them reflexive and insiders/outsiders in their societies.

Chapter 7

Conclusion

> ... the intellectual's provisional home is the domain of an exigent, resistant, intransigent art into which, alas, one can neither retreat nor search for solutions. But only in that precarious exilic realm can one first truly grasp the difficulty of what cannot be grasped and then go forth to try anyway.
>
> (Edward Said)

> To leave traces in the history of the French language – that's what interests me. I think that if I love this language like I love my life, and sometimes more than certain native French do, it is because I love it as a foreigner who has been welcomed, and who has appropriated this language for himself as the only possible language for him. Passion and hyperbolization. All the French of Algeria share this with me, whether Jewish or not ...
>
> (Jacques Derrida)

Edward Said underlined the relationship between empire, geography and culture, suggesting that these were drawn together by 'overlapping territories and intertwined histories'. He reminds us that 'even as we must fully comprehend the pastness of the past, there is no way in which the past can be quarantined from the present' (1993: 2). The past and the present, Said points out, not only imply each other but also are linked inextricably. This book has attempted to examine how the postcolony has influenced the theorists under review, for, it is vital that theoretical work 'formulate the relationship between empire and culture' (71). Read in this way, it is essential that the Maghrebin influences are traced in the theoretical works of these thinkers. This book is not an exposition of origins or even a redefining of the question of 'origins'.[1] Rather, it is aimed at recognising the importance and fluidity of borders that have been rigidly imposed between the postcolony and the metropole.

Recent developments within postcolonial theory have sought to explore the place of the West and its defining influence in forging the postcolony, recognising that neither the former nor the later could be reified. Postcolonial theory has been particularly conscious of breaking down imperial binaries that privilege the West as the progenitor of progress and the postcolony as the repository of backwardness and underdevelopment. Furthermore, the very notion that there is a singular modernity has been widely criticised with a deeper understanding articulated through the notion of alternative modernities.

Nevertheless, in a recent review of *Postcolonialism: An Historical Introduction*, Sarika Chandra and Neil Larsen take Robert Young to task for suggesting that post-structuralism has connections with the global South. They suggest that this 'means nothing more than that, one, Derrida invented post-structuralism; two, that he happened to have been born in Algeria; and three, that he at one point boarded a ship and went to France' (2006: 205). What they fail to recognise is the centrality of overlapping territories and intertwined histories. Indeed, they miss the point that there is a 'crossing of routes that proposes transversal passages through the Western topos, leading to a wider and perhaps unfamiliar constellation' (Chambers 2008: 133). It is precisely the possibility of forging new constellations that has made the postcolonial project so vital – it seeks to continuously destabilise the West's very own ontologies.

Iain Chambers has sought to understand the complexities of Mediterranean crossings, to try to understand how the region has been defined and redefined as a result of the political vagaries of a particular time. He explains how the African axis of the Mediterranean has been marginalised whilst proposing that it represents 'a composite historical site that interpellates, interrogates and interprets the potential sense of Euro-America and the modernity and progress it presumes to represent' (34). Put another way, for at least the last five hundred years, the Mediterranean has become 'the site of an ongoing and unfolding critique of the "progress" … that constitute[s] "our" modernity' (42). For Chambers, his particular positioning of the Mediterranean is 'not proposed simply to recover a forgotten past and set the record straight'. Rather, it seeks to capture the 'resistance of a past that persists, even when it is deliberately forgotten and denied' (141–42). The icons of theory explored in this book, insiders and outsiders, specular and syncretic intellectuals, have actively engaged in such crossings. They travelled to the margins and produced a theoretical sophistication that is unparalleled. They challenged the very orthodoxy that defined theory that preceded them. In so doing, they opened up possibilities that have redefined disciplines and knowledge production itself.

Despite this, postcolonial theory has far too often been characterised as epistemologically indebted to post-structuralism and postmodernism. As R. Radhakrishnan points out:

> … the ongoing collaborations between postcoloniality and poststructuralism have been particularly fraught. To those exponents of history and historiography who would consider poststructuralism to be by far a bad dream, the very term *postcoloniality* has come to signify a way of dealing with history by not really dealing with it. In the name of a purely epistemological or theoretical coalition, the 'after' after colonialism and

> the 'after' after structuralism have come together in what seems to be a rebellion without a cause.
>
> (2008: 4)

Whilst the prefix 'post' suggests a temporal rupture, it has been conceptualised generally as a manner of superseding the structural, the modern and the colonial. It is clear that the one cannot be demarcated from the other. Despite the efforts of postcolonial theorists who sought to formulate a different conception of the postcolony in light of the legacy of colonialism, they were charged with being third-world intellectuals who operated from within the first world. Further, it was argued that postcolonial theorists drew simply upon the tools of post-structuralism and postmodernism which were largely irrelevant to the needs of the peoples of the postcolonial world.

Once again, the forms of knowledge production and the boundaries between these seemingly disparate worlds were being drawn. Moreover, the authenticity of this new conceptualisation was being denigrated by the classic formulation that nothing original could emanate from the postcolony. Even though there was so much angst over post-structuralism and postmodernism, the postcolonial at best could only be a mere by-product.

This form of representation of the postcolony was exemplified just a few years ago when the former United States Ambassador to Kenya, Smith Hempstone, claimed that 'Kenya, like most African countries, came half-baked from history's oven. It had slept through the Renaissance and the Reformation, missed the American, French and industrial revolutions, was still fixated on bride-price and circumcision rites (male and female) when the nuclear age dawned. Somehow, it had occurred to nobody to invent the wheel' (Hempstone 1995: 50). The postcolony which was incapable of even inventing the wheel had no capacity to produce subjects that were able to generate original ideas that were, it seems, the exclusive preserve of Europeans.

This self-belief in European cultural superiority was predicated on the logic of the civilising mission that necessitated the invention of the other. As Hélène Cixous explains:

> … if there were no other, one would invent it. Besides that is what masters do: they have their slaves made to order. Line for line. They assemble the machine and keep the alternator supplied so that it produces all the oppositions that make economy and thought run … The paradox of otherness is that, of course, at no moment in History is it tolerated or possible as such. The other is there only to be reappropriated, recaptured, and destroyed as other.
>
> (Cixous and Clement 1986: 71)

The attacks on postcolonialism, it seemed to me, continued to reflect that desire of creating otherness albeit this time theoretically. There was little capacity to recognise the complexities of identity formation that necessarily occurs in postcolonial subjects. The fact that postcolonial subjects were challenging the boundaries under which they had been constructed and contained must not be overlooked. The exclusionary and inclusionary lines of belonging were being redrawn. As Donna Haraway points out, 'boundaries are drawn by mapping practices; "objects" do not pre-exist as such. Objects are boundary projects. But boundaries shift from within; boundaries are very tricky. What boundaries provisionally contain remains generative, productive of meanings and bodies. Siting (sighting) boundaries is a risky practice' (Haraway 1989: 201).

Reflecting on the colonial roots of the foremost exponents of post-structuralism and postmodernism, it became clear to me that they were located within boundaries erected to demarcate them from the postcolony and the metropole. Although they had a 'filiative' and an 'affiliative' relationship with the postcolony their colonial roots were never acknowledged as being central to their theoretical work. Unlike their postcolonial counterparts, these thinkers were seen simply as French intellectuals. The post-structuralist and postmodernist thinkers considered in this book – including Jacques Derrida, Hélène Cixous, Louis Althusser, Pierre Bourdieu, Michel Foucault and Jean-François Lyotard – were either born in Algeria or spent a considerable time in the Maghreb.

The colonisation of Algeria, and in particular the events surrounding the Algerian War, remain engrained deeply within the French imagination. These events defined an entire generation, with the names Jean-Paul Sartre, Albert Camus and Frantz Fanon being inseparable from the struggle for Algerian liberation. These three thinkers were the precursors to the post-structuralist and postmodernist revolution. A key question that has persistently preoccupied me, as I have worked through this book, has been the centrality of Algeria. Why have other colonial projects, such as that of the British, not produced a similar confluence of thinkers who have had such a profound impact on theory? Why have intellectuals with an affiliation to British colonies, such as Ireland, India, Kenya and Zimbabwe, not had a similar impact on contemporary theory? Algeria was designated as an extension of France and this differentiated it from every other French colony. Unquestionably, it was France's most intimate other and was regarded as its most prized colonial possession. Within the French colonial experience, there is no equivalent of such a large number of intellectuals being affiliated with a single colony – intellectuals who have indeed dominated theory as have these post-structuralists and postmodernists. Despite its promise of a greater France that would extol the universal values of the French Revolution, it is in Algeria that the French colonial project was exposed for all its brutality and violence.

In his discussion of 'traveling theory', Edward Said has pointed out that:

> Like people and schools of criticism, ideas and theories travel – from person to person, from situation to situation, from one period to another.

> Cultural and intellectual life are usually nourished and often sustained by this circulation of ideas, and whether it takes the form of acknowledged or wholesale appropriation, the movement of ideas and theories from one place to another is both a fact of life and a usefully enabling condition of intellectual activity.
>
> (Said 1993: 226)

Said cites as examples of this phenomenon the way in which Eastern ideas of transcendence were imported into Europe and the translation of European ideas of society into Eastern societies. Said was interested in tracking how theory moved from one context or situation to another and the manner in which it was locally inflected. This process is analogous to what James Clifford terms 'travelling cultures' where 'cultural action, the making and remaking of identities, takes place in the contact zones, along the policed and transgressive intercultural frontiers of nations, peoples, and locales' (1997: 7). Said uses the example of Lukacs and his student Goldmann to illustrate how theory travels. In Goldmann's hands, Lukacs' ideas are transformed, necessarily because he was not writing as someone intimately involved in the struggle of the Hungarian Soviet Republic of 1919. Rather, Goldman appropriated these ideas as an expatriate historian at the Sorbonne. The transformation, in Said's example continues when Lukacs' ideas, through Goldman, cross the Channel and are further transformed by Raymond Williams. As Said notes, when theory travels, it can 'quickly acquire the status of authority within the cultural group, guild, or affiliative family' (1983: 247).

In the work of the French post-structuralist and postmodern theorists, it is not merely a matter of theory travelling. It is about belonging and not belonging in both French and Algerian culture, of occupying that in-between space, as part of their own alterity that inevitably makes its way into their writings. Their profound influence on contemporary thought needs to be contextualised against the backdrop of Algeria and the experience of colonisation. It is their sense of exile, of being on the margins that enables them to challenge Western theory from within its own intellectual heritage. It is, in short, the spectre of Algeria that continues to mark their work.

There is little doubt that the thinkers examined in this book are doubly inscribed as both insiders and outsiders. This makes them well positioned to undertake the project of a 'critical ethnography of the West' (Young 2001a: 397). They were all border intellectuals, albeit specular or syncretic, who were located in that interstitial space between the postcolony and France. Each, in their own way, forces us back to Algeria, only to remind us of the need to transcend that particular boundary.

It is my contention that, in order to understand the project of French post-structuralism, it is imperative both to contextualise the African colonial experience and to highlight the Algerian locatedness, identity and heritage of its leading proponents. It seems appropriate to see Althusser, Bourdieu, Camus, Cixous, Derrida, Fanon, Foucault, Lyotard, Memmi and Sartre as Franco-Maghrebians. Collectively, not only havc they challenged French colonialism and its ideas of cultural superiority but they have also rendered the prevailing theoretical orthodoxy wanting. These Franco-Maghrebians with their roots in Algeria have had a profound impact on virtually all the disciplines of the humanities and the social sciences. As expounded in the work of these intellectuals, post-structuralism and postmodernism ultimately must be seen through the lens of the postcolonial.

Notes

1 Introduction

1 This list of those who have been associated with, or who have dealt with or written about Algeria is extensive although by no means exhaustive and includes Robert Randou, Jules Roy, Jules Lecoq, Rene-Jean Clot, Francois Bonjean, Marie Cardinal, Jean Pierre Millecam, Marcel Moussy, Musette Auguste Robinet, Jean Pelegri, Sadia Levy, Sarah Bernhardt, Paul Morand, Jean Amrouch, Elissa Rhais, Andre Rosfelder, Emmanuel Robles, Eugene Delacrois, Dominique Ingres, Charles Julien, Aime Dupuy, Andre Gide, Albert Camus, Fernand Braudel, Louis Althusser, Hélène Cixous, Bernard-Henry Levy, Jacques Berque, Isabelle Adjiani, Yves Saint-Laurent, Jean Lacouture, Jacques Attali and of course Jacques Derrida.

2 It is important to note, however, Ahmad's own trajectory. He is an academic who works in one of India's most prestigious institutions, has worked and works in Western universities and published his book *In Theory* (1992) with a British publisher.

3 For a critique of JanMohamed's characterisation of Said, see Ashcroft and Ahluwalia (2001). An obvious limitation is the binary nature of the syncretic and specular intellectuals, which are not always easy to differentiate in practice.

4 The phrase 'mind of winter', Edward Said points out, is one used by Wallace Stevens. The status of exile has been captured recently in the writings of Julia Kristeva. She writes:

> You will have understood that I am speaking the language of exile. This language of the exile muffles a cry, it doesn't ever shout. … Our present age is one of exile. How can we avoid sinking into the mire of common sense, if not by becoming a stranger to one's own country, language, sex and identity? Writing is impossible without some kind of exile.
>
> (quoted in Ashley and Walker 1990: 259)

5 For example, John Bevereley, along with several colleagues, launched a Latin American Subaltern Studies Project. In his Subalternity and Representation, he examines the relationship between subalternity and representation by analyzing the ways in which that relationship has been played out in the context of Latin American studies (Bevereley 1999).

6 For a critical engagement with the project of alternative modernities, see Harootunian (2002) and Knauft (2000).
7 It is important to note that Laura Chrisman has argued that Gilroy's book was a 'sign of the times', in which he was responding to rather deterministic accounts of slavery and the African diaspora. See Chrisman (1997: 51).

2 Algeria and Colonisation

1 Also see (Canny 1976; Seth 2007).
2 For further details on the Jewish community see Julien (1964) and Abu-Nasr (1987).
3 For further details see Ageron (1991); Confer (1966); Cooke (1973); Julien (1964); Vatin (1974); and Yacono (1973).
4 See Gallisot (1987); Kaddache (1980); Stora (2001); and Wolf (1969).
5 See Lustick (1993); Martini (1997); Nora (1961); Prochaska (1990); Sivan (1979); and Weitzer (1990).

3 Sartre, Camus and Fanon

1 This has resonance with Althusser's antihumanism, which will be explored in Chapter six.
2 Fanon's biographical details can be found in Caute (1970). Also, see Gendzier (1973); Hansen (1977); Bulhan (1985) and Gordon *et al.* (1996). For a good discussion of the gender issue in Fanon's work, see Moore-Gilbert (1996).
3 For a detailed analysis of the negritude writers, see Ahluwalia (2001a).
4 For a detailed account of Spivak's 'strategic essentialism', see Childs and Williams (1997) and Moore-Gilbert (1997).
5 For a detailed analysis of Sartre's influence, see Trotter (1999).
6 For an excellent insight into the origins of anti-humanism, see Hindess (1996: 79–98).
7 Susan Buck-Morss has observed that Fanon uses European philosophy as a weapon against European (white) hegemony, interpreting the master-slave dialectic both socially (using Marx) and psychoanalytically (using Freud) in order to theorize the necessity of violent struggle by Third World nations to overcome colonial status and to reject the hypocritical humanism of Europe, attaining equal recognition in terms of their own cultural values. Martinique-born Fanon would perhaps have been the closest to seeing the connection between Hegel and Haiti, but it was not his concern. (2000: 849)
8 It is important to take note of David Macey's point about Fanon and the question of violence. He writes that the 'negative emphasis on the theme of violence is probably a reflection of the American reception and of the way in which Fanon is read by Hannah Arendt in her book *On Violence'* (2000: 22).
9 On postcolonial transformation, see Ashcroft (2001); Ahluwalia (2001a).
10 The idea that this humanism is separate from Sartre's is one that Neil Lazarus finds difficult. For Lazarus, Fanon never places such a new humanism and he argues that the conclusion of *The Wretched of the Earth* should be read as 'manifestly Sartrean' (Lazarus 1999: 178).

4 Derrida

1 A town hall document dated October 21, 1871, confirms that Georgette Safar's grandfather 'born in Algiers during the year eighteen hundred and thirty-two fulfills the conditions for citizenship' prescribed by the 1871 decree, and 'has declared that he takes the name of Safar as family name and as first name that of Mimoun'. Seven witnesses had vouched for the parents of 'the above named', who had 'just signed in Hebrew'. They 'had been established in Algeria before eighteen hundred and thirty'. Until the Cremieux decree of 1875, the 'indigenous Jews' of Algeria were not French citizens. They would lose their citizenship and become indigenous again under the Vichy government (Bennington and Derrida 1993: 325).
2 For a detailed analysis of this, see Mamdani (1996); Ahluwalia (2001b).
3 Frantz Fanon, in *A Dying Colonialism* (1989), examined the Jewish population in Algeria at some length. Writing at the height of war, when the FLN was trying to attract support from minorities, he was particularly concerned to show that the Algerian Jewish population was not homogenous and sought to explain their diversity through a socioeconomic analysis.
4 For a detailed analysis of the negritude movement, see Ahluwalia (2001a).
5 Derrida reflects further on this in his last interview. See (Derrida 2007).

6 Althusser, Bourdieu, Foucault and Lyotard

1 For details on the postcolony, see (Ahluwalia 2001a; Mbembe 2001).
2 For a detailed analysis of interpellation see (Ferretter 2006).
3 For an excellent reflection on the problems with Althusser from one of his strongest adherents, see (Hindess 2007).
4 For a detailed account of Bourdieu's early days in Algeria and his fieldwork, see (Bourdieu 2004).
5 As Richard Jenkins points out: 'apart from *Algeria 1960*, he has drawn extensively upon this material in *Outline of a Theory of Practice* and its successor, *The Logic of Practice* (Jenkins 2002: 36).
6 These writings have all been translated and included in (Afary and Anderson 2005).
7 It is important to note that Robbie Duschinsky has pointed out the importance of Heidegger on Foucault. Duschinsky argues:

> It is my contention that the resemblance of language between Heidegger's account of the Nazi movement and Foucault's account of the Iranian revolution is indicative of a similar misreading of contemporary events, caused by the seductive desire to see in a contemporary radical movement the solution to their theoretical problems and a possible path out of the cage of Western metaphysical thought (554–55).

7 Conclusion

1 This project is not about a recuperation of the sort undertaken by Martin Bernal's *Black Athena* (1987), which accused nineteenth-century Europe of having committed a deception by explicitly denying its debt to Egyptians and Semites in the development of ancient Greece.

Bibliography

Abun-Nasr, Jamil M. (1987) *A History of the Maghrib in the Islamic Period*, Cambridge: Cambridge University Press.

Afary, Janet and Kevin Anderson. (2005) *Foucault and the Iranian Revolution*, Chicago: University of Chicago Press.

Ageron, Charles-Robert. (1991) *Modern Algeria: A History from 1830 to the Present*, Trenton, NJ: Africa World Press.

Ahluwalia, Pal. (1995) *Plantations and the Politics of Sugar in Uganda*, Kampala: Fountain Publishers.

—— (2001a) *Politics and Post-Colonial Theory: African Inflections*, London: Routledge.

—— (2001b) 'When Does a Settler Become a Native?: Citizenship and Identity in a Settler Society', *Pretexts*, Vol. 10, No. 1, pp. 63–73.

—— (2003) 'Fanon's Nausea: The Hegemony of the White Nation', *Social Identities*, Vol. 9, No. 3, pp. 341–56.

—— (2009) 'On Late Style: Edward Said's Humanism', in Ranjan Ghosh, *Edward Said and the Literary, Social and Political World*, London: Routledge.

Ahluwalia, Pal and Nursey-Bray, Paul. (1997) 'Frantz Fanon and Edward Said: Decolonisation and the Search for Identity', in Pal Ahluwalia and Paul Nursey Bray (eds) *Postcolonialism: Culture and Identity in Africa*, New York: Nova Science Publishers.

Ahluwalia, Pal and Zegeye, Abebe (2001) 'Travelling Cultures', Text to *Imperial Ghetto*, photographs by Omar Badsha, Pretoria: South Africa History Online.

Ahmad, Aijaz. (1992) *In Theory: Classes, Nations, Literatures*, London: Verso.

—— (1995) 'The Politics of Literary Postcoloniality', *Race and Class*, No. 36, Vol. 3, pp. 1–20.

Aldrich, Robert. (1996) *Greater France: A History of French Overseas Expansion*, London: Macmillan.

Alessandrini, Anthony (ed.). (1999) *Frantz Fanon: Critical Perspectives*, London: Routledge.

Althusser, Louis. (1965) Lire Le Capital, Paris: Francois Maspero.

—— (1969) *For Marx*, trans. Ben Brewster, London: Penguin Books.

—— (1970) *Reading Capital*, trans. Ben Brewster, London: Verso.

—— (1993) *The Future Lasts Forever: A Memoir*, trans. Richard Veasey, Oliver Corpet and Yann Moulier Boutand (eds), New York: The New Press.

Aneja, Anu. (1993) 'The Medusa's Slip: Hélène Cixous and the Underpinnings of Ecriture Féminine', *Lit*, Vol. 4, pp. 17–27.

Appadurai, Arjun. (1996) *Modernity at Large: Cultural Dimensions of Globalization*, Minneapolis: University of Minnesota Press.

Appiah, Kwame Anthony. (1993) *In My Father's House: Africa in the Philosophy of Culture*, Oxford: Oxford University Press.

Apter, Emily. (1997) 'Out of Character: Camus's French Algerian Subjects', *MLN*, Vol. 112, No. 4, pp. 419–516.

Aranson, Ronald. (2004) *Camus and Sartre: The Story of a Friendship and the Quarrel that Ended it*, Chicago: University of Chicago Press.

Armbruster, C. (1983) 'Hélène Clarice Nouvelle Voix', *Contemporary Literature*, Vol. 24, No. 2, pp. 145–57.

Ashcroft, Bill. (2001) *Post-Colonial Transformation*, London: Routledge.

Ashcroft, Bill and Ahluwalia, Pal. (1999) *Edward Said: The Paradox of Identity*, London: Routledge.

—— (2001) *Edward Said*, London: Routledge.

Ashley, Richard and R.B.J. Walker. (1990) 'Introduction: Speaking the Language of Exile: Dissident Thought in International Studies', *International Studies Quarterly*, No. 34, Vol. 3, pp. 259–68.

Azar, Michael. (1999) 'In the Name of Algeria: Frantz Fanon and the Algerian Revolution', in Anthony Alessandrini (ed.) *Frantz Fanon: Critical Perspectives*, London: Routledge.

Badiou, A. (2005) *Metapolitics*, trans. Jason Barker, London: Verso.

Baker, Robert. (1993) 'Crossings of Levinas, Derrida and Adorno: Horizons of Nonviolence', *Diacritics*, Vol. 23, No. 4, pp. 12–41.

Barber, Michael D. (2001) 'Sartre, Phenomenology and the Subjective Approach to Race and Ethnicity in *Black Orpheus*', *Philosophy and Social Criticism*, Vol. 27, No. 3, pp. 91–103.

Bartlett, Elizabeth Ann. (2004) *Rebellious Feminism: Camus's Ethic of Rebellion and Feminist Thought*, London: Macmillan Palgrave.

Bataille, G. (1985) *Visions of Excess: Selected Writings, 1927–1939*, Allan Stoekl (ed.) and trans., Minneapolis: University of Minnesota Press.

—— (1991) *The Accursed Share: An Essay on General Economy*, Vol. 1, trans. R. Hurley, New York: Zone Books.

Bennington, Geoffrey (2000) 'Double Tonguing: Derrida's Monolingualism', *Tympanum*, Vol. 4, pp. 1–12.

Bennington, Geoffrey and Derrida, Jacques. (1993) *Jacques Derrida*, Chicago: Chicago University Press.

Benson, Bruce Ellis. (2000) 'Traces of God', *Books and Culture*, September 2000, Vol. 6, No. 5, pp. 42–45.

Bernal, Martin. (1987) *Black Athena: The Afroasiatic Roots of Classical Civilization*, Piscataway: Rutgers University Press.

Bernasconi, Robert. (1996) 'Casting the Slough: Fanon's New Humanism for a New Humanity', in Gordon, L.R., Sharpley-Whiting, D.T. and White, R.T. (eds) *Fanon: A Critical Reader*, Oxford: Blackwell.

Bertens, Hans. (1995) *The Idea of the Postmodern*, London: Routledge.
Bevereley, John. (1999) *Subalternity and Representation*, Durham: Duke University Press.
Bhabha, Homi. (1986) 'Introduction', in Frantz Fanon, *Black Skin, White Masks*, London: Pluto Press.
Birchall, Ian. (2004) *Sartre Against Stalinism*, New York: Berghahn Books.
Bourdieu, Pierre. (1962) *The Algerians*, Boston: Beacon Press.
—— (1977) *Outline of a Theory of Practice*, Cambridge: Cambridge University Press.
—— (1986) 'The Struggle for Symbolic Order: An Interview with Pierre Bourdieu', *Theory, Culture and Society*, Vol. 3, No. 3, pp. 37–51.
—— (1990) *The Logic of Practice*, London: Polity.
—— (1998) Practical Reason. On the Theory of Action, Standford: Stanford University Press.
—— (2000) 'Making the Economic Habitus: Algerian Workers Revisited', trans. Richard Nice and Loïc Wacquant, *Ethnography*, Vol. 1, No. 1, pp. 17–41.
—— (2004) 'Algerian Landing', *Ethnography*, Vol. 5, No. 4, pp. 415–43.
Bourdieu, Pierre and Eagleton, Terry. (1994) 'Doxa and the Common Life: An Interview', in S. Zizek (ed.) *Mapping Ideology*, London: Verso.
Buck-Morss, Susan. (2000) 'Hegel and Haiti', *Critical Inquiry*, Vol. 26, No. 4, pp. 821–65.
Bulhan, Hussein Abdilahi. (1985) *Frantz Fanon and the Psychology of Oppression*, New York: Plenum Press.
Butler, J. (1993) 'Endangered/Endangering: Schematic Racism and White Paranoia', in R. Gooding-Williams (ed.) *Reading Rodney King: Reading Urban Uprising*, New York: Routledge.
Calarco, Matthew R. (2000) 'Derrida on Identity and Difference: A Radical Democratic Reading of The Other Heading', *Critical Horizons*, Vol. 1, No. 1, pp. 51–69.
Calhoun, Craig. (2006) 'Pierre Bourdieu and Social Transformation: Lessons from Algeria', *Development and Change*, Vol. 37, No. 6, pp. 1403–15.
Camus, Albert. [1989] (1942) *The Stranger*, trans. Matthew Ward, New York: Vintage Books.
—— (1996) *The First Man*, trans. David Hapgood, New York: Vintage Books.
Canny, N.P. (1976) *The Elizabethan Conquest of Ireland: A Pattern Established 1555–76*, Hassocks, Sussex: Harvester.
Carroll, David. (1997) 'Camus's Algeria: Birthrights, Colonial Injustice and the Fiction of a French-Algerian People', *MLN*, Vol. 112, No. 4, pp. 517–49.
Caute, D. (1970) *Fanon*, London: Fontana.
Césaire, Aimé. [1972] (1950) *Discours sur le Colonialisme*, Paris: Présence Africaine.
Chakrabarty, D. (1992) 'Postcoloniality and the Artifice of History: Who Speaks for 'Indian' Pasts?', *Representations*, Vol. 37, pp. 1–26.
—— (2000) *Provincializing Europe: Postcolonial Thought and Historical Difference*, Princeton: Princeton University Press.
—— (2002a) *Habitations of Modernity*, Chicago: University of Chicago Press.

Chakrabarty, Dipesh and Dube, Saurabh. (2002) 'Presence of Europe: An Interview with Dipesh Chakrabarty', *The South Atlantic Quarterly*, Vol. 101, No. 4, pp. 859–68.

Chamberlain, M.E. (1985) *Decolonization: The Fall of the European Empires*, Oxford: Basil Blackwell Ltd.

Chambers, Iain. (2008) *Mediterranean Crossings: The Politics of an Interrupted Modernity*, Durham: Duke University Press.

Chandra, Sarika and Larsen Neil. (2006) 'Postcolonial Pedigrees', *Cultural Critique*, Vol. 62, pp. 197–206.

Chaterjee, Partha. (1997) *Our Modernity*, Dakar: CODESRIA/SEPHIS.

Childs, P. and Williams, P. (1997) *An Introduction to Post-Colonial Theory*, London: Prentice Hall.

Chrisman, Laura. (1997) Journeying to Death: A Critique of Paul Gilroy's *The Black Atlantic Crossings*, Vol. 1, No. 2, pp. 82–96.

Cixous, Hélène. (1973) *Portrait du Soleil*, Paris: Denoel.

—— [1977] (1991) *Coming to Writing and Other Essays*, Deborah Jenson (ed.) and trans. Sarah Cornell, Ann Liddle and Susan Sellers, Cambridge Mass.: Harvard University Press, 1991.

—— (1980) 'The Laugh of the Medusa', in Elaine Marks and Isabelle de Courtivron (eds) *New French Feminisms*, Brighton: New Harvester.

—— (1981) 'Castration or decapitation', trans. Annette Kuhn, *Signs*, Vol. 7, No. 1, pp. 41–55.

—— (1986) *Inside*, trans. Carol Barko, New York: Schocken Books.

—— (1988a) 'Extreme Fidelity', trans. Ann Liddle and Susan Sellers in Susan Sellers, *Writing Differences: Readings From the Seminar of Hélène Cixous*, Milton Keynes: Open University Press.

—— (1988b) 'Tancrede Continues', trans. Ann Liddle and Susan Sellers in Susan Sellers, *Writing Differences: Readings From the Seminar of Hélène Cixous*, Milton Keynes: Open University Press.

—— (1989) 'A Realm of Characters', in Susan Sellers (ed.) *Delighting the Heart: A Notebook by Women Writers*, London: The Women's Press.

—— (1998) *Stigmata: Escaping Texts*, London: Routledge.

—— (1999) *Osnabrück*, Paris: Des femmes.

—— (2002) 'The Book as One of Its Own Characters', *New Literary History*, Vol. 33, pp. 403–34.

—— (2003) 'Letter to Zohra Drif', *College Literature*, Vol. 30, No. 1, pp. 82–90.

—— (2004a) *Hélène Cixous: The Writing Notebooks*, trans. and ed. Susan Sellers, London: Continuum.

—— (2004b) *Portrait of Jacques Derrida as a Young Jewish Saint*, trans. Beverley Bie Brahic, New York: Columbia University Press.

—— (2006) *Reveries of the Wild Woman*, trans. Beverley Bie Brahic, Evanston: Northwestern University Press.

—— (2006a) *Insister of Jacques Derrida*, trans. Peggy Kamuf, Stanford: Stanford University Press.

—— (2007) *Hélène Cixous: Manhattan Letters From Prehistory*, trans. Beverley Bie Brahic, New York: Fordham University Press.

Cixous, Hélène and Clément, Catherine (1986) *The Newly Born Woman*, trans. Betsy Wing. Manchester: Manchester University Press.

Cixous, Hélène and Calle-Gruber, Mireille (1997) *Rootprints: Memory and Life Writing*, London: Routledge.

Cixous, Hélène and Derrida, Jacques (2001) *Veils*, trans. Geoffrey Bennington, Stanford: Stanford University Press.

Clegg, I. (1971) *Workers' Self Management in Algeria*, New York: Monthly Review Press.

Clifford, James. (1997) *Routes: Travel and Translation in the Late 20th Century*, Cambridge: Harvard University Press.

Cohen, William B. (2003) 'The Algerian War and the Revision of France's Overseas Mission', *French Colonial History*, Vol. 4, pp. 227–39.

Confer, Vincent. (1966) *France and Algeria: The Problem of Civil and Political Reform, 1870–1920*, Syracuse, NY: Syracuse University Press.

Conley, Verena Andermatt. (1984) *Hélène Cixous: Writing the Feminine*, Lincoln: University of Nebraska Press.

—— (1991a) 'Hélène Cixous', in Sartori, Eva Martin and Zimmerman, Dorothy Wynne (eds) *French Women Writers: A Bio-Bibliographical Sourcebook*, New York: Greenwood Press.

—— (1991b) 'Introduction', in H. Cixous (ed.) *Readings: The Poetics of Blanchot, Joycem Kafka, Kleist, Lispector and Tsvetayeva*, trans. Verena Andermatt Conley, Minneapolis: University of Minnesota Press.

Cooke, James J. (1973) *New French Imperialism 1880–1910: The Third Republic and Colonial Expansion*, Hamden, CT: David & Charles Archon Books.

Cresswell, Tim. (2002) 'Bourdieu's geographies: in memoriam', *Environment and Planning D: Society and Space*, Vol. 20, pp. 279–382.

Dane, Robyn. (1994) 'When Mirror Turns Lamp: Frantz Fanon as Cultural Visionary', *Africa Today*, 2nd Quarter, pp. 70–91.

David, Catherine. (1988) 'An Interview with Derrida', in Wood, David and Bernasconi, Robert (eds) *Derrida and Différance*, Evanston, IL: Northwestern University Press.

Davidson, B. (1978) *Let Freedom Come: Africa in Modern History*, Boston: Little, Brown and Company.

Davies, Tony. (1997) *Humanism*, London: Routledge.

Davis, Robert Con. (1999) 'Cixous, Spivak and Oppositional Theory', in Jacobus, Lee A. and Barreca, Regina (eds) *Hélène Cixous: Critical Impressions*, Amsterdam: Gordon and Breach Publishers.

Derderian, Richard L. (2002) 'Algeria as a *Lieu de Mémoire*: Ethnic Minority Memory and National Identity in Contemporary France', *Radical History Review*, No. 83, Spring, pp. 28–43.

Derrida, Jacques. (1974) *Glas*, Paris: Galilée.

—— (1976) *Of Grammatology*, trans. Gayatri Spivak, Baltimore: Johns Hopkins University Press.

—— (1978) *The Post Card: From Socrates to Freud and Beyond*, trans. Alan Bass, Chicago: University of Chicago Press.

—— (1981a) *Dissemination*, trans. Barbara Johnson, Chicago: University of Chicago Press.

—— (1981b) *Positions*, trans. Alan Bass, Chicago: University of Chicago Press.

—— (1982) *Margins of Philosophy*, Brighton: Harvester.

—— (1986) 'Racism's Last Word', in Harry Louis Gates (ed.) *'Race', Writing and Difference*, trans. Peggy Kamuf, Chicago: University of Chicago Press.

—— (1989) 'How Not to Speak', in Sanford Budick and Wolfgang Iser (eds), trans. Ken Frieden, *Languages of the Unsayable*, New York: Columbia University Press.

—— (1992) *The Other Heading: Reflections on Today's Europe*, trans. Pascale-AnneBrault and Michael B. Naas, Bloomington: Indiana University Press.

—— (1994) *Specters of Marx: The State of the Debt, the Work of Mourning, and the New International*, trans. Peggy Kamuf, New York: Routledge.

—— (1995) *The Gift of Death*, trans. David Wills, Chicago: University of Chicago Press.

—— (1995) *Points ... Interviews, 1974–1994*, Elisabeth Weber (ed.), Stanford: Stanford University Press.

—— (1998) *Monolingualism of the Other, or the Prosthesis of Origin*, trans. Patrick Mensah, Stanford, CA: Stanford University Press.

—— (2001) *The Work* of *Mourning*, Brault, Pascale-Anne and Nass, Michael (eds), Chicago: University of Chicago Press.

—— (2002) *Acts of Religion*, Gil Anidjar (ed.), New York: Routledge.

—— (2002) 'Hostipitality', in Gil Anidjar (ed.), *Acts of Religion*, New York: Routledge.

—— (2006) *H.C. for Life, That is to say ...* , trans. Laurent Milesi and Stefan Herbrechter, Stanford: Stanford University Press.

—— (2007) *Learning to Live Finally: An Interview with Jean Birnbaum*, trans. Pascale-Ann Brault and Michael Naas, Hoboken, New Jersey: Melville House Publishing.

Derrida, Jacques and Attridge, D. (1991) *Acts of literature*, London: Routledge.

Deutscher, Penelope. (1998) 'Mourning the Other, Cultural Cannibalism, and the Politics of Friendship (Jacques Derrida and Luce Irigaray)', *Differences*, Vol. 10, No. 3, pp. 159–84.

Dianteill, Erwan. (2003) 'Pierre Bourdieu and the Sociology of Religion: A Central and Peripheral Concern', *Theory and Society*, Vol. 32, pp. 529–49.

Dirlik, Arif. (1994) 'The Postcolonial Aura: Third World Criticism in the Age of Global Capitalism', Critical Inquiry, 20, Winter, 1994, pp. 328–56.

—— (1996) 'The Aura of Postcolonialism: Third World Criticsm in the Age of Global Capitalism', in P. Mongia (ed.) *Contemporary Postcolonial Theory*, London: Arnold.

Dubey, Madhu. (1998) 'The "True Lie" of the Nation: Fanon and Feminism', *Differences*, Vol. 10, No. 2, pp. 1–29.

Dufourmantelle, Anne and Derrida, Jacques. (2000) *Of Hospitality*, trans. Rachel Bowlby, Stanford: Stanford University Press.

Duschinsky, Robbie. (2006) ' "The First Great Insurrection Against Global Systems" Foucault's Writings on the Iranian Revolution', *European Theory of Social Theory*, Vol. 9, No. 4, pp. 547–58.

Elliot, Gregory. (1987) *Althusser: The Detour of Theory*, London: Verso.

Eribon, Didier. (1991) *Michel Foucault*, trans. Betsy Wing, Cambridge, MA: Harvard University Press.

Fanon, Frantz. (1965) *A Dying Colonialism*, London: Penguin.

—— (1967) *The Wretched of the Earth*, Harmondsworth: Penguin.

—— (1970) *Toward the African Revolution*, Harmondsworth: Penguin.

—— (1986) *Black Skin, White Masks*, London: Pluto Press. With an introduction by Homi Bhabha.

—— (1989) 'Algeria Unveiled', in *Studies in a Dying Colonialism*, trans. Haakon Chevalier, London : Earthscan Publications.

—— (1989) *Studies in a Dying Colonialism*, trans. Haakon Chevalier, London: Earthscan.

Ferretter, Luke. (2006) *Louis Althusser*, London: Routledge.

Fields, Belden. (1984) 'French Maoism', *Social Text*, No. 9/10, Spring-Summer, pp. 148–77.

Fisher, C. (1999) 'Cixous' Concept of 'Brushing' a Gift', in Jacobus, Lee A. and Barreca, Regina (eds) *Hélène Cixous: Critical Impressions*, Amsterdam: Gordon and Breach Publishers.

Forbes, Jill. (2000) 'Bourdieu's Maieutics', *Substance*, Issue 93, Vol. 29, No. 3, pp. 22–42.

Fort, Bernadette. (1997) 'Theater, History Ethics: An Interview with Hélène Cixous on *The Perjured City, or the Awakening of the Furies*', *New Literary History*, Vol. 28, No. 3, pp. 425–56.

Foucault, Michel. [1961] (1967) *Madness and Civilisation: A History of Inanity in the Age of Reason*, trans. R. Howard, New York: Pantheon.

—— [1962] (1986) *Raymond Roussel*, Paris: Gallimard.

—— [1963] (1973) *The Birth of the Clinic: An Archaeology of Medical Perception*, trans. A.M. Sheridan Smith, New York: Pantheon.

—— [1969] (1972) *The Archaeology of Knowledge*, trans. A.M. Sheridan Smith, New York: Pantheon.

—— [1966] (1973) *The Order of Things: An Archaeology of the Human Sciences*, trans. A. Sheridan, London: Tavistock.

—— [1975] *Discipline and Punish: The Birth of the Prison*, New York Pantheon.

—— [1976] (1978) *The History of Sexuality, Vol. I An Introduction*, trans. Robert Hurley, New York: Pantheon.

—— (1980) 'Two Lectures', in C. Gordon (ed.) *Power/Knowledge*, Brighton: Harvester.

—— [1984] (1985) *The History of Sexuality, Vol. II: The Use of Pleasure*, trans. Robert Hurley, New York: Pantheon.

—— [1984] (1986) *The History of Sexuality, Vol. III: The Care of the Self*, New York: Pantheon.

—— (1991) 'Governmentality', in Graham Burchell, Colin Gordan and Peter Miller (eds) *The Foucault Effect: Studies in Governmentality*, Chicago: University of Chicago Press.

—— (1999) 'Michel Foucault and Zen: A Stay in a Zen Temple', in Jeremy Carrette (ed.) *Religion and Culture: Michel Foucault*, London: Routledge.

—— (2003) 'Society Must be Defended', Lectures at the Collège De France 1975–1976, trans. David Macey, New York: Picador.

Fourny, Jean-François. (2000) 'Bourdieu's Uneasy Psychoanalysis, *Substance*, No. 93, pp. 103–12.

—— (2000) 'Introduction', *Substance*, No. 93, pp. 3–6.

Gallisot, René. (1987) *Maghreb-Alg'erie, Class et Nation, Tome I*, Paris: Arcant'ere Editions.

Gandhi, Leela. (1998) *Postcolonial Theory: A Critical Introduction*, New York: Columbia University Press.

Garrett, Paul Michael. (2007) 'Making social work more Bourdieusian: why social professions should critically enagage with the work of Pierre Bourdieu', *European Journal of Social Work*, Vol. 10, No. 2, pp. 225–43.

Gasbarrone, Lisa. (1994) ' "The Locus for the Other": Cixous, Bakhtin and Women's Writing', in Karen Hohne and Helen Wussow (eds) *A Dialogue of Voices: Feminist Literary Theory and Bakhtin*, Minneapolis: University of Minnesota Press.

Gates, Henry Louis. (1991) 'Critical Fanonism', *Critical Inquiry*, Vol. 17, No. 3, pp. 457–70.

Gendzier, Irene. (1973) *Frantz Fanon: A Critical Study*, New York: Pantheon Books.

Geras, Norman. (1987) 'Post-Marxism?', *New Left Review*, Vol. 163, pp. 40–82.

Gerrasi, John. (1989) *Jean-Paul Sartre: Hated Conscience of His Century*, Chicago: University of Chicago Press.

Gilbert, Sandra. (1986) 'Introduction: A Tarantella of Theory', in H. Cixous and C. Clément (eds) (1986) *The Newly Born Woman*, trans. Betsy Wing, Manchester: Manchester University Press.

Gilroy, P. (1993) *The Black Atlantic: Modernity and Double Consciousness*, Cambridge, Mass.: Harvard University Press.

Goankar, Dilip. (1999) 'Alternative Modernities', *Public Culture*, Vol. 11, No. 1, pp. 1–18.

Goldberg, David and Quayson, Ato (eds) (2002) *Relocating Postcolonialism*, Oxford: Blackwell Publishers.

Gordon, L.R. (1996) 'Tragic Revolutionary Violence', in Gordon, L.R., Sharpley-Whiting, D.T. and White R.T. (eds) (1996) Fanon: A Critical Reader, Oxford: Blackwells.

—— and White R.T. (eds) (1996) *Fanon: A Critical Reader*, Oxford: Blackwells.

Haddour, Azzedine. (2001) 'Introduction: Remembering Sartre', in Jean-Paul Sartre, *Colonialism and Neocolonialism*, London: Routledge.

Hall, Stuart. (1990) 'Cultural Identity and Diaspora', in Jonathan Rutherford (ed.) *Identity: Community, Culture, Difference*, London: Lawerence and Wishart.

—— (1995) 'Negotiating Caribbean Identities', *New Left Review*, No. 209, January/February, pp. 3–14.

Hanchard, Michael. (1999) 'Afro-Modernity: Temporality, Politics and the African Diaspora', *Public Culture*, Vol. 11, No. 1, pp. 245–68.

Handelman, Susan A. (1982) *The Slayers of Moses: The Emergence of Rabbinic Interpretation in Modern Literary Theory*, Albany, NY: SUNY Press.

—— (1983) 'Jacques Derrida and the Heretic Hermeneutic', in Krupnick, Mark. (ed.) *Displacement: Derrida and After*, Bloomington: Indiana University Press.

Hanrahan, Mairéad. (2003) 'Of Three-Legged Writing: Cixous's *Le jour où je n'étais pas lá'*, *French Forum*, Vol. 28, No. 2, pp. 99–113.

Hansen, Emmanuel. (1977) *Frantz Fanon: Social and Political Thought*, Columbus: Ohio State University Press.

Haraway, Donna. (1989) 'Situated Knowledges: The Science Question in Feminism and the Privilege', in *Simians, Cyborgs and Women*, New York: Routledge.

Harootunian, Harry. (2002) 'Quartering the Millennium', *Radical Philosophy*, No. 116, pp. 21–29.

Harris, Leonard and Johnson, Carolyn. (1996) 'Foreword', in Gordon, L.R., Sharpley-Whiting, D.T. and White, R.T. (eds) *Fanon: A Critical Reader*, Oxford: Blackwells.

Harrison, Bernard. (1999) ' "White Mythology" Revisited: Derrida and His Critics on Reason and Rhetoric', *Critical Inquiry*, Vol. 25, pp. 505–34.

Hempstone, Smith. (1995) 'Kenya a Tarnished Jewel', *The National Interest*, winter, pp. 50–57.

Henry, Paget. (1996) 'Fanon, African and Afro-Caribbean Philosophy', in Gordon, L.R., Sharpley-Whiting, D.T. and White, R.T. (eds) *Fanon: A Critical Reader*, Oxford: Blackwell.

Hiddleston, Jane. (2005) 'Derrida, Autobiography and Postcoloniality', *French Cultural Studies*, Vol. 16, No. 3, pp. 291–304.

Hindess, Barry. (1996) 'No end of Ideology', *History of Human Sciences*, Vol. 9, No. 2, pp. 79–98.

Hutcheon, Linda. (1989) 'Circling the Downspout of Empire: Post-Colonialism and Postmodernism', *Ariel*, Vol. 20, No. 4, pp. 149–75.

—— (1994) 'The Post Always Rings Twice: The Postmodern and the Postcolonial', *Textual Practice*, Vol. 8, No. 2, pp. 205–39.

JanMohamed, A. (1983) *Manichean Aesthetics: The Politics of Literature in Colonial Africa*, Amherst: University of Massachusetts Press.

—— (1992) 'Worldliness-Without-World, Homelessness-as-Home: Toward a Definition of the Specular Border Intellectual', in Michael Sprinker (ed.) *Edward Said: A Critical Reader*, Oxford: Blackwell.

Jenemann, David. (2007) *Adorno in America*, Minneapolis: University of Minnesota Press.

Jenkins, Richard. [1992] (2002) *Pierre Bourdieu*, London: Routledge.

Jenkins, Tim. (2006) 'Bourdieu's Béarnais Etnography', *Theory, Culture, and Society*, Vol. 23, No. 6, pp. 45–72.

Johnson, Barbara. (1981) 'Translator's Introduction', in Jacques Derrida, *Dissemination*, trans. Barbara Johnson, London: Athlone Press.

Johnson, Douglas. (1993) 'Introduction', in Louis Althusser, *The Future Lasts Forever: A Memoir*, trans. Richard Veasey, Oliver Corpet and Yann Moulier Boutand (eds), New York: The New Press.

Jones, Ann Rosalind. (1985) 'Inscribing Femininity: French Theories of the Feminine', in Gayle Greene and Cordelia Kahn (eds) *Making a Difference: Feminist Literary Criticism*, London Methuen.

Judy, Ronald. (1996) 'Fanon's Body of Black Experience', in Gordon, L.R., Sharpley-Whiting, D.T. and White, R.T. (eds) *Fanon: A Critical Reader*, Oxford: Blackwell.

Julien, Charles-Andr'e. (1964) *Histoire de l'Algérie Contemporaine. Les Débuts 1830–70*, Paris: Presses Universitaires de France.

Kaddache, Mahfoud. (1980) *Histoire du Nationalisme Algérien: Question Nationale et Politique Algérienne 1919–1951*, Tome I et II. Algiers: S.N.E.D.

Kaiwar, Vasant. (2004) 'Towards Orientalism and Nativism: The Impasse of Subaltern Studies', *Historical Materialism*, Vol. 12, No. 2, pp. 189–247.

Kauppi, Niilo. (2000) 'The Sociologist as Moraliste: Pierre Bourdieu's Practice of Theory and the French Intellectual Tradition', *Substance*, Vol. 29, No. 3, No. 93, pp. 7–21.

Kearney, Richard. (1984) *Dialogues with Contemporary Continental Thinkers*, Manchester: Manchester University Press.

Keller, David. (2001) 'Deconstruction: Fad or Philosophy?', *Humanitas*, Vol. XIV, No. 2, pp. 58–75.

Khapoya, Vincent. (1998) *The African Experience: An Introduction*, Upper Saddle River, NJ: Prentice Hall.

Kirshner, Lewis. (2003) 'The Man Who Didn't Exist: The Case of Louis Althusser', *American Imago*, Vol. 60, No. 2, pp. 211–39.

Knauft, Bruce (ed.). (2002) *Critically Modern. Alternatives, Alterities, Anthropologies*, Bloomington: Indiana University Press.

Kohn, Margaret. (2008) 'Empire's Law: Alexis de Tocqueville on Colonialism and the State of Exception', *Canadian Journal of Political Science*, Vol. 41, pp. 255–78.

Krais, Beate. (2000) 'The Gender Relationship in Bourdieu's Sociology', *Substance*, Vol. 29, No. 3, pp. 53–67.

Kritzman, Lawrence. (1997) 'Camus's Curious Humanism or the Intellectual in Exile', *MLN*, Vol. 112, No. 4, pp. 550–75.

Kronick, Joseph G. (2000) 'Philosophy as Autobiography: The Confessions of Jacques Derrida', *MLN*, Vol. 115, pp. 997–1018.

Kruks, Sonia. (1996) 'Fanon, Sartre and Identity Politics', in Gordon, L.R., Sharpley-Whiting, D.T. and White, R.T. (eds) *Fanon: A Critical Reader*, Oxford: Blackwells.

Krupnick, Mark. (ed.) (1983) *Displacement: Derrida and After*, Bloomington: Indiana University Press.

Laclau, Ernesto and Chantal Mouffe. (1985) *Hegemony and Socialist Strategy: Towards a Radical Democratic Politics*, London: Verso.

Lane, Jeremy F. (2004) *Pierre Bourdieu: A Critical Introduction*, London: Pluto Press.

Law, John. (2000) 'On the Subject of the Object: Narrative, Technology and Interpellation', *Configurations*, Vol. 8, No. 1, pp. 1–29.

Lawlor, Mary. (1959) *Alexis de Tocqueville in the Chamber of Deputies: His Views on Foreign and Colonial Policy*, Washington: Catholic University of America Press.

Lazarus, Neil. (1999) *Nationalism and Cultural Practice in the Postcolonial World*, Cambridge: Cambridge University Press.

Le Sueur, James D. (2001) *Uncivil War: Intellectuals and Identity Politics During the Decolonization of Algeria*, Philadelphia: University of Pennsylvania.

Lenoir, Remi. (2006) 'Scientific Habitus Pierre Bourdieu and the Collective Intellectual', *Theory, Culture and Society*, Vol. 23, No. 6, pp. 25–43.

Leonard, Miriam. (2000) 'Creating a Dawn: Writing Through Antiquity in the Works of Hélène Cixous', *Arethusa*, Vol. 33, No. 1, pp. 121–48.

Lie, Sissel. (1999) 'Life Makes Text from My Body: A Reading of Hélène Cixous' *La Venue à l'Écriture*', in Jacobus, Lee, A. and Barreca, Regina (eds) *Hélène Cixous: Critical Impressions*, Amsterdam: Gordon and Breach Publishers.

Lloyd, David and Paul Thomas. (1998) *Culture and the State*, London: Routledge.

Lowy, Michael. (1973) *The Marxism of Che Guevara*, New York: Monthly Review Press.

Lustick, Ian. (1993) *Unsettled States, Disputed Lands: Britain and Ireland, France and Algeria, Israel and the West Bank-Gaza*, Ithaca, NY: Cornell University Press.

Lyotard, Jean-François. (1984) The *Postmodern Condition: A Report on Knowledge*, trans. Geoff Bennington and Brian Massumi, Minneapolis: University of Minnesota Press.

—— (1988) *The Differend: Phrases in Dispute*, trans. Georges Van Den Abeele, Manchester: Manchester University Press.

—— (1988b) *Peregrinations: Law, Form, Event*, New York: Columbia University Press.

—— (1993) *Political Writings*, trans. Bill readings and Kevin Paul Geiman, Minneapolis: University of Minnesota Press.

Lyotard, Jean-François and Jean-Loup Thebaud. (1985) *Just Gaming*, trans. Wlad Godzich, Minneapolis: The University of Minnesota Press.

Macey, David. (1994) *The Lives of Michel Foucault*, London: Vintage.

—— (2001) *Frantz Fanon: A Biography*, New York: Picador Books.

MacMaster, Neil. (2002) 'The Torture Controversy (1998–2002): Towards a "New History" of the Algerian War?', *Modern and Contemporary France*, Vol. 10, No. 4, pp. 449–59.

—— (2003) 'The Torture Controversy (1998–2002): Towards a "New History" of the Algerian War?', *Modern and Contemporary France*, Vol. 10, No. 4, pp. 449–59.

Majumdar, Margaret A. (1995) *Althusser and the End of Leninism?* London: Pluto Press.

Maley, William. (2001) 'Review of Jacques Derrida, Monolingualism of the Other', *Textual Practice*, Vol. 15, No. 1, pp. 123–34.

Malpas, Simon. (2003) *Jean-François Lyotard*, London: Routledge.

Mamdani, Mahmood. (1996) *Citizen and Subject: Contemporary Africa and the Legacy of Late Colonialism*, Princeton: Princeton University Press.

—— (2001) *When Victims Become Killers: Colonialism, Nativism and the Genocide in Rwanda*, Oxford: James Currey.

Manners, Marilyn. (1999) 'Hélène Cixous Names Woman, Mother Other: "A Feminine Plural Like Me" ', in Lee A. Jacobus, and Regina Barreca (eds) *Hélène Cixous: Critical Impressions*, Amsterdam: Gordon and Breach Publishers.

Marrouchi, Mustapha. (1997) 'Decolonizing the Terrain of Western Theoretical Productions', *College Literature*, Vol. 24, No. 2, pp. 1–34.

Martini, Lucienne. (1997) *Racines de Papier: Essai sur l'Expression Litteraire de l'Identité Pieds-Noirs*, Paris: Publisud.

Maton, Karl. (2003) 'Reflexivity, Relationism, and Research: Pierre Bourdieu and the Epistemic Conditions of Social Scientific Knowledge', *Space and Culture*, Vol. 6, No. 1, pp. 52–65.

Mauss, M. (1969) *The Gift: Forms and Functions of Exchange in Archaic Societies*, trans. I. Cunnison, London: Cohen and West Ltd.

Mbembe, Achille. (2001) *On the Postcolony*, Berkeley: University of California Press.

McRobbie, Angela. (2002) A Mixed Bag of Misfortunes? Bourdieu's Weight of the World', *Theory, Culture and Society*, Vol. 19, No. 3, pp. 129–138.

Megill, Allan. (1985) *Prophets of Extremity: Nietzsche, Heidegger, Foucault, Derrida*, Berkeley: University of Berkeley Press.

Micha, René. (1977) 'La Tête de Dora sous Cixous', Review of Hélène Cixous' *Dedans* (1969), *Le Troisème Corps* (1970), *Portrait du Soleil* (1973), *La Jeune née* (1975), *Portrait de Dora* (1976) and *La* (1976), *Critique*, Vol. 33, No. 357, pp. 114–21.

Miller, James. (1993) *The Passion of Michel Foucault*, New York: Anchor Books.

Mills, Sara. (2003) *Michel Foucault*, London: Routledge.

Moi, Toril. (1985) *Sexual/Textual Politics: Feminist Literary Theory*, London: Methuen.

Montag, Warren. (1999) 'Spirits Armed and Unarmed: Derrida's Specters of Marx', in Michael Sprinker (ed.) *Ghostly Demarcations: A Symposium on Jacques Derrida's Specters of Marx*, London: Verso.

Moore-Gilbert, Bart. (1996) 'Frantz Fanon: En-gendering Nationalist Discourse', *Women: A Cultural Review*, Vol. 7, No. 2, pp. 125–35.

—— (1997) Postcolonial Theory: Contexts, Practices, Politics, London: Verso.

Morrissey, L. (1999) 'Derrida, Algeria' and 'Structure, Sign and Play', *Postmodern Culture*, Vol. 9, No. 2, pp. 1–5.

Motard-Noar, Martine. (1995) 'Hélène Cixous', in William Thompson (ed.) *The Contemporary Novel in France*, Gainseville: University Press of Florida.

—— (1999) 'Reading and Writing the Other: Criticism as Felicity', in Lee A. Jacobus, and Regina Barreca (eds) *Hélène Cixous: Critical Impressions*, Amsterdam: Gordon and Breach Publishers.

Nancy, Jean-Luc. (1991) *The Inoperative Community*, Peter Connor (ed.), Minneapolis: University of Minnesota Press.

Naylor, Philip C. (2000) *France and Algeria: A History of Decolonization and Transformation*, Gainesville: University of Florida.

Nederveen Pieterse, Jan and Parekh, Bhiku. (1995) *The Decolonization of the Imagination: Culture, Knowledge and Power*, London: Zed Books.

Nora, Pierre. (1961) *Les Français d'Algérie*, Paris: Julliard.

Norris, Christopher. (1987) *Derrida*, Cambridge: Harvard University Press.

O'Brien, Conor Cruise. (1970) *Albert Camus: Of Europe and Africa*, New York: Penguin.

Ofrat, G. (2001) *The Jewish Derrida*, trans. Peretz Kidron, Syracuse: Syracuse University Press.

Olson, Alan. (1984) 'The Shape of Modern French and German Philosophy', *Int Phil Rel* Vol. 15, pp. 173–79. Review Essay.

Onwuanibe, Richard. (1983) *A Critique of Revolutionary Humanism: Frantz Fanon*, St. Louis: Green.

Paolini, Albert. (1999) *Navigating Modernity: Postcolonialism, Identity and International Relations*, Boulder: Lynne Rienner Publishers.

Parry, Benita. (1994) 'Resistance Theory/Theorising Resistance or Two Cheers for nativism', in F. Barker, P. Hulme and M. Iversen (eds) *Colonial Discourse/Postcolonial Theory*, Manchester: Manchester University Press, pp. 172–96.

—— (2004) *Postcolonial Studies: A Materialist Critique*, London: Routledge.

Phillips, Caryl. (1991) Cambridge, London: Bloomsbury.

Picard, Anne-Marie. (1999) 'Le Père de l'écriture: Writing Within the Secret Father', in Jacobus, Lee A. and Barreca, Regina (eds) *Hélène Cixous: Critical Impressions*, Amsterdam: Gordon and Breach Publishers.

Pitts, Jennifer. (2000) 'Empire and Democracy: Tocqueville and the Algerian Question', *Journal of Political Philosophy*, Vol. 8, No. 3, pp. 295–318.

Powell, Jason. (2006) *Jacques Derrida: A Biography*, London: Continuum.

Presbey, Gail. (1996) 'Fanon on the Role of Violence in Liberation: A Comparison with Gandhi and Mandela', in Gordon, L.R., Sharpley-Whiting, D.T. and White, R.T. (eds) *Fanon: A Critical Reader*, Oxford: Blackwell.

Prochaska, David. (1990) *Making Algeria French: Colonialism in Bone, 1870–1920*, Cambridge: Cambridge University Press.

—— (2003) "That Was Then, This Is Now: *The Battle of Algiers* and After", *Radical History Review*, No. 85, Winter, pp. 133–49.

Quayson, A. (2000) *Postcolonialism: Theory, Practice or Process*, Cambridge: Polity Press.

Radhakrishnan, R. (2008) *History, the Human and the World Between*, Durham: Duke University Press.

Readings, Bill. (1993) 'Foreword: The End of the Political', in Jean-François Lyotard, *Political Writings*, trans. Bill readings and Kevin Paul Geiman, Minneapolis: University of Minnesota Press.

Reed-Danhay, Deborah. (2002) 'Remembering Pierre Bourdieu 1930–2002', *Anthropological Quarterly*, Vol. 75, No. 2, pp. 375–80.

—— (2005) *Locating Bourdieu*, Bloomington: Indiana University Press.

Reid, David. (1997) 'The Rains of Empire: Camus in New York', *MLN*, Vol. 112, No. 4, pp. 608–24.

Resch, Robert Paul. Althusser and the Renewal of Marxist Social Theory. Berkeley: University of California Press, c1992 1992. http://ark.cdlib.org/ark:/13030/ft3n39n8x3/ retrieved from www.usc.edu/dept/complit/typanum/4/khor.html
Richter, M. (1963) Tocqueville on Algeria, *Review of Politics*, Vol. 25, pp. 362–98.
Robbins, Derek. (1991) *The Work of Pierre Bourdieu*, Boulder:Westview Press.
—— (2002) 'Pierre Bourdieu, 1930–2002', *Theory Culture and Society*, Vol. 19, No. 3, pp. 113–16.
Robbins, Jill. (1995) 'Circumcising Confession: Derrida, Autobiography, Judaism', *Diacritics*, Vol. 25, No. 4, pp. 20–38.
Rosenfeld, Michael. (1998) 'An Interview with Jacques Derrida', *Cardozo Life*, Fall 1998.
Rudey, John. (1992) *Modern Algeria: The Origins and Development of a Nation*, Bloomington: Indiana University Press.
Running-Johnson, Cynthia. (1999) 'The Self and the "Other(s)" in Cixous' *Sihanouk*', in Jacobus, Lee A. and Barreca, Regina (eds) *Hélène Cixous: Critical Impressions*, Amsterdam: Gordon and Breach Publishers.
—— (2001) 'Cixous's Left and Right Hands of Writing in *Tambours sur la digue* and *Osnabrück*', *French Forum*, Vol. 26, No. 3, pp. 111–22.
Rushdie, Salman. (1991) *Imaginary Homelands*, New York: Penguin
Rye, Gill. (2002) 'New Women's Writing in France', *Modern and Contemporary France*, Vol. 10, No. 2, pp. 165–75.
Said, Edward. (1978) *Orientalism*, New York: Vintage.
—— (1983) *The World, The Text and the Critic*, Cambridge, MA: Harvard University Press.
—— (1984) 'The Mind of Winter: Reflections on a Life in Exile', *Harpers*, No. 269, September, pp. 49–55.
—— (1993) *Culture and Imperialism*, London: Chatto and Windus.
—— (1994) *Representations of the Intellectual*, London: Vintage.
—— (2000) 'Invention, Memory and Place', *Critical Inquiry*, Vol. 26, No. 2, pp. 175–92.
—— (2004) *Humanism and Democratic Criticism*, Houndsmills, Basingstoke: Palgrave Macmillan.
Salgado, Raquel Scherr. (1997) 'Memoir at Saint-Brieuc', *MLN*, Vol. 112, No. 4, pp. 576–94.
Salusinszky, Imre. (1987) *Criticism in Society*, London: Routledge, Keegan and Paul.
Samers, Michael. (1997) 'The Production of Diaspora: Algerian Emigration From Colonialism to Neo-Colonialism', *Antipode*, Vol. 29, No. 1, pp. 32–64.
San Juan, E. (1998) *Beyond Postcolonial Theory*, New York: St. Martin's Press.
Sankovitch, Tilde A. (1988) *French Women Writers and the Book: Myths of Access and Desire*, *Syracuse*, New York: Syracuse University Press.
Sartre, Jean-Paul. (1943) *Being and Nothingness*, Paris Gallimard.
—— (1965) Anti-Semite and Jew, New York: Shocken.
—— (2001) *Colonialism and Neocolonialism*, trans. by Azzedine Haddour, Steve Brewer and Terry McWilliams, London: Routledge.

Sarup, Madan. (1993) *An Introductory Guide to Post-Structuralism and Postmodernism*, second edition, London: Harvester Wheatsheaf

Schmitt, Carl. (1985) *Political Theology: Four Chapters on the Concept of Sovereignty*, trans. George Schwab, Cambridge: MIT Press.

Schrift, Alan D. (2001) 'Logics of the Gift in Cixous and Nietzsche: Can We Still Be Generous?', *Angelaki*, Vol. 6, No. 2, pp. 113–23.

Schwarz, H. and Ray, S. (eds) (2000) *Blackwell Companion to Postcolonial Studies*, Oxford: Blackwell Publishers.

Scott, David. (1995) 'Colonial Governmentality', *Social Text*, No. 43, Autumn, pp. 191–220.

—— (1999) *Refashioning Futures: Criticism after Postcoloniality*, Princeton: Princeton University Press.

Sekyi-Otu, Ato. (1996) *Fanon's Dialectic of Experience*, Cambridge: Harvard University Press.

Sellers, Susan. (ed.) (1988) *Writing Differences: Readings From the Seminar of Hélène Cixous*, Milton Keynes: Open University Press.

—— (1994) *The Hélène Cixous Reader*, London: Routledge.

—— (1996) *Hélène Cixous: Authorship, Autobiography and Love*, London: Polity.

Seth, Sanjay. (2004) 'Reason or Reasoning? Clio or Siva?', *Social Text*, Vol. 22, No. 1, pp. 85–101.

—— (2007) *Subject Lessons: The Western Education of Colonial India*, Durham: Duke University Press.

Shiach, Morag. (1991) *Helene Cixous: A Politics of Writing*, London: Routledge.

Sivan, Emmanuel. (1979) 'Colonialism and Popular Culture in Algeria', *Journal of Contemporary History*, Vol. 14, No. 1, pp. 21–53.

Smith, Paul. (1988) *Discerning the Subject*, Minneapolis: University of Minnesota Press.

Sorum, Paul C. (1997) *Intellectuals and Decolonization in France*, Chapel Hill: University of North Carolina Press.

Spivak, Gayatri. (1976) 'Introduction', in Jacques Derrida, *Of Grammatology*, trans. Gayatri Spivak, Baltimore: Johns Hopkins University Press.

Sprinker, Michael. (ed.) (1992) *Edward Said: A Critical Reader*, Oxford: Blackwell.

—— (1999) *Ghostly Demarcations: A Symposium on Jacques Derrida's Specters of Marx*. London: Verso.

Stanton, Domna C. (1980) 'Language and Revolution: The Franco-American Disconnection', in Hester Eisenstein and Alice Jardine (eds) *The Future of Difference*, Boston: Hall.

Starling, Roger. (2002) 'Addressing the Dead: Of Friendship, Community and the Work of Mourning', *Angelaki*, Vol. 7, No. 2, pp. 107–24.

Stephens, M. (1991) Deconstructing Jacques Derrida, *Los Angeles Times Magazine*, 21 July.

Stern, Richard. (1991) 'Derridiarry', *LRB*, 15 August, pp. 20–22.

Still, J. (1999) 'The Gift Hélène Cixous and Jacques Derrida', in Jacobus, Lee A. and Barreca, Regina (eds) *Hélène Cixous: Critical Impressions*, Amsterdam: Gordon and Breach Publishers.

Stone, Martin. (1997) *The Agony of Algeria*, New York: Columbia University Press.

Stora, Benjamin. (1993) *Histoire de la Guerre d'Algérie, (1954–62)*, Paris: La Découverte.

—— (2001) *Algeria 1830–2000: A Short History*, trans. Jane Marie Todd, Ithaca: Cornell University Press.

Sturrock, John. (1998) *The Word From Paris: Essays on Modern French Thinkers and Writers*, London: Verso.

Swartz, David. (2002) 'In memoriam: Pierre Bourdieu 1930–2002', *Theory and Society*, Vol. 31, pp. 547–53.

Syrotinski, M. (2007) *Deconstruction and the Postcolonial: At the Limits of Theory*, Liverpool: University of Liverpool Press.

Szeman, Imre. (2000) 'Ghostly Matters: On Derrida's *Specters*', *Rethinking Marxism*, Vol. 12, No. 2, pp. 104–16.

Talmor, Sascha. (1995) 'Albert Camus's Last Book – Le Premier Homme', *History of European Ideas*, Vol. 21, No. 5, pp. 675–87.

Tocqueville, Alexis De. (2001) *Writings on Empire and Slavery*, trans. Jennifer Pitts (ed.), Baltimore and London: Johns Hopkins University Press.

Todd, Oliver. (1997) *Albert Camus: A Life*, trans. Benjamin Ivry, New York: Carroll & Graf Publishers, Inc.

Triulzi, Alessandro. (1996) 'African Cities, Historical Memory and Street Buzz', in Iain Chambers and Lidia Curti (eds) *The Post-colonial Question: Common Skies, Divided Horizons*, London: Routledge.

Trotter, David. (1999) 'Fanon's Nausea', *Parallax*, Vol. 5, No. 2, pp. 32–50.

Turner, Lou. (2002) '(e)Racing the Ego: Sartre, Modernity and Fanon's Theory of Consciousness', *Parallax*, Vol. 8, No. 2, pp. 46–53.

Vatin, Jean-Claude. (1974) *L'Algérie Politique: Histoire et Société*, Paris: Armand Colin.

Venn, Couze. (2000) *Occidentalism: Modernity and Subjectivity*, London: Sage.

Vincent, Julien. (2004) 'The Sociologist and the Republic: Pierre Bourdieu and the Virtues of Social History', *History Workshop Journal*, No. 58, Autumn, pp. 129–48.

Wa Thiong'o Ngugi. (1993) *Moving the Centre: The Struggle for Cultural Freedoms*, London: Heinemann.

Wacquant, Loïc. (2004) 'Following Pierre Bourdieu into the field', *Ethnography*, Vol. 5, No. 4, pp. 387–414.

Wandel, Torbjor. (2001) 'The Power of Discourse: Michael Foucault and Critical Theory', *Cultural Values*, Vol. 5, No. 3, pp. 368–82.

Watkin, William. (2002) 'Friendly Little Communities: Derrida's Politics of Death', *Strategies*, Vol. 15, No. 2, pp. 219–37.

Weber, Elizabeth. (ed.) (1995) *Points ... Interviews 1974–1994*, Stanford, CA: Stanford University Press.

Wehrs, Donald R. (2004) 'Sartre's Legacy in Postcolonial Theory or, Who's Afraid of Non-Western Historiography and Cultural Studies?', *New Literary History*, Vol. 34, 2004, pp. 761–89.

Weitzer, Ronald. (1990) *Transforming Settler States: Communal Conflict and Internal Security in Northern Ireland and Zimbabwe*, Berkeley: University of California Press.

Welsh, Sarah Lawson. (1997) '(Un)belonging Citizens, Unmapped Territory: Black Immigration and British Identity in the post-1945 Period', in Stuart Murray (ed.) *Not on any Map: Essays on Postcoloniality and Cultural Nationalism*, Exeter: University of Exeter Press.

West, Cornel. (1990) 'The New Cultural Politics of Difference', in Russell Ferguson, Martha Gever, Trinth T. Minh-Ha, Cornel West (eds) *Out There: Marginalization and Contemporary Cultures*, Cambridge: MIT University Press.

Wise, Christopher. (2001) 'Deconstruction and Zionism: Jacques Derrida's Specters of Marx', *diacritics*, Vol. 31, No. 1, pp. 56–72.

Wolf, Eric. (1969) *Peasant Wars of the Twentieth Century*, New York: Harper & Row.

Wood, Nancy. (1998) 'Remembering the Jews of Algeria', *Parallax*, Vol. 4, No. 2, pp. 169–83.

Wortham, Simon. (2000) 'Anthologizing Derrida', *Symploke*, Vol. 8, No. 1–2, pp. 151–63.

Yacine, Tassadit. (2004) 'Pierre Bourdieu in Algeria at War: Notes on the Birth of an Engaged Ethnosociology', *Ethnography*, Vol. 5, No. 4, pp. 487–509.

Yacine, Tassadit and Racevskis, Roland. (1999) 'Is a Genealogy of Violence Possible?', *Research in African Literatures*, Vol. 30, No. 3, pp. 23–35.

Yacono, Xavier. (1973) *Histoire de la Colonisation Française*, Paris: PUF.

Young, Robert. (1990) *White Mythologies: Writing History and the West*, London: Routledge.

—— (2001a) *Postcolonialism: An Historical Introduction*, Oxford: Blackwells.

—— (2001b) 'Sartre: the "African Philosopher" ', in Jean-Paul Sartre, *Colonialism and Neocolonialism*, London: Routledge.

Zaborowski, Holger. (2000) 'On Freedom and Responsibility: Remarks on Sartre, Levinas and Derrida', *The Heythrop Journal*, Vol. 41, No.1, pp. 47–65.

Zack, Lizabeth. (2002) 'Who Fought the Algerian War? Political Identity and Conflict in French-Ruled Algeria', *International Journal of Politics, Culture and Society*, Vol. 16, No. 1, pp. 55–97.

Index